An Introduction to Gestalt

Multidimensional wavelengths
cellular vs unfinished subconscious

An Introduction to Gestalt

Charlotte Sills, Phil Lapworth
and Billy Desmond

Cellular memory
↓
pinpoint in this life
sometimes cannot
≠ logical
↓
protocol

locate it - feel get the message

Separate, alone

wholeness — Completion
being   Run their course

↗ *aware t release*

historical experience
unfinished business
↓
desire to bring to
completion
if don't deye
us how
present
Focused
on Now

SAGE

Los Angeles | London | New Delhi
Singapore | Washington DC

Los Angeles | London | New Delhi
Singapore | Washington DC

SAGE Publications Ltd
1 Oliver's Yard
55 City Road
London EC1Y 1SP

SAGE Publications Inc.
2455 Teller Road
Thousand Oaks, California 91320

SAGE Publications India Pvt Ltd
B 1/I 1 Mohan Cooperative Industrial Area
Mathura Road
New Delhi 110 044

SAGE Publications Asia-Pacific Pte Ltd
3 Church Street
#10-04 Samsung Hub
Singapore 049483

Editor: Alice Oven
Assistant editor: Kate Wharton
Production editor: Rachel Burrows
Copyeditor: Kate Scott
Proofreader: Jill Birch
Indexer: David Rudeforth
Marketing manager: Tamara Navaratnam
Cover design: Wendy Scott
Typeset by: C&M Digitals (P) Ltd, Chennai, India
Printed by MPG Books Group, Bodmin, Cornwall

Library of Congress Control Number: 2011938473

British Library Cataloguing in Publication data

A catalogue record for this book is available from
the British Library

Mixed Sources
Product group from well-managed
forests and other controlled sources
www.fsc.org Cert no. SA-COC-1565
© 1996 Forest Stewardship Council

ISBN 978-1-4462-0727-7
ISBN 978-1-4462-0728-4 (pbk)

Contents

About the Authors

Charlotte Sills is a practitioner and supervisor in private practice, a tutor at Metanoia Institute and a tutor and supervisor of coaching at Ashridge Business School. She is the author and co-author of many books and articles on therapeutic work.

Phil Lapworth is a counsellor, psychotherapist and supervisor in private practice near Bath and has written extensively in the field of counselling and psychotherapy.

Billy Desmond is a Gestalt psychotherapist, supervisor, executive coach and organisational development consultant. He is a tutor and consultant at Ashridge Business School and the Head of Gestalt Department at Metanoia Institute.

PART I
BACKGROUND

1

A Brief History of Gestalt

In this first chapter we will provide some context to the emergence of Gestalt therapy and Gestalt as a philosophy for living our daily lives. If you are new to Gestalt, we suggest that you turn first to Part II. This will give you a better idea of the immediacy of the Gestalt approach. Later, you could return to Part I in order to see where it all came from.

The Gestalt approach to therapy was first developed by Frederick Perls (known as Fritz) with his wife, Laura, and other colleagues, in particular Paul Goodman. They brought together a number of different psychological concepts and approaches to develop a method of working with people that was a major challenge to the traditional models of the time, and one that was in tune with the anarchic and free-thinking, anti-establishment mood of the 1960s. Goodman in particular held a view that Gestalt therapy was not to be limited to the individual. He believed therapy had a responsibility to be inclusive of the wider social environment to facilitate the creation of social institutions that support the human potential for growth, compassion, freedom and connection. Since its inception, there have been many developments and refinements of its central theories. Indeed, it continues to develop, as Gestalt theorists and practitioners continue the tradition of questioning fixed models, and looking at what *is* rather than what is thought to be.

A concept central to the Gestalt approach is *wholeness*. In fact the word 'Gestalt' roughly translates from German as 'an organised whole'. It emphasises looking at whole and integrated experiences – be they communities, organisations, groups, objects or individuals – rather than dissecting them into their analysable parts. For example, one could analyse a root, stem, leaf, petal, stamen and pistil, but this would not capture the totality of the flower growing in a garden. In therapy, we can explore a person's feelings, thoughts and sensations but we also need to consider the whole of the individual and their relationships with their family, community and the society they live in. The essential message is that *the whole is more than the sum of its parts.* It is only by attending to the whole that we can also understand the parts. We will be talking more about wholeness later in this book. For the moment you, the reader, are faced with the first major Gestalt of the book – that of the approach itself. It is made up of many and diverse parts which together constitute the unique whole of Gestalt.

The story of Gestalt therapy starts with Fritz Perls. He was born in Berlin and lived in Germany until 1933. His early life experiences – being a Jew in a non-Jewish area, his anti-Fascist views, his rebellious personality as well as his many areas of study – were all later to affect the approach he developed. After qualifying in medicine, he began training as a Freudian psychoanalyst, which he completed in Vienna in 1928. During this time, and afterwards, he underwent several analyses himself. His psychoanalytical training had enormous influence on his later ideas. Many psychoanalytic concepts form the foundation of the Gestalt approach. These include the belief that our childhood experiences affect our adult lives; that 'pathological' behaviour has a meaning that may be unconscious but that can be brought into awareness; that humans have natural drives; and that people have an innate tendency towards homeostasis or equilibrium.

Perls was especially influenced by those theorists, sometimes known as 'interpersonal psychoanalysts', who were developing and expanding Freud's ideas towards a more person-centred and holistic approach to clients. These theorists included Fromm, Adler and Sullivan, and more radical analysts such as Reich, who was developing his theory that human problems are manifested not just psychologically but also physically, in 'body armour', and whose work focused on the body and the importance of cathartic expression.

At the same time, Perls was also interested in other movements in Germany, including Gestalt psychology, from which the name Gestalt psychotherapy derives. He married a Gestalt psychologist, Lore Posner (later known as Laura Perls), who taught him much and who contributed greatly to his subsequent work. From Gestalt psychology Perls drew many of his ideas on perception: our perception is geared to seeing wholes, and making sense of the world in whole images or experiences; what is more, of all the potential stimuli we could notice at any moment, we will tend to focus on those which make up a 'whole' relevant to us at that moment according to our perceived needs. For example, the hungry man, faced with a wide variety of items in the kitchen, will notice the bread, cheese and butter, because they will immediately suggest 'sandwich' to him. It might be only later that he sees the note his wife has left him saying his supper is in the fridge. A greater awareness of the situation could have helped him in his quest for food. The same applies in organisational life. In our current times of change, people in organisations feel anxious, fearing for their job security. To alleviate this they focus only on the task, keeping busy but forgetting to attend to their relationships with colleagues where there may be the possibility of support that could prove to be beneficial for them, the task and the organisation as a whole. This focus on immediate need has enormous implications for us in our lives, and certainly in therapy and coaching.

Another major idea from Gestalt psychology was the 'Zeigarnick effect'. Zeigarnick, a psychologist, first drew attention to the phenomenon that is commonly known as 'unfinished business'. If we have only some of the elements of a situation or Gestalt, we will have a natural urge to provide the rest in our minds, in order to have completeness. We 'fill in the gaps'. For example, if we write 'elephan' here, you will probably automatically add a 't' in your mind. We are unsatisfied with incompleteness, and things that are not finished for us. Whether they are events, conversations, feelings or even our sense of ourselves, they seem to haunt us in our personal and professional lives and have the potential to stop us focusing wholeheartedly on what is happening in the present. This is often a reason why individuals come to therapy or coaching.

For example, Jacqui, a chief executive of a national charity was finding it difficult to focus on getting the five-year strategy engagement process underway. She was pre-occupied and feeling unusually apathetic. In coaching she became aware the last time she initiated such a process it was very unsatisfactory, but she never had an opportunity to reflect on and understand the reasons it did so. Once she attended to this historic event and made some sense of it, she felt energised and called a meeting of her board to initiate the strategy process.

Perls studied existential philosophy, which was also to influence his work. He was very affected by the existential notion that human beings, though connected to each other and to every living being, are, in another sense, fundamentally separate and alone. This sense of individual aloneness is a sort of freedom that we do not usually acknowledge, imagining ourselves bound to other people in a variety of ways. Being aware of that freedom can lead to anxiety and despair. But it can also lead to another sort of freedom – the freedom of living authentically without false constraints and obligations, taking responsibility for one's own personal meaning. In Gestalt therapy the idea of responsibility is often presented as 'response-ability', where individuals have the choice, freedom and ability to respond to situations with awareness. Earlier, we were stressing the importance of wholeness; here we are emphasising the separateness of existentialism. It is interesting that both wholeness and separateness are central to Gestalt, where the dance of dependence, independence and interdependence is promoted in the work. The tension between our fundamental connectedness and our sense of individual agency can be seen in the development of two different streams of Gestalt (see below).

Perls was also involved with phenomenology, the study of perception – things as they appear to be. Phenomenology offers a method of becoming aware of and understanding the meanings we are making. It stresses that the only truth we can know is that which is happening in the present moment. This leads to the importance of the 'here and now', which we will expand upon later.

In 1933, the Perls left Germany and after a year in Holland moved to South Africa. Following their exposure to Kurt Goldstein's (1940) organismic theory in Germany they became interested in the ideas of holism put forward by Jan Smuts (1996 [1926]), the then South African prime minister, in his book *Holism and Evolution*. Holism underlines the interconnectedness of all things, as does Lewin's (1952), field-theory and these have become fundamental in Gestalt. Field-theory is the bedrock of the approach. It stresses that everything has a context and nothing can be understood separate from its context. Holism also focuses on the natural drive of humans to make wholes and therefore connects well with Perls' views on working in a Gestalt way.

In South Africa also, Fritz and Laura wrote *Ego, Hunger and Aggression* (Perls, 1992 [1947]). Based on Freudian and other theories, the book was the first to put forward Perls' innovative ideas about therapy. It takes the activity of eating (biting, chewing, spitting out, swallowing, digesting) as a metaphor for a person's relationship to the world. Aggression is described as a healthy drive to reach out and take from the world. This book introduced many of the ideas that became core elements of Gestalt Therapy in the 1950s and 1960s.

Fritz and Laura Perls left South Africa in 1946, when, mainly owing to dissatisfaction with the political situation, they moved to New York. Fritz Perls was then 53.

In America they worked with many people who were to be important in the growth of Gestalt therapy, amongst them the philosopher and writer, Paul Goodman, who along with Laura and Fritz is seen as one of the co-founders of Gestalt therapy. Perls also met Paul Weiss, who introduced him to Eastern spiritual traditions and philosophies. Perls was particularly attracted to Zen Buddhism with its emphasis on awareness being the path to enlightenment. The importance of 'awareness in the present moment' complemented the ideas gleaned from existentialism and phenomenology.

Finally, in exploring the roots of Gestalt, it is important to mention the theatre, which had always been a love of Perls. With his penchant for the dramatic, he was very drawn to the work of Moreno, the originator of psychodrama, although the two men did not get on personally. In Part III of this book, you will see how Gestalt ways of working can sometimes use the dramatic to heighten the potency of the experience.

Between 1946 and his death in 1970, Perls and his colleagues were involved in the founding and establishing of Gestalt therapy, with important centres in New York, Cleveland, Esalen in California and Cowichan in Canada. His lifetime of travelling made him unwilling to settle in one place, so every few years he moved on to found another centre, leaving his followers to continue the work.

A Fork in the Path

At this point, as Mackewn writes (1994: 105), 'two distinct branches grew out of this integrative and dynamic beginning'. One of these was led by Fritz Perls. He became famous for what he called his 'circuses', where he demonstrated his unique and charismatic form of therapy to full lecture theatres, inviting participants to come and sit centre-stage in 'the hot seat' to work with him. Perls was widely admired and revered for his innovative and iconoclastic ideas and methods. However, while he was described by some people as tender, generous and sensitive, he was much criticised by others for his high-handedness, his arrogance and the abrasive and confrontational manner which could often seem persecutory to his trainees. All in all, the man – like the therapy he founded – was an intriguing, multifaceted whole. If you wish to read more about Perls and the work he did, see Clarkson and Mackewn (1993).

Earlier, we described the tension in Gestalt practice between existential connectedness and a sense of ultimate aloneness. This first branch of Gestalt heavily focused on individual experience and agency. The second branch of Gestalt therapy put more emphasis on existential connectedness as well as retaining more of the rich diversity of sources. Mackewn (1994) lists Gestaltists such as Laura Perls, Fromm, Simkin, Erving and Miriam Polster and Kepner as being significant in the growth of Gestalt in the 1960s and 1970s. Additionally, the philosophical tradition of Gestalt therapy is also worth noting, embodied in the work of Laura Perls who studied with the existential theologian Paul Tillich, a German protestant, and the philosopher Martin Buber, a German Jew (Serline and Shane, 1999). Laura presented Gestalt therapy as an existential and phenomenological approach beyond technique, emphasising the experiential and co-created relationship. Since then, they and others have gone on to develop it further, in terms both of theory and of practice. This has evolved into what has become known as 'relational' Gestalt therapy. Although Gestalt therapy has always had a focus on relationship to self and other at its core, the emphasis on relational mutuality has been placed in the foreground. This is what Paul Goodman would have called 'social therapy', where person and environment are interdependent. It is a vital and continuing source of many recent international trends and growing edges, where we as individuals, groups and organisations are embedded, connected and participate in the wider world in which we live.

Gestalt in the World

In these few short pages it has been impossible to convey the depth and complexity of the development of the Gestalt approach or the profound effect that it has had on the practice of counselling and psychotherapy. The year 1977 saw the founding of the American *The Gestalt Journal*, a forum for Gestaltists to debate and develop their ideas. Over the course of the last three decades, Gestalt has taken a significant place amongst therapeutic approaches in Europe, and European writers are making important contributions to the development of the Gestalt approach. The excellent *British Gestalt Journal* was started in 1991 and is one of 11 Gestalt journals in the English language today. Additionally there are several national and international organisations whose aim is to promote Gestalt in counselling, psychotherapy, coaching, and organisational development. These associations, such as the United Kingdom Association for Gestalt Therapy (UKAGT), European Association for Gestalt Therapy (EAGT) and Association for the Advancement of Gestalt Therapy (AAGT), are underpinned by many of the principles we have mentioned above, and encourage novel ways of working that challenge practitioners to take the Gestalt orientation and way of living into the wider world.

Gestalt in Organisations

In 1954, Edwin and Sonia Nevis established the Gestalt Institute of Cleveland and in the 1960s Sonia started the process of translating individual Gestalt therapy theory and praxis to couples, families and eventually small groups and teams. Edwin and Sonia established the Gestalt International Study Centre where the Gestalt approach was enshrined in the Cape Cod training programme. This provided the platform for the application of Gestalt therapy theory and principles to organisation development, with Edwin Nevis writing a seminal book, *Organisational Consulting: A Gestalt Approach* (Nevis, 1987).

The integration of Gestalt therapy theory is now evident in many consulting and educational organisations who offer coaching and organisational development interventions to corporate, public and third sector institutions.

It is from the work of many of these recent Gestaltists (to which reference will be made in the text) as well as of Fritz and Laura Perls, Paul Goodman and their early collaborators that we have drawn the ideas found in this book.

2

An Overview of Gestalt Principles and Recent Developments

As we have seen, the practice of Gestalt has grown from a synthesis of many approaches and philosophies and Gestalt theory itself is an example of a Gestalt: each element standing on its own, yet part of the integrated theory and practice of Gestalt. The Gestalt understanding of human beings is based upon a number of principles as shown in Figure 2.1 which we will explore further in Part II of this book.

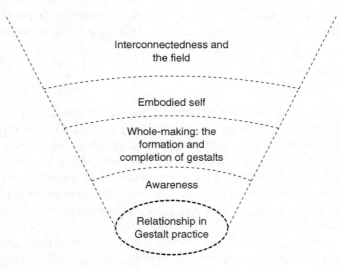

Interconnectedness and
the field

Embodied self

Whole-making: the
formation and
completion of gestalts

Awareness

Relationship in
Gestalt practice

Figure 2.1 Gestalt Principles

The Relationship in Gestalt Practice

Principle of Human Value

People are intrinsically neither good nor bad. We are what w
The implication for the Gestalt practitioner is that we move away
towards confirming the client's self-discovery and self-realisation. We adopt an attitude of awe and wonderment, refraining from categorising, diagnosing or labelling
as these reify and reduce a person. It is also a process where we need to hold a stance
of genuine curiosity in the other as a unique person.

The Here-and-Now Principle

'Here' means at the present place and 'now' means at the present time. People experience the past through remembering in the here and now, and imagine the future
through anticipating in the here and now. We can only be in the present. In the
present there is no past and the future has not yet occurred. Being present requires
the therapist, executive coach and organisational consultant to be fully available,
accepting the current unfolding moment-to-moment experience of the relationship.

Working in the 'here and now' is an invitation to come home to 'being' rather
than 'doing'. H.L. Mencken, in *The Little Zen Companion* (1994), said: 'We are here
and it is now. Further than that, all human knowledge is moonshine.'

Awareness

Principle of Self-awareness

Often we go through life on 'automatic pilot', using non-conscious, learned patterns
to free our minds to engage with things that need our attention. This is a natural and
necessary way of being, but can sometimes create problems. It can take the vibrancy
and immediacy out of experience and be self-limiting or damaging. People have the
potential to be aware of their emotions, thoughts, sensations and perceptions. In order
to make changes in ourselves and our lives (and that is what our clients want to do
when they come to see us), we need to develop a freedom to choose new ways of
feeling, thinking and doing. Such change can only be brought about by our awareness
of our current (and perhaps habitual) ways of being. This awareness in itself can bring
about spontaneous change. For instance, a client directing his awareness to a tension
in his body can sometimes experience a sudden realisation of a previously repressed
feeling which can then be expressed.

Principle of Self-responsibility

People are proactive as well as reactive. They determine their own responses to the world. As we become aware that it is we ourselves who are feeling, thinking and behaving, we take responsibility for choosing how we are, rather than believing 'That's just the way I am. I can't do anything about it.' With self-responsibility comes an increased sense of agency and possibility. We are responsible (response-able), for determining our actions based on our values, beliefs and context. Self-responsibility is a social-relational process that takes account of self, the other and the wider environment, and not only an intra-personal, self-referencing affair.

Principle of Self as Process

The self in Gestalt therapy is viewed and experienced as constantly changing as a result of the ongoing process of being influenced and influencing the world we live in. This process perspective of self has similarities to the Buddhist idea of a constantly changing self.

Taking a Gestalt view, we describe 'Self' as the current experience of 'being-in-the-world-with-others' (an expression borrowed from Heidegger, 1962). The self we experience at any particular moment inevitably brings patterns of relating that have been established in the past, but it is then affected and shaped by our current needs and the response of the environment. Therefore, the self we are emerges of and from our context. For example, Paul, a client with a history of childhood emotional neglect, arrives to therapy on time for the first time in three months, but still remains somewhat withdrawn in the session. Here, Paul is trying to get what he needs from contact with the psychotherapist but this is as much as he can manage for the moment. So, his self is changing, while at the same time, his enduring pattern of withdrawing in case he experiences further neglect still prevails.

Whole-making: Formation and Completion of Gestalts

Principle of Figure and Ground

In our contact with the environment we vary our focus of perception. Some things will stand out while others remain in the background. In our earlier example, we described a hungry man. As he stood in the kitchen, the ground of his visual experience was the whole of the kitchen. Of all the things in the kitchen, it was the items which meant 'sandwich' that became figure. It is this ability to identify figures of interest that are aspects of the ground, which enables attention to be focused on determining our needs.

Principle of Satisfaction of Needs

People have innate needs and a natural capacity and drive to meet them. For instance, the need for companionship seems to be universal and most people manage to find enough friends to satisfy that need. Clients often come to therapy with some early developmental needs that were unmet by their primary care givers, with the hope that these needs can be fulfilled. John came to therapy feeling depressed and withdrawn. It emerged that he and his therapist needed to work with unfinished business from John's childhood where the love and affirmation he so desired as a young boy was not available from his parents. An aspect of the work required these needs to be experienced in the here and now of the co-created therapeutic relationship where John could both allow himself to be fully aware of this old pain and also receive the healing warmth and attention of the therapist.

Principle of Wholeness

A person is a whole: body, emotions, thoughts, sensations, movements, perceptions and context. They all function interrelatedly to create this whole. This is antithetical to the Western emphasis on dualities such as mind–body, head–heart, individual–group, or person–environment. A graphic example of this is that of the hospital patient who may be 'the kidney case in bed three' but is actually Mary Jones, a young, scared, brown–eyed, witty mother of two, from a beautiful village – and much more besides.

Principle of Completion

People have a natural tendency to complete experiences, be they events, feelings, thoughts or actions. An unfinished experience or Gestalt will preoccupy us and prevent us from living fully in the present. If you have ever had the experience of wishing you had said something to someone who has died, you will know how 'unfinished business' can haunt you. Or, if you've been in a work situation where you've been holding something back for fear of rebuttal, you may be aware of the energy it takes away from being focused. Often, there is a burgeoning desire or wish to get it 'off your chest'.

Embodied Self

Principle of Embodiment

Perls famously said 'Lose your mind and come to your senses.' He was remarking on the fact that 'civilised man' spends much of his time thinking or worrying about the past and the future and ignoring the existential truth that he is embodied in space and time, in the present. Mind and body become separated and preference is given to the rational mind. Thus, we lose the ability to stay grounded in ourselves and the integrity of our senses. This leaves us hesitating to trust our somatic experiences. However, if we are true to our own experience, which includes both body and mind, that is the foundation for being in the world with integrity.

Principle of Multiple Ways of Knowing and Experiencing

This principle acknowledges that human beings can access understanding of their experiences by trusting, for example, their bodily, imaginative and expressive ways of knowing as well as cognitive and emotional ways. Sarah, an experienced senior leader of a large charity, arrives at a coaching session feeling anxious about her new post as Chief Executive. Her coach holds a belief from the outset that she has the capacity within her to understand, address and make changes that will enable her to lead in a way that is congruent and truthful for her. In this instance, the coach invites Sarah to draw a coloured picture that reflects her experience, to help access a more expressive and bodily way of knowing what successful leadership looks like for her.

Interconnectedness and the Field

Principle of Interrelatedness

People are part of their environment or 'field' and cannot be understood separate from that field (Lewin, 1952). Experience always involves our contact with and relationship to our surroundings. Gestaltists believe that authentic relationships with others enable growth: not that we should define ourselves in relation to others but that we find ourselves through that relationship. Clearly, the therapy and coaching relationship can provide just such an opportunity. This relationship with others includes our wider ecological relationship with the environment.

Principle of Organismic Self-regulation

Self-regulation is the natural tendency of humans to maintain a state of equilibrium in the interaction between the organism and the environment. The concept originates from the work of scientist and philosopher Kurt Goldstein. Self-regulation occurs physiologically, for example, in sweating when we are hot to keep our temperature steady. In Gestalt (e.g. Beaumont, 1993), the term 'self-organisation' extends the idea of an organismic tendency to include the functions of thinking, meaning-making and organising ourselves and our world. Thus self-regulation/organisation would include 'letting off steam' when angry, smiling when happy, withdrawing when feeling over-stimulated and seeking stimulation when bored. Self-organisation occurs through interactions with self and others, as well as being determined by the quality of contact a person has with the wider society and environment.

Part II of this book will expand upon these principles as they apply to Gestalt theory, while Part III will focus upon what actually happens between practitioners and their clients.

Recent Trends in Gestalt Therapy

In the 1960s, Perlsian Gestalt therapy had a dramatic, confrontational feel to it. Clients took 'the hot seat', not so much to be invited to increase awareness of themselves, but to be precipitated into it, with powerful interventions and techniques. The cultural revolution of that era urged people to throw off their old restrictions and allegiances in order to 'do their own thing', regardless of what others thought. This individualistic philosophy ignored the fact that individuals are necessarily involved in relationships and with the wider field of their society and environment. However, since the early days, and stemming more from the 'second branch' of Gestalt (Mackewn, 1994), there has been a change in emphasis in Gestalt practice, locating relationship at the heart of therapeutic work. Amongst others, Rogers (1951), Buber (1958 [1923]), the Object Relations School, Self psychologists and Intersubjectivists, have had a profound influence on the practice of Gestalt. The work of Hycner and Jacobs (e.g. 1995, 2008), Lichtenberg (e.g. 1990), the Polsters (e.g. 1974, 2009), Staemmler (e.g. 1993, 1999), Yontef (e.g. 1993) (to name a few) and more recently, writers such as Brownell (e.g. 2008), Gaffney (e.g. 2009), Joyce and Sills (2001/2010), Philippson (e.g. 2001, 2009), Spagnuolo Lobb (e.g. 2005), Wollants (2012) and Wheeler (e.g. 2000, 2009) have significantly influenced Gestalt theory towards a relational and field theoretical perspective.

These developments have also highlighted the limitation of the developmental theory described by Perls as the activity of suckling, biting, chewing, digesting (1992 [1947]: 126–7), a process broadly based on the perspective that humans self-regulate. Such a theory is insufficient when considering child development from a relational field-orientated perspective, as it fails to address the relational intersubjectivity between a child and its primary caregiver shown by recent findings in neurobiology (see e.g. Schore, 2003; Stern, 1985) to be key to the development of healthy functioning.

What is more, there were further changes in Gestalt methodology as Gestaltists recognised that while the more dramatic techniques could sometimes have immediately powerful effects, they did not always produce long-lasting beneficial changes in clients. On the contrary, sometimes the assault on the person's way of being could be experienced as very unsettling and undermining. Significant, long-lasting change seemed to be more associated with the respectful and attentive contact between therapist and client, where, perhaps for the first time, a client may have the experience of being in a relationship where they are truly seen and heard. Consequently, there has been increasing focus on the importance and significance of the relationship between therapist and client; a developing belief amongst practitioners that the individual can only be understood in relation to his situation; and an understanding that true growth and healing can only take place in a relationship.

Gestalt today is as vibrant a mix as it always was. At its heart is the therapeutic relationship and a method of exploring and increasing awareness in the co-created dialogue. Within the context of this therapeutic relationship, the Gestaltist may invite the client to expand their limitations in a variety of ways that are uniquely Gestalt, focusing on the 'safe emergency' of experimentation. It is some of this exciting mix that we hope to convey in the following pages.

Additional Reading

Mackewn, J. (1997) *Developing Gestalt Counselling*. London: Sage.

PART II
GESTALT THEORY

3

The Relationship in Gestalt Practice

We believe that the health and growth of human beings are best facilitated in the context of a relationship. Probably the most important thing a practitioner can offer to clients is a willingness to see, hear and accept them as they are, without preconception, expectation or judgement. By paying respectful attention to our clients' thoughts, feelings and behaviour, we invite them to do the same for themselves. We encourage them to become aware of themselves and express themselves as fully as they are able at that time. We act as a witness and in so doing provide confirmation of who they are. As Joseph Zinker said: 'Our deepest, most profound stirrings of self-appreciation, self-love and self-knowledge surface in the presence of the person whom we experience as totally accepting' (1975: 92).

Sometimes we may think we need to offer our clients sophisticated techniques or theoretical insights, but the therapeutic relationship may be the first time that our clients have experienced being truly attended to and heard – and this experience of confirmation can be the most healing feature of the work. In fact, as we said in Chapter 2, numerous research studies (e.g. Asay and Lambert, 1999; Martin et al., 2000, or, for a full summary, see Cooper, 2008; Wampold, 2001), including major meta-studies of positivist research, point to the quality of the therapeutic relationship, alongside the client's motivational and social factors, as the key determinant of effectiveness in psychotherapy, rather than the method, mode or theoretical orientation. After all, we are born from relationship, and as infants we are born into relationship with the world. Mackewn (1994) emphasises that the power to heal lies not in the therapist or even in the client alone but in what happens between them. It is the quality of this between-ness in the relationship where the source of healing and growth occurs. Our function as relationally orientated practitioners invites particular attention to this co-created between, and Clarkson reminds us not to take this lightly as 'the responsibility is awesome' (2003: 25).

Why is the relationship so important? One reason is simply the presence of 'other'. Gestalt therapy and coaching is not about changing people or telling them what they ought to do. We trust that it is an innate drive of human beings to be oriented towards health. It is not even about encouraging them to change themselves. It is about holding hope for the person's potential and all that a person can become. Gestaltists believe that human beings – even those in distress – are best able to grow and take charge of their lives by becoming more aware of who they *are* in all their needs and wants, feelings and thoughts, ambivalences and conflicts, what they say and what they do. Only then can they feel responsible for their own lives and make choices in order for them to find the best resolutions to their problems.

If a person is to have a better awareness of who they are, they must have a clear sense of 'I': what is 'me' and what is 'not me'. Have you ever been in a flotation tank? You are immersed in warm (body temperature) water in the dark and the quiet; it is hard to tell where your body ends and the water begins. You begin to feel as if you were at one with the universe. This may be an experience close to that of a baby inside a womb. You have some sensation inside you, but no sense of the size, shape or position of your body and limbs – no clear sense of yourself. In order for us to feel ourselves as solidly separate, we need to have something that is obviously 'not us' impinging upon us, touching our boundary. This is how we describe the self in Gestalt: the process of contacting that occurs at the boundary between the organism and its environment. This boundary is not only physical. Psychologically, a clear sense of ourselves happens in the same way. A person can only define himself as 'I' and have a solid sense of who that is, when that 'I' is in relation to something or someone which is 'Not–I', even though, paradoxically, *the self that is experienced* is inevitably shaped by the encounter. No discussion of the relational in Gestalt practice can exclude this unique perspective of self: the self is relational, and emerges within a given situation. Self is a function of the situation, continually in process, where aspects of the self are enduring over temporal, spatial and cultural dimensions. The Gestalt perspective of self as a process and function of its environment is still novel in psychotherapy models, where the emphasis is often more on enduring structure.

Self as Process and Function Emerges from Relationship

Self is a process of making contact through which we manage our context by adaptation or 'creative adjustment' (Perls, 1969: 45) to the environment; a process where certain aspects of a person's total experience become figural and other aspects become unnoticed in the ground. In Chapter 2, we linked the repeating pattern of contact to a person's (probably early) learned way of getting his needs met. However, if this pattern is not rigid, the process of relating in the present can also be '. . . the means for changing oneself and one's experience of the world' (Polster and Polster, 1974: 101).

Gordon Wheeler is an articulate advocate for understanding the self in social context and relationships. He says that we understand our selves within intersubjective matrixes of other selves. Our individual expression of self emerges from '. . . our own process out of a field [context] which includes the inner worlds of other selves' (2000: 109). In other words, we have multiple selves depending on the context. For example, we experience ourselves as different when we are with our boss than with our children or our best friend or alone on a mountain top. The self emerges and becomes known only in relationship to our environment and other person(s), even if the others are actually internalised in our imagination. We will explain this unique perspective in a little more detail.

This process of making contact emerges *of* and *from* the situation (in other words, it is part of and also a result of the situation) that we are co-creating, and *changes moment to moment*, while aspects also *endure over time*. For example, right now I (Billy) am immersed in writing. Looking out the window, I momentarily become captivated, pausing to see and make contact with the burnt orange sky of twilight. My skin is tingling, and excitement emerges where I feel connected to the outside world. I am moved, my torso, and facial muscles feel soft, eyes tearful with awe at such beauty. My felt sense of self, being interconnected to the wider world after being moved by nature, is an experience of self that endures over time: in that moment, incorporating the memory of my experience of previous sunsets over the course of my life.

In comparison, my experience of self two hours previously was different. I was writing an email to an old friend whom I hadn't seen for over six months. I was feeling a sense of loneliness and told him that I wanted to see more of him as I find his presence in my life enriching. I noticed a feeling of longing and hope emerging as, in his reply, he suggested that we consider meeting sooner rather than later. Here, I felt the loneliness was my experience of self as I sat to write my email, which then changed to longing and hope in the next moment upon his suggestion of meeting. Here, my self was spontaneously and creatively adapting during our moment-to-moment email exchange to facilitate meeting a person I cared for and enjoyed.

In summary, the self is born of relationship and emerges from relational encounters over the duration of our lives. The self as process is the capability we possess to respond spontaneously in our contact with the environment and to develop the capacity to creatively adjust to meet our needs. Self changes moment to moment *and* has enduring aspects over time, across cultures and in its environment. The self includes one's ongoing identity, one's here-and-now embodied experience of being, and also the capacity to separate one's own experiences from another, to reflect and to choose.

Healthy and Unhealthy Relational Contact

'Healthy' Relational Contact

Although it seems somewhat prescriptive, we want to articulate some parameters of healthy functioning that are implicit in Gestalt philosophy and principles. In general terms, healthy people think and feel positively about themselves much of the time. They have satisfying relationships and find ways of using their life in satisfying and creative ways. They are spontaneous in their contact, responding fluidly and creatively in their environment. Healthy people are actively involved with other people and the environment, relating rather than reacting, aware of their needs and taking responsibility for meeting them creatively and constructively while remaining aware and respectful of others and the environment.

Relating ≠ Reacting

Part of being healthy is the ability to manage one's feelings and to support oneself in times of stress as well as to recognise the need for the support of others. This means the development of mutually interdependent relationships as opposed to ones of dependence, independence or exploitation.

Healthy people also take responsibility for the choices they make in life and for the meaning they make of their lives. Awareness of themselves and their environment is intrinsic to this responsibility (we will say more about awareness in Chapter 4). Healthy people experience themselves and the world and make appropriate and creative adjustments informed by their awareness.

As you will see as you read this book, awareness is not a laborious process of perpetual or obsessional navel-gazing. The Gestalt view of healthy awareness emphasises immediacy of contact with others and the environment without the 'baggage' of the past or the future. That is not to say that the past or future is not relevant. It is an inevitable part of peoples' contact with one another and their environment, in so far as it is remembered, experienced and lived in the here and now. Healthy people have the capacity to live fully in the present with all the aliveness and vibrancy that implies. This does not mean being happy all the time but being alive and in contact with others and the environment with a whole range of feelings, thoughts and actions. A healthy person feels sad, angry, excited or scared and fully expresses those feelings in appropriate ways.

In his book, *Creative Process in Gestalt Therapy* (1977), Zinker suggests that, in the course of therapy, a person:

- moves towards greater awareness of himself – his body, his feelings, his environment;
- learns to take ownership of his experiences, rather than projecting them onto others;
- learns to be aware of his needs and to develop skills to satisfy himself without violating others;
- moves towards a fuller contact with his sensations, to savour all aspects of himself;
- moves towards the experience of his power and the ability to support himself;
- becomes sensitive to his surroundings, yet protected within situations which are potentially destructive or poisonous;
- learns to take responsibility for his actions and their consequences;
- feels comfortable with the awareness of his fantasy life and its expression.

Naranjo (1970) gives a list of healthy injunctions regarding desirable ways of experiencing, including:

- Live in the 'now';
- Live in the 'here' in the immediate situation;
- Accept yourselves as you are;
- See your environment and interact with it as it is, not as you wish it to be;
- Be honest with yourselves;
- Express yourselves in terms of what you want, think, feel, rather than manipulate self and others through rationalisations, expectations, judgements and distortions;

- Experience fully the complete range of emotions, the unpleasant as well as pleasant;
- Accept no external demands that go contrary to your best knowledge of yourself;
- Be willing to experiment, to encounter new situations;
- Be open to change and growth.

We would also add that in the therapy or coaching relationship a person has the opportunity to develop the capacity to hold the tension between being inseparably interconnected with the wider world and at the same time sufficiently autonomous to take responsibility for him or herself.

All the above aspects of health are ideals. In this sense, health is a process of development towards these ideals – a continuing process, not just throughout therapy or coaching but throughout life. As in life, self-development is usually a cyclical or spiralling rather than a linear process, coming back to the same issues perhaps, but at a different level or angle such that our experience is deeper and our contact with the world more choiceful. This, we hope, increases the likelihood of ongoing healthy relationships with self, others and the wider environment.

'Unhealthy' Relational Contact

In using the term 'unhealthy' we are not seeking to disapprove of the quality of individuals' relational contact. We all adapt or creatively adjust our contact, to create a way of interacting with our environment that served us well historically, even though it may not now meet our needs. In other words, we all have disturbances of one form or another which may block our achievement of these ideals of healthy relationships. Gestalt practice directly addresses these disturbances as we move towards our objective of psychological health. In this section, we consider some of the common patterns which prevent us from living our life to the full.

- We may be over-dependent upon environmental support, becoming passive and undirected, waiting for others to look after us or to tell us what to do. Alternatively, we may live in an over-independent way, rebelling against the demands of others or refusing to participate in the 'give-and-take' of relationships.
- We may limit our range of experiences by suppressing our sensations, feelings or thoughts so that we are out of contact with our real selves.
- We may disown parts of ourselves by clinging to a specific self-image. A useful concept here is the yin and the yang: two opposite types of energy, the two sides to each situation or state of being. Gestalt describes this concept as 'polarities'. Every quality has its opposite quality. Sometimes, however, we are attached to the idea of ourselves as being a particular way, for example, calm, kind or gentle. We are unwilling to 'own' the inevitable 'other side of the coin' which may be boisterous, selfish or rough. Polster and Polster (1974) stated that individuals are a never-ending sequence of polarities. It is the therapist's task to support the client making contact with both polarities in a flexible way.
- We may be either stuck at one end of a polarity or constantly swinging to extremes without the subtler, flexible gradations of experience in between. Thus we miss

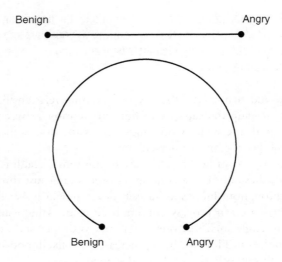

Benign   Angry

Benign   Angry

Figure 3.1 Polarities

the 'point of creative indifference' (Friedlander, 1918): the mid-point between the polarities when we approach the world without investment or prejudice, open to any experience and any possibility. Figure 3.1 depicts polarities first as a line with opposite extremes and secondly as a circle with the two polarities very near each other. The latter illustrates the phenomenon of the violent switch from one polarity to another when suddenly they do not seem far apart (as in the benign person who perhaps rarely gets angry but becomes immediately aggressive when he does).

- We may be acting from habit, unaware of the options we have in any given situation. We react to the world from fixed patterns based on expectations formed in past experiences. Our relationships, instead of being grounded in the honest exchange of thoughts, feelings and wants, are distorted by prejudices, hopes and old beliefs.
- We may be 'acting out' our lives rather than living them, spending energy outside the here and now, dwelling on, or even living psychologically in the past or the future. At any given moment we may be concentrating, not on what is happening to us in the present, but on memories of what has passed or on concerns for what may be going to happen. Or we may be saying, 'I wish I knew what Jim is doing now,' focusing on the 'there', rather than on our own surroundings, the 'here'. We may reject who we are and strive constantly to be somebody else. We may cling to the familiar and smother our natural drive for growth.

In the relational branch of the Gestalt approach, greater emphasis is placed upon the interconnectedness of individuals with their surroundings, including awareness of the environment and responsibility within that context (see Afterword). If we do not attend to these things, we are not in good contact with ourselves, others or the environment. An unhealthy relational dynamic becomes a fixed gestalt where the present becomes a misty place devoid of clear figures and the excitement of the moment.

In summary, health is the natural state to which we are born. Consider a healthy young child: aware, lively, flexible, creative, adaptable, responsible, relational. Unhealthy contact is any interruption, disturbance or rigidity in these qualities. We will now introduce the concept of dialogue as an attitude we can hold in our connection with others that supports the development of healthy and full contact.

Dialogue: A Person-to-Person Meeting

Sustained dialogue is a characteristic of intimate interactions between people where we truly experience the other in all their sameness and difference to us. According to the existentialist philosopher, Martin Buber (1965a), dialogue between person and person manifests in relationship with the potential for healing and growth. In the dialogue both parties are changed in the between-ness of the encounter, which is greater than sum of the individuals.

In Gestalt, the quality of the between-ness that is experienced in the relationship between client and practitioner is defined by what Buber called 'I–Thou' and 'I–It' dimensions of relating. These are two primary attitudes a person can assume in relation to other individuals, their environment and the world.

In describing the I–Thou attitude of relating, Buber (1965a) struggled to identify what it was that caused people to grow and become the finest they could be. He decided (as others, such as Carl Rogers, have done) that the development of 'person-hood' could only come out of an authentic meeting between two people who encounter each other as openly and non-defensively as they can, in the full awareness both of their individual separateness and of their connection. The I–Thou relationship is a genuine meeting of person to person and a '... stance of genuinely being interested in the person we're interacting with as a *person*' (Hycner, 1991: 6; emphasis in original).

Buber also talked about another form of relationship, which he referred to as I–It relating. In this form of relating, we approach the people and things as if they were objects or functions whose existence is for us to affect, control or manipulate. (Equally, we may feel as if 'It' affects, controls, or manipulates us.) In ordinary living we must, of course, often relate to the world in this way in order to focus on our own needs, wants or plans. Hycner informs us that 'an I–It stance is a *necessary* aspect of human living' (1991: 6; emphasis in original). A frequent example is when we assume what a person is like (for example, from the way they look) and relate to them as if they were our image of them. This may be a correct image based on good observation or intuition, or it may be purely based on the fact that we expect the person to treat us in the way someone else has treated us – for instance our parents, teachers, or friends. This is what is called transference, because we 'transfer' our experiences from the past into the present. In either case, it is I–It relating because it is based on our expectations rather than the here-and-now experience of the person.

We are very likely to adopt an I–It stance when the other person is in a particular role in relation to us, and we focus on the role instead of the person. For example, a social work manager, Sally, is reviewing cases. She phones Sophia, one of the team, to clarify some details. This is done with courtesy, efficiency and with a real clarity on the outcomes required. Here Sally is in an I–It mode of relating to carefully complete an important task. Later, Sophia sees Sally for supervision of a particularly challenging and sensitive client case. Sally is open, empathetic and able to fully immerse herself in the case and Sophia's experience as if it was her very own. Sophia feels seen, heard and understood. At this point, she no longer experiences Sally as her manager, but as a person who is deeply interested in her and her whole experience. The relationship has become I–Thou. There is a qualitative difference in the encounter.

Our sense of self as a person emerges from our context, which includes the quality of our relational encounters. A life lived without the meeting of person to person would be sterile and, according to Buber, could not truly give us a sense of our real selves. Jacobs says: 'The I–It mode is vitally necessary for living, the I–Thou for the realisation of personhood' (1989: 26), and quotes Buber as saying: 'Without It a human being cannot live but whoever lives with only that is not human.' We all need to spend much of our time in the I–It mode of relating to organise our lives. In describing the therapeutic relationship, Jacobs uses the term 'dialogic process' to refer to the essential movement between the two modes of relating. The therapeutic relationship offers a special opportunity to engage with another human being in the I–Thou relationship in order to become our fullest selves. But it is worth noting that the I–Thou mode is a position we can hold – not something we can create.

Clearly, the therapy situation is a very particular form of meeting. Though the personal growth of both therapist and client is possible, we must be aware that our clients are not there for *our* growth. We are both there with an agreed focus: the growth and development of the client. Our satisfaction must come from commitment to this task. In this sense, therefore, there is not mutuality within the relationship. Here is an interesting paradox. We have said that, in terms of intention, there is not mutuality. This means that in the wider context of the therapy or coaching situation, the relationship must be I–It. But this does not prevent a very real meeting from taking place. Within the therapeutic relationship, the practitioner holds a continuum between I–It and I–Thou. It is our task to approach clients with an I–Thou *attitude* or *intention*. We believe also that the client's growth involves developing the capacity for a fully mutual relationship.

Clients coming into therapy or coaching are unlikely to engage in an I–Thou relationship immediately. Indeed, most who come to see a therapist will do so at a time of difficulty or distress; they will see their therapist perhaps as a potential problem solver, or even a 'magician' who will make them feel better. Some may rarely have had the experience of being fully aware of themselves in the present moment. Even those who have frequently had such experiences are likely to approach the therapist or coach at first from an I–It position. This is only natural and applies also to the practitioner. Before meeting, both will have created images, fantasies and expectations regarding each other based on past experiences. Importantly, the practitioner will bracket (see Chapter 9) these preconceptions, referring to them only in the service of understanding the client. As soon as they meet, she will make herself available to engage with the client in an I–Thou attitude. It is a practitioner's task at this point to facilitate the client in developing his here-and-now awareness. The client, naturally, will take time to adjust to the new setting and the new situation, gradually moving from an I–It relationship to more frequent moments of I–Thou dialogue. This may happen in the first session, but some clients will take longer – weeks, or for therapy clients, even months or years.

To reiterate, we are not suggesting that the practitioner will never use an I–It way of relating to her client. On the contrary, in our roles we will use the I–It mode much of the time. To be constantly in I–Thou mode would not only be impossible but would mean that we never *thought* about our clients within sessions (reflective self-supervision) or outside the sessions (external supervision). Both of which are I–It.

It is our responsibility to use our professional knowledge and experience within these relational encounters with clients as well as outside them. For instance, in a therapy session, the client says he feels dreadfully depressed and cannot sleep, the therapist may be aware of a moment of anxiety and particular concern. A 'priority' figure emerges: 'Could this client be so severely depressed as to need medical help; could he even be a danger to himself?' It is important to find out what other 'symptoms' there are. The therapist approaches the client with the express strategic plan of clarifying her judgement. For this period, the therapist is inevitably relating in an I–It way, as she is not simply giving herself to the emerging moment, she is steering the conversation.

In Part III of this book, we describe a variety of techniques or ways of thinking about and using Gestalt theory. In order to facilitate their effective use, we have to be relating in an I–It way. However, the therapist's intention is always that these interventions will arise out of having been in real dialogue with the client, and never just 'applied'.

Different Relational Interactions Required for Effective Relationships

role

This fluidity of types of relationship extends to many different kinds of communicating and interacting. Nevis et al. (2003) suggest both strategic (I–It) and intimate (I–Thou) interactions are required. We will illustrate these in the following example.

A chief executive of a national charity is working with her executive team on the five-year strategy that trustees will review. The chief executive has engaged in both individual conversations and group workshops to ensure all voices are represented from each of the organisation's directorates. The intention of this approach was to foster a sense of care for each other and attain a better understanding of what they do, by listening attentively and being genuinely curious about what each person was thinking and feeling. Here, each person, regardless of role, length of service or power, was open to being influenced and influencing. A mutuality of exchange was experienced in their relating and when significant differences emerged there was a commitment to sustained dialogue. Additionally, a stance of creative indifference was taken where people withheld the pull to be invested in any particular outcome and new awareness and insights were attained. This seemed to further enhance the quality of the five-year strategy. These were 'intimate interactions' (Nevis et al., 2003): forms of communication, verbal or non-verbal, that encourage closeness between people, where exchange is spontaneous and mutuality is experienced in the relational encounter with inequality of status or power of role suspended.

Two months into the work, a sense of urgency becomes palpable in the executive team. Cuts in funding have just been announced and membership donations are in decline. The trustees have requested to review the work two weeks early. Decisions are required and time is running out! The chief executive, after some further consultation, decides on a way forward to ensure the strategy document and plan is completed on schedule. In the next executive team meeting, she explains her intentions and then hears from others before clearly articulating the way forward with a decisiveness and firmness in her voice. Some team members who are not fully in agreement choose to remain silent as they acknowledge the importance of an expedient choice and the executive decision-making power and responsibility of the chief executive. These types of interactions where the focus is on the task, where dialogue may be robust, interruptive, abrupt and where unpopular decisions are made are described by Nevis et al. (2003) as 'strategic interactions'.

They advocate that both intimate and strategic interactions seek to maintain connection between all persons involved. It is necessary to recognise that there is a distinction in these interactions; mutuality and empathy are experienced in the intimate interactions; while in the strategic interactions, the attitude is an acknowledgement of authority, or recognition of the role of a person as a function of a particular situation.

Both types of relational interaction are necessary for the development of authentic and genuine relationships that can withstand ruptures and encourage reflective and reflexive learning. The dialogic relationship, a stance where the practitioner moves between I–It and I–Thou modes of relating, is a major factor in the quality of support that is experienced for all persons in the relationship. (See Chapter 10 for further discussion of this issue.)

4

Awareness

Awareness is at the heart of both the theory and practice of Gestalt counselling. Gary Yontef says: 'In Gestalt therapy, *the only goal* is *awareness*' (Yontef and Simkin, 1989: 337; emphasis in original). Awareness is the full recognition of our experience: of what we are feeling, thinking and doing in the present moment and what is happening around us as it is happening. Erving and Miriam Polster (1974: 211) state that awareness is '. . . a continuous process for keeping up to date with one's self' and Yontef describes it as: '. . . a form of experience that may be loosely defined as being in touch with one's own existence, with *what is*' (1993: 144; emphasis in original). Put like this, it sounds obvious and not particularly extraordinary. How can this theoretical concept of something that is ever present and readily accessible to us when needed, be the heart of Gestalt?

In the following pages we will expand upon this deceptively simple concept of awareness and offer the reader an opportunity to recognise how very little we are really aware in our normal day-to-day living and how enriching an increase in awareness can be. But first, let us be clear on what we mean. Awareness means noticing what emerges within us without judgement; it is not the same as introspection. Perls et al. describe introspection as a deliberate turning of attention to what we are doing, feeling and planning '. . . in an evaluating, correcting, controlling, interfering way' which prevents their appearance in awareness (1972 [1951]: 75). Being fully aware of ourselves means knowing ourselves and living our lives in a richer way. It means being in the present, which, by definition, is new every moment. Experiences and perceptions are more vivid and powerful. Interactions which may have become semi-ritualised through habit take on a newness and immediacy. We are in touch with ourselves and the reality of the world around us.

Being aware also includes reclaiming aspects of ourselves which we have lost through disuse (such as intuition, bodily sensations) or repression (such as feelings or thoughts which seemed unacceptable). Often this disowning is an 'unconscious' process, a creative adjustment to meet our needs which may have served us well in the past but, out of awareness, may dull or limit our ability to respond with choice and spontaneity. Therapy or coaching can help people to reverse the disowning. As Erving and Miriam Polster (1974: 236) put it, 'we try to bring into awareness that self which has been "betrayed"'. Today, mindfulness techniques heightening awareness of what a person is sensing, feeling and thinking in the here-and-now, are being offered as a therapeutic intervention for individuals suffering from depression and other problems, with much success.

Perls said that the only way really to experience life is in the present. The past remembered or replayed in the present becomes part of the here-and-now in the retelling or re-enacting of the experience. Therefore, if we become aware of how we operate in the present, including our historical and habituated creative adjustments, we will have the living process in the room, and can take responsibility for what we are doing, become aware of our needs and restore choice to our lives. When our awareness is fully in the present, we have the potential to deal effectively with situations as they occur, rather than according to old habits which may not be meeting our needs.

Perls (1969) identified three zones of awareness. We add a fourth, given our understanding of the healthy Gestalt self-in-relationship. They are inextricably linked and overlap but for the purpose of explaining them clearly we will treat each one separately:

1 *The inner zone:* awareness of the body, bodily sensations of all kinds, proprioceptions and feelings. Polster and Polster (1974) indicate that becoming aware of our bodily sensations supports the emergence of expression and action rather than immediately jumping to what we think we *should* say, feel or do.

2 *The outer zone:* awareness through the five senses and also through talking and moving. Gestaltists call these the 'contact functions' as in order to make contact fully with someone or something we need to look, listen, see, hear, talk, touch, move, taste and smell.

3 *The middle zone:* awareness of fantasies, thoughts and imaginings. This is, of course, part of our inner world, but Perls called it the middle zone to highlight that one of its roles is to mediate between the other zones – making sense of each. The middle zone, therefore, is vitally important to us. It is more highly developed than in any other mammal. It can be enormously creative and inventive. Yet it can be the source of problems. Perls believed that many difficulties were caused by people living too much in the middle zone of remembering, imagining, dreaming and rationalising. Remember that he exhorted us to 'lose our minds and come to our senses', evoking the inner and outer zones. Inviting clients to raise their awareness of these two zones and experience them fully is crucial. However, helping them to become aware of the limitations and distortions of their middle zone and to harness the creativity and ingenuity of that zone is also a significant part of Gestalt practice.

4 *The co-creating zone:* this zone of awareness emerges from the 'between-ness' of one person in contact with another in response to the most important event in the field or situation. It is the zone where new awareness is attained from the relational encounter and the wider context, which both persons bring to the encounter; but it is often held out of awareness. It is the development of awareness of self and other. When people deeply resonate with each other's experience, a new feeling may emerge that belongs not only to one or the other but to *both* the relationship *and* wider relational field. When they share and respond to each other's ideas, new ones are created by the dialectic – the conversation of difference. This may be the zone where shared intimacy, metaphor or insight illuminates a historical event that was previously held out of awareness. Or a private struggle is seen to be connected

to the wider relational context. This zone of awareness highlights our interconnect-edness, our sense of self as constantly changing and being changed in relationship to aspects of the field in comparison to a perspective of self as independent from its environment.

Heightening awareness in these four zones supports us experiencing the fullness and beauty of life, while also holding the potential to transform and heal painful and discomforting experiences.

But enough of *talking* about these zones: we invite you to learn by *experience* as we take you on an exploration of your awareness zones.

Awareness of the Inner Zone

The Physical

Take a few moments to become aware of the position of your body at this moment. Notice which parts of your body are relaxed and which are tense. Notice any involuntary 'micro-movements' and be aware of how they may develop. Notice areas of discomfort of which you had not been aware. Move your shoulders a little and notice how your muscles in this area feel different. Are any other parts of your body affected by the movement? Stretch an arm or a leg and again notice the changes in your bodily sensations.

Find a comfortable place where you can sit or lie down and be undisturbed for a few minutes. Close your eyes and concentrate on your breathing and the rise and fall of your chest and stomach as they expand to fill with air. Now slowly exhale. Breathe deeply and slowly a few times and then be aware of settling into a rhythm of breathing that is comfortable for you. Then focus your awareness on your right foot; be aware of its shape and solidity. As you breathe in, tense the muscles in your toes and foot, then, as you breathe out, let your muscles relax and let the tension flow out. Become aware of your right calf. Again, tighten the muscles in it as you breathe in and relax them as you breathe out. Do the same for your knee, your thigh and your buttock. Do the same for your other leg. Then continue the process slowly around your body – your back, genitals, stomach, chest, shoulders, arms, hands, neck, face and head. Now see if you can become aware of your heart beating and your digestive organs working. Focus again on your breathing and stay aware of your whole body. If you become aware of passing thoughts or external distractions, simply notice them and let them go. Continue to sit or lie in that state of relaxed awareness for a few minutes.

Feelings and Emotions

You may already have become aware of your emotions during the last exercise as they are intrinsically bound up in your body. Often people report having different feelings in different parts of their bodies. Some people who are not accustomed to recognising their feelings and emotions also, not surprisingly, have difficulty in rec-ognising the bodily sensations to which they are connected. They may need help in naming feelings that they have and using them as a signal to themselves about their experience.

How are you feeling now? Notice what you do in order to find out what you are feeling, how you turn your awareness to yourself, what you use as indicators. You may not be feeling a strong feeling, but you will be feeling something, some version or combination of the basic feelings of happiness, sadness, anger and fear – although you may not use those names. Usually we use words like OK, fed up, excited, bored, homesick, anxious, depressed and so on. There are countless nuances of feeling. For simplicity, we invite you to explore your experience of the basic ones.

Happiness

Remember a time when you felt really happy. Try to recapture that experience in the present. Be aware of how your body feels when you are happy: you may feel tingling energy in your limbs, a lightness in your step, your face may be alert, you may want to smile.

Sadness

Now remember a time of sadness. Do you feel heavy in your chest or stomach or face, a prickling behind your eyes?

Anger

Now remember the last time you were angry. What were you angry about? How do you know when you are angry? Your shoulders, arms and hands may get tense as if you were ready for a fight. You may feel your face get hot, your jaw tense and teeth clench.

Fear

Think of something of which you are frightened. Where do you feel fear? Often people feel it as a leaden tension in the stomach, somewhat nauseous, or a fluttering in the chest. You may feel short of breath and you may be aware of the blood draining from your face. Your eyes may widen.

Anxiety

Think of a time when you were anxious about something. What were you anxious about? What did you notice in your body? Sometimes, people notice their palms become sweaty, or experience a feeling of slight breathlessness or restlessness where it may be difficult to remain still. Notice whether your anxiety is a natural part of living — what Koestenbaum and Block (2001: 124–5) call existential anxiety; an aspect of healthy functioning that 'reveals our truth of what it means to be human'. Or is it 'neurotic anxiety', an avoidance of that existential truth, resulting in unhealthy contact? Or an 'anxiety about anxiety', which interrupts our contact with full experience — usually by replaying unhelpful thoughts to ourselves.

Many of our strong feelings, when part of a here-and-now experience, are often noisy and wet. We shout, cry, scream or laugh. We express them naturally and they finish quite soon. In a continuing situation like bereavement, the feelings finish after they are expressed but come again, in waves. Sometimes, however, we get into a feeling 'habit' where we may repeatedly repress our feeling or express a tired, familiar feeling rather than respond freshly to an experience. In Chapter 6 we address these habituated responses in more detail as 'fixed gestalts'.

Now imagine that you are stuck in a traffic jam on your way to the station. Your train leaves in 20 minutes and you are crawling along at a snail's pace. What are you feeling? Where in your body? Is this a familiar feeling for you at times of difficulty or stress? One of your 'feeling habits'?

Aroused Curiosity

We believe that curiosity is a drive with which we are born. The neuroscientist Panksepp (1998) includes 'seeking' as one of the seven genetically ingrained emotional circuits, and his description of seeking can be seen as akin to curiosity. We have only to watch the activities of a baby to see how innate is the desire to reach out, to explore the world and how each new discovery is greeted with wonder. It is curiosity that stimulates the infant to learn to crawl as they spot an attractive new object and mobilise themselves to go towards it.

When did you last feel curious about something? What bodily sensations went with that curiosity? Try and re-experience them now. Do you feel an arousal of excitement in your chest or your stomach, energy in your limbs, quickening breath and heartbeat?

Awareness of the Middle Zone

In this area of our inner world are words and images as well as fully formed thoughts. Again, take a few minutes to sit comfortably. Close your eyes if you wish. Let yourself be aware of any thoughts, memories or fantasies that you have. Try not to get 'attached' to any of them. Simply notice them and let them go. Do not force them or shape them. Do not censor them, or, if you do, just be aware of that too, and move on. Notice how many of your thoughts are memories, or plans for the future, rather than fresh awareness in the here and now. These are part of, and necessary to, our everyday living but we can sometimes be astonished at how little of our thinking is truly a response to the present moment.

Like feelings, sometimes our thoughts become habituated. Creative adjustments that once served us well become hindrances to awareness of our current reality. Are you aware of recurring themes in your thoughts? Return to the fantasy about being stuck in the traffic jam. Along with your feelings, are you aware of any associated thoughts or images, such as: 'I'm so stupid, I should have left earlier,' or, 'Why does this always happen to me?' or, 'I can just imagine my boss's face'? Are any of these responses familiar in times of difficulty? If so, they may be part of the habitual responses or fixed gestalts that we mentioned earlier.

Awareness of the Outer Zone

We are asking you to do the following seven activities as you sit where you are now. However, we invite you to do them regularly in a variety of situations and to notice how your experience of the present moment changes when you do this. You could do the exercises with a friend and compare your experiences – noticing what you have noticed.

Seeing

Look up from this book. What do you see? Notice the shapes of the things or people around you. Notice their colour and size, their distance and closeness, whether their outlines and details are clear or indistinct. If you are in a room, look at the corners. What do you see? Now look at your hands. Really study the shape, the lines, any hairs, scars, freckles or veins. We often talk of knowing something 'like the back of our hands' but are you sure that you would be able to recognise your hand amongst a lot of other hands?!

Listening

Close your eyes. Pay attention to what you hear. Notice differences in pitch, volume, tone, proximity and intensity. Can you hear the sound of your breathing? You will notice that there are many sounds of which you were not previously aware or which you had incorporated into the background. If we let ourselves be aware of all the noises in our life, it would be difficult to concentrate on anything else.

Touching

Move around your environment, touching and feeling the different objects there. Notice whether they are hot or cold, rough or smooth, angular or rounded. With your eyes closed, pick up an object and feel it all over. Do this as if you are exploring it for the first time. Notice how much information you get from your fingers.

Now explore your left hand with your right hand and be aware of the sensations in both.

Now notice the places where your body meets the environment. Feel the pressure of the chair under you, and your feet on the floor. Notice if there are any draughts or wind and the way your skin feels.

Tasting

Find something edible and small like a raisin, a piece of cheese or bread. Sit down and close your eyes. Put the morsel in your mouth and very slowly begin to eat it. Notice how your salivary glands begin to work and how the texture of the food changes in your mouth. Is it crunchy and rough or smooth and slippery? Notice whether you prefer to chew or to suck and pay minute attention as your taste buds respond. Is the food bitter or sweet, salty or bland? Does the taste change in any way? Let yourself be aware if you feel the urge to swallow quickly and resist it for a few moments. Then swallow and feel the food as it goes down your throat into your stomach.

Probably, like us, you usually eat with much of your awareness involved elsewhere. By paying attention to what you put into your body in this way, you can transform your eating experience.

Smelling

Move around your environment, picking things up and smelling them. You may be surprised how many things have a smell. Smell a jar of coffee, an orange, a loaf of bread, different plants. Be aware whether the smells are sharp and pungent or sweet and perfumed, stale and musty or fresh and clear. Lick the back of your hand and then smell it. Notice the scent of your own skin.

Talking

Experiment with finding seven different ways to say: 'I have a suggestion for you.' Try varying the pitch, the tone, the intonation of your voice; try whispering; try project-ing from your belly to the back of the proverbial lecture hall.

Moving

This time imagine that you have a client sitting opposite you and find several different ways of conveying a message to the client by the way you are sitting. Use body posture, position, angle, muscle tone, facial expression and so on.

Finally, allow yourself to be aware of *all* your senses. There are no rules and there is no 'right' way of doing this. Simply be aware of the sights, sounds, textures, smells, tastes and motions you are experiencing at this moment. Allow your awareness to flow between your senses.

Practice with a Partner

With a partner, start by observing each other and take it in turns to speak. State what you see without interpretation: 'I am aware of the collar of your jacket as it curves over your neck. I am aware of your eyes as you look at me and I notice how blue they are. Now I am noticing you smiling and looking away from me. I am aware of the little lines at the side of your mouth and now I am noticing how your body is curled in the chair,' and so on. Then focus on what your partner is saying: 'I am aware of you speaking quite fast. I am aware of you noticing more about my face than my body. I am aware of you noticing colours and I am now aware that your voice is soft,' and so on. You may find this exercise surprisingly intimate and yet all you are doing is bringing to your awareness, and verbalising, some of the many things we may usually take for granted. Explore each other's hands by touch, and be aware of yourself as giver and receiver.

Awareness of the Co-creating Zone

Again, we invite you to do this with someone you know. Sitting across from each other, have a conversation about an issue that is still somewhat unresolved, yet important to one of you. As you converse notice what is happening for you at the other three zones as you are interacting with each other. What happens to the other person when you make an intervention, and then what happens to you in response. Are there recurring feelings, thoughts or bodily responses that seem unique to this encounter? After 15 minutes, pause and share your experiences of any metaphors, bodily movements, sounds, words, phrases, or even snatches of song that seemed particular to this encounter. Resume and repeat and see if anything else emerges. For example, in a therapy session with Paulo, the therapist was aware of a recurring metaphor of a veil, and she felt a strong desire to move from her chair, make herself small and hide. Once she was as confident as she could be that her feelings belonged to their relationship and not her unfinished business, she shared these with him. It deeply resonated with him as he also was starting to slightly pull away his chair. The veil reminded him of a time when he was eight, when he would hide in case he would be 'discovered' when guests arrived at his parents' house. This seemed related for him to his current struggle to come out as gay at work as he feared rejection. In this zone it is important to be aware of and sensitive to the quality of the relationship and the context before expressing what we are aware of.

Practice Combining the Zones

This exercise can enhance the natural flow of your moment-by-moment awareness. Find a comfortable place to sit and let yourself monitor the focus of your awareness as it changes and shifts. Use the introduction, 'Now I am aware . . .' to describe your experience. Again, there is no right or wrong way of doing this exercise: your experience is your experience. Simply notice whatever you are aware of, including your distractions, and move on without criticism or judgement of yourself. For example, 'Now I am aware of a wisp of cloud above a tree-top. Now I am aware of wondering if it is going to rain. Now I am aware of remembering the washing hanging on the line. Now I am aware of my teeth pressing together. Now I am aware that I am cold. Now I am aware of feeling amused at doing this exercise,' and so on.

Notice which types of awareness are most strong or frequent for you. Do you spend more time in your inner zone, your middle or your outer zone? Which of your senses do you use most? Is your inner awareness of bodily sensations, thoughts or feelings? Again, you may notice that it is quite hard to stay fully aware in the present moment. You may follow some train of thought and forget to be aware for some time. If so, just notice when you become aware again and move on. Similarly, you may find yourself unaccountably wanting to stop the exercise or censor some of your awareness. Just notice this also – 'I am aware of avoiding something' and stay with your experience.

Here is an exercise in structuring your awareness. Start with noticing something in your outer zone, then move to the inner or middle zone for your next awareness. Use the format, 'I see/hear/smell/etc. and I feel [this may be a sensation or emotion] . . . and I think'. For example, 'I see the poster for the concert and I feel excited and I think I will take a friend to the concert' or 'I hear a clinking in the street and I think that it is probably the milkman . . . I think about breakfast and I feel hungry.'

Now do this exercise with a partner. For instance, 'I see you raise your eyebrows and I think you are expecting something from me and I feel anxious as I think I don't know what you want . . . I notice you are leaning forward now and I feel warm towards you and I think you like me . . . I hear you laugh and I feel happy and I think I am enjoying doing this exercise with you.' Be aware of how you make meaning of your experiences. This is the work of the middle zone. In discussing the exercise afterwards with your partner, notice if any metaphors arose, or sensations were stirred in you as you interacted with each other that may resonate with the wider relational, cultural or environmental field, historic or present. This is the zone of co-created awareness. You also may discover that you have a propensity to notice particular things and that there are certain themes to your meaning-making. In Part III of this book, we will look at ways in which awareness of this kind can be helpful to your clients.

Our last exercise focuses on another important element of awareness: those things of which we choose to remain unaware. Again, do this exercise by yourself and then with a friend. Become aware of your experiences as before, but this time say, 'I am aware of . . . and what I left out was . . .'. You may even experiment with saying, 'I am aware that I am avoiding noticing . . .'. You may be surprised at what you notice now that you have brought other elements into your awareness.

Heightening Awareness to Facilitate Change

As Gestalt practitioners, we endeavour to connect with our clients in a dialogic process moving between both I–It and I–Thou modes of relating. Within the co-created relationship we aim to heighten clients' awareness. Concomitantly, we heighten our own awareness of how we configure ourselves in relationship to each unique client and each particular situation. However, our primary focus is in supporting our clients' development of an autonomous awareness that will facilitate change.

Clients often arrive feeling stuck and unable to change. In Gestalt, uniquely, we facilitate the development of clients' awareness, trusting the organismic self-regulation of individuals to change. This is the paradoxical theory of change (Beisser, 1970) that supports us to work with clients being or becoming aware. Beisser says that people change when they embrace who they truly are, not when they try to become who they believe they 'should' be. He asserts: 'change does not take place through a coercive attempt by the individual or by another person to change him, but it does take place if one takes the time and effort to be what he is – to be fully invested in his current positions' (1970: 77). This theory of change is applicable to groups and communities as well as to individuals. Too often, our desire to change is based on doing something differently and what that would look like. For example: I want to be more assertive in a meeting and I decide that I need to speak up more, or I want to become fitter and I will go to the gym three times a week. They are good intentions, but often we fail to realise these and then may feel disappointed.

If we have a desire to change then using the paradoxical theory of change we first need to be genuinely curious and inquire into our current experience fully. We need to befriend aspects of ourselves that hitherto may have been kept out of awareness or disowned, often for the best of reasons. It is by heightening our experience of what *is*, and bringing all these aspects of ourselves into full awareness that change can occur, even though this may be uncomfortable. Yontef says awareness is a 'form of experiencing. It is the process of being in vigilant contact with the most important events in the individual/environmental field, with full sensory-motor, emotional, cognitive and energetic support' (1993: 179).

Being able to move seamlessly between modes of directed and undirected awareness (Nevis, 1987) may support this process. Directed awareness is the intentional exploration of a particular aspect of experience that is figural. Undirected awareness is the process of being fully available to the here-and-now without any predetermined outcome in mind, noticing phenomena as they emerge through all four zones of awareness. In effect it is the individual sensing into the field of which they are part and in which they are interconnected (see Chapter 7). Both of these modes, as in our previous exercises, focus on heightening awareness, not on guiding or having an intention to change a person.

In summary, the paradoxical theory of change supports us in heightening our clients' awareness, which can facilitate change that is sustaining and integrated. We do this from a stance of trusting our clients' innate ability for growth, which leads to the expression of how to be and what to do with choice and responsibility.

Reflections on Awareness

1 Awareness is *here* – at this place, and *now* – at this time. We can only be aware in the present moment. We may use thoughts and images to dwell upon the past or the future but 'aware' experience can only be in the present.

2 Awareness can be divided into awareness of the external world (the outer zone) and our internal world (the inner zone and the middle zone) and our interconnected world (co-created zone). Awareness of contact between our inner and outer worlds leads to increased knowledge of who and how we are and greater vividness of experience.

3 The flow of awareness is uneven. We move our attention from zone to zone, sometimes in a flow of associations, sometimes in response to sudden distractions and changes in stimuli.

4 Potentially, there are innumerable elements of which we can become aware at any one moment. We may have a general, wide-ranging awareness of several of these elements or we may focus more sharply upon one element. We organise the many stimuli in our world into what in Gestalt are called 'figures', allowing the rest to become 'ground'. Healthy living lies in making 'lively' figures and being aware of the choices we are making in doing so. We will come back to this important concept in subsequent chapters.

5 As we become aware of different elements in our world, we make meaning out of them. It is important to be aware of the meanings we are making in order to widen our options of choice.

We end this chapter with three inspiring quotations:

Awareness is huge. It's like asking, 'What is a person?' 'What is the meaning of life?' (Zinker, 1990)

To work holistically you need to be aware of your own whole person in relationship to clients, paying attention to all your reactions and responses. (Mackewn, 1997: 47)

The aim of life is to live, and to live is to be aware – joyously, drunkenly, serenely, divinely aware. (Henry Miller, cited by Schiller, 1994)

Additional Reading

Kolodny, R. (2004) 'Why awareness works and other insights from spiritual practice', *British Gestalt Journal*, 12 (2): 92–9.

5

Embodiment

In Gestalt, we pay particular attention to awareness of our bodily presence and the physical incorporation and containment of our emotions and thoughts. This is a pillar of the Gestalt view of health, now fully supported by recent neuroscientific findings as a key factor in human growth and transformation (e.g. Siegel, 2010). When embodying experience, our bodies are alive and vibrant in the present moment. We are aware of our internal bodily sensations, physical expressions, gestures and posture, as well as the spontaneous nature of these in our responses to other people and the environment.

In our Western society, body experience is often considered as something separate from the 'self' of the person, as reflected in Descartes' dictum 'Cogito ergo sum' (I think therefore I am), where 'I', as a person, am defined by my intellect, leaving emotions and body aside. Even our education systems teach children 'to live only with cognitive rationality and with the powers of the intellect' (Palmer, 1997: 43), while the body and relationships are rarely attended to. Our language also limits our ability to integrate the body. At best, we are inclined to say 'my body' or 'the body', locating the body as something separate from the self. James Kepner points out that there is no single word to say 'I–Body' (1993: 7). Instead, we tend to describe our body as an object, 'something that happens to me, rather than the "me that is happening"' (ibid.). From a Gestalt perspective, this separation does not fit comfortably with our holistic approach which affirms the whole person and his or her whole context. Leaving our bodies out of our living experience is to dull our senses, dampen our awareness and limit our opportunities for growth and development. Ignoring the way a client holds himself as he walks into the room, and sits at the beginning of a session, is potentially to miss how he is organising the whole of himself in his current situation. For example, Ozlem, Jim's coach, noticed how, uncharacteristically, he hurried into the room and seemed to 'fall into' the chair. He began to speak about the sense he made of the previous session, which did not seem congruent with his body posture. His forehead was tight and his eyes were darting about as if he was scanning the room. He spoke through clenched teeth. Ozlem was also attending to her own bodily experiences as she saw Jim. She noticed her heart racing and one of her feet on tiptoe as if she was ready to move. She invited Jim to notice his breathing and describe what he was experiencing in his body. By doing so, Jim became aware of his tightened jaw and his increasing body temperature, which he connected to his unexpressed anger at the preceding board meeting where he'd had to 'bite his tongue' when some controversial decisions were made about an important project. If Ozlem had ignored Jim's bodily expressions, the session might have been very different and less effective.

In this example, Jim's feelings were clearly associated with a somatic experience. This bodily experience is also our inner zone of awareness (Chapter 4), where our emotional life has a bodily affect. Of course, from a Gestalt holistic perspective, these are accompanied by thoughts (middle zone of awareness) and movement (outer zone of awareness) – each part of a whole reflected in each other.

The emphasis of embodiment is on integrating bodily experiences. Perls' dictum 'lose your mind and come to your senses' was a call for people to inhabit the fullness of the here-and-now embodied experience. A person's body is not an instrument but an integral part of who he or she is. Laura Perls reminded us what is important is to 'be a body' not the 'use of the body' (1992: 210). In some therapeutic approaches, attending to our physical self is seen as *adding* a bodily perspective to help improve the effectiveness of the work. However, in Gestalt, our body process is 'not just an addition to the "real stuff" . . . it is *intrinsic* to everything human' (Kepner, 2003: 11; emphasis in original). Embodiment is the whole person.

Integrating the Body

Strictly speaking, we mean 're-integrating' the body, as from any observation of babies and infants it is clear that they are bodily affective in their very state of being. It is something that as older children and adults we have lost – indeed, that has disintegrated. A person's experience becomes split into the thinking and verbalising 'I', which is given priority over the somatic, non-verbal and affective 'It'. It is rare for a person to greet a friend with the words, 'I feel a tingling on my neck and down my spine, as I am delighting in seeing you now!' The more usual is a gesture, like a handshake or a kiss on each cheek with a 'hello' or 'nice to see you'. With awareness of this splitting, we have opportunities to redress this imbalance and re-own our visceral and somatic experiences as part of the immediacy of our whole lived bodies. After all, we cannot fully live and relate other than as embodied beings.

Conor, a successful call-centre manager, sought therapy as he was 'feeling down' and could not understand why. He was unaware of his bodily experience but Jeff, his therapist, noticing his compressed posture and lowered head, invited Conor over the next few weeks to focus on his bodily self. In one session Conor noticed that he was pressing himself down to become smaller. Jeff invited him to stay with his bodily awareness and pay attention to his feelings. Conor then recalled that as a teenager he was frequently reprimanded by his father for not achieving higher grades at school. He felt pressured and gradually started to withdraw from contact. Up to this moment he had disowned his bodily experiences and feelings of anger towards his father for pressing and pushing him to improve.

It is not uncommon for clients to disown somatic aspects of themselves. They often arrive to therapy and coaching with unfinished business, where the past is present in the here-and-now of their whole embodied experience, preventing them from moving freely into the future. As in the example with Conor, therapists and coaches can support their clients to become more aware of the history that is carried in their lived bodies in the here-and-now. However, it is important when working from an embodied perspective that practitioners are sensitive to the possibility of shame. Developing a trusting working relationship, building support and appropriately pacing the work are critical in a world where the body is sometimes objectified. We believe the practitioner can enable this to happen by sensitively working in an integrated way with the internal somatic sensations, the outer bodily posture and gestures, and the body in movement, of both client and practitioner. In a moment we attempt to elaborate on each of these, aware that, constrained by the structure of our language, we are once again compartmentalising the different aspects of bodily experience.

Internal Somatic Sensations   *Re-awakening senses*

The internal bodily sensations and associated feelings (inner zone of awareness) are part of a person's embodied experience. We are continually experiencing bodily sensations in relationship to one another. Sometimes, a person keeps these sensations out of awareness as they are associated with feelings deemed unacceptable to the person. Inviting clients to pay attention to their bodily sensations and notice what they are feeling can help reawaken awareness.

Therapist and coach are part of the co-created relationship and each will be noticing his or her own bodily sensations and feelings in the here-and-now. Neuroscience, in particular the study of mirror neurons, shows how a person's body resonates with another's. If a client is struggling to pay attention to his internal somatic sensations and associated feelings, the practitioner may heighten awareness by informing the client of his or her own bodily experience. For example, Paul was talking about being bullied in a very matter-of-fact way. Mary, the therapist, told Paul: 'I am aware that I am tightening my chest, my heart is racing and I am sitting on the edge of my chair. I feel scared for you as you tell me this.' Paul then informed Mary how he was always ready to run at a moment's notice as he was constantly fearful of being hurt in the school playground.

Outer Bodily Gestures, Response and Posture

Our verbal relating is usually accompanied with physical gestures. The gesture of one person evokes responses in the other person who then reciprocates with a gesture. Therapists and coaches can see how clients are holding their physical bodies in response to the here-and-now interactions happening in the relationship. Of course, clients also see how a therapist or coach is responding in this co-created process of relating. Paying attention to the smallest of gestures, or a body posture, can open up a joint inquiry within the relationship. Sometimes these physical manifestations are replaying a historical experience or some unfinished business that is given bodily expression in the here-and-now of the relationship. Anna was explaining the details of her family relationships in the session. As she spoke, she flicked her wrist outwards on a couple of occasions. The therapist invited her to repeat the flick of her wrist and notice what she was sensing and feeling in her body. Anna flicked her wrist a few times and noticed that she was feeling restricted, and wanted to push somebody away. She then became angry and tearful as she became aware of a time when an older cousin had made sexually suggestive remarks to her as a teenager and she felt too frightened to tell him to 'go away and leave her alone'.

There are times when we notice that a client's gestures seem to be communicating something different from what they are saying. Here, the practitioner may feel somewhat confused as different feelings and bodily sensations are evoked in her as she listens intently to what her client is saying. Paul was exploring a particular bullying incident in the session. He was grimacing, his forehead furrowed, his eyes narrowed and his face looked pale, yet he spoke in a joking and light-hearted manner. Mary reflected back what she noticed. To heighten awareness, she invited him to pay attention to his internal somatic responses and describe what he was sensing and feeling. When Paul attended to his sensations he realised in that moment with Mary he felt scared. He experienced Mary as powerful with her straight and upright posture. By comparison, he felt small in stature and noticed he was withdrawing his body inwards as if trying to disappear.

In some cases, with well-supported clients, a therapist or coach may ask for permission to 'try on' the body posture of a client (Clemmens, personal communication, 2008; Frank, 2001). This requires a strong working relationship, and the practitioner needs to have a high level of bodily awareness. Once he has agreement, he 'tries on' his client's posture, inviting the client to instruct him so that his posture faithfully reflects that of his client. Then the practitioner sensitively reports back his sensations and feelings from this position. He asks the client to inform him of what he notices and to pay attention to his own internal sensations and feelings. Conor was looking small in his stature, his stomach drawn inwards, his torso concave and his head slightly turned to one side, while his eyes looked wide open and alert. Jim, the therapist, took on this posture and then reported back his somatic experience saying, 'I find it difficult to breathe and I feel small. I feel threatened by you, yet I can see every move you make from here.' Conor started to recognise that his difficulty in being assertive was partly due to the fact that he did not use his breathing to support himself. He then experimented with moving his body to find a way of supporting himself when feeling anxious or threatened.

Body in Movement

Movement of the body is required to change our experience. Extending the repertoire of movement with awareness supports the possibility of greater choice for clients when responding to their current life situation. Words are not always required. In fact, words may only get in the way of developing new awareness and understanding. Kennedy (2005: 111) points out that if a person's intention is to change, 'only the movement of the body can turn that idea into reality'. For example, Joe wants to get fit because he wants a healthier lifestyle and wants to remain well. This will not happen for Joe by thinking alone. His desire requires movement. Joe must get out of bed in the morning and go to the gym or for a run. This is an obvious example, but in fact any change involves movement. Layla had been avoiding contact with her new manager ever since their disastrous first meeting. She was aware that she was treating him the way she had treated her powerful and dominating father. She wanted to somehow face them both about their different needs and different working style but feared a confrontation. In order to change her behaviour, Layla had to move – seek out her manager, look him in the eye and ask him to listen to her concerns. She noticed herself straightening up as she took the risk of meeting him face to face.

In Gestalt therapy and coaching the process of inviting movement emerges out of what occurs in the here-and-now relationship. It is kinaesthetic movement with awareness. The movement is dependent on the client's needs, the presence of the therapist and the current life situation seeking resolution. Kathy was struggling to find words to describe the situation with her boyfriend, and her leg was gently swinging. The therapist invited her to exaggerate the swinging until it became a kick. They explored what it was like both to kick out and to swing her leg gently. The therapist asked her if any of this was related to her experience with her boyfriend. Kathy noted that when her experience was not being listened to, she sat there sulking like a teenager but inside she was furious and wanted to lash out. The work then continued to explore how Kathy could get her needs met in the therapy relationship, as a way of addressing her lover relationship.

In the therapeutic relationship, therapists pay attention to both the client's and their own embodied experience. Many of the patterns of movement people use to organise their experience are established in the early years of life (Frank, 2001). Some have become habituated and this may impede a client's possibility for change. Every movement pattern is a response to the relational environment of the time. It is made part of the whole person but is not necessarily assimilated in a way that produces balance and harmony. In a therapy group, George announced to others that his father had died over the weekend. George sat rigidly and spoke in a flat tone. The therapist was aware that George's posture was in part due to the pain he experienced as an ill child when his parents repeatedly told him that 'boys don't cry' and also that he was a 'strong, brave fellow'. George was 'acceptable' for being self-sufficient and not showing his emotion even though he was at times scared and lonely. The therapist suggested that he explore the other polarity of his embodied experience. He agreed. She invited the group to stretch out their arms and hold the palms of their hands open as offers of support. She asked George to pay attention to his body and invited him to move. To offer support to this new movement the therapist stood alongside George as he slowly ambled around the group. He then moved towards a male member of the group and placed his palm into his. He allowed himself to feel the support of the man's hand. He noticed his body softening, his back becoming more flexible as he allowed himself to feel the support. He also noticed his eyes becoming tearful and full of sadness. This was the first time in his life that George could allow himself to feel the support of others and not feel judged for his softness and emotional expression.

Expressive and creative movement is also a way of heightening embodied awareness of the story of our lives, including past, present and future longings. Expressive movement may involve inviting clients to exaggerate particular body gestures or postures and pay attention to what they are sensing and feeling in their bodies. Also, clients may be invited to move in the room as a way of giving expression to what they experience now and what they hope for in the future. In a coaching session, Tina was struggling to make a decision about a new internal job offer. She felt stuck. Jim, her coach, invited her to choose two places in the room, one place to represent her current role and the other to represent the new role. He then invited her to imagine each of these roles. He subsequently invited her to slowly move to both places in turn and report back what she was experiencing in her body, as well as to verbalise her experience. This facilitated Tina to become aware of energy and excitement for her current job. She discovered meaningfulness and satisfaction in this job and felt comfortable with refusing the offer of the new role. She was also better able to articulate why this was so.

Embodied Whole Includes our Cultural Context

We are all born into a society that in general supports our arrival and holds hopes for our future. From the moment of birth (and some believe in our mother's womb), we exist as living bodies in relationship to other living bodies within a socio-cultural context. Both cultural history and social structures influence bodily phenomena (Clemmens and Bursztyn, 2005). Typical physical gestures, movements and sensations are part of our culture, and are embodied in different ways for people of different ethnicities, genders and sexualities. These are often assimilated into our living bodies out of awareness. It is important that the therapist or coach fosters the conditions necessary for cultural embodied experience to be brought into awareness. This is particularly necessary for our 'disembodied cultures', where the body is often dis-owned and not seen as an intrinsic part of our living body experiences.

Eros is an aspect of our embodied experience that is also culturally bound and frequently misunderstood. In much of our Western culture the erotic tends to be associated with sexual feelings and behaviour. However Eros is something more than that. It also includes a person's capacity for loving engagement, care and desire. In this sense, Eros is present as part of the relational encounter and, from a Gestalt perspective, it may be experienced as liveliness, energy and excitement in our bodies when we are with a friend, or a person we are attracted to in some way. When there is a physical attraction between people it may also be experienced in erogenous zones. Sometimes people's sexuality and sexual feelings are disowned and in such instances, our disem-bodied culture, which includes family and society, does not provide a sufficiently supportive environment to allow for the healthy integration and appropriate expres-sion of the associated sensations and feelings.

For some clients, Eros is an aspect of their experience that needs to be reawakened. In others, the work involves discovering how to unravel ways of relating that have become inappropriately sexualised. For instance, Tim informed his therapist that he invariably had sexual feelings towards adults of both sexes with whom he had expe-rienced relational closeness and intimacy. As a teenager he had been sexually abused by a close friend of his parents. When he tried to stop the abuse he was cruelly manip-ulated and blamed. It seemed that Tim's habitual response of sexualising relationships was a way for him not to feel rejected and repulsed. The boundaries between intimacy, affection and sexual desire were not discriminated. As another example, Ann, a lesbian, presented in counselling with little bodily awareness. She grew up in a conservative family and community. Her family rejected her when she 'came out'. As a teenager living in a homophobic and sexist environment she never experienced support for her same-sex desires and love. Her creative adjustment was to hide her feelings and disown aspects of her bodily desires and feelings, as these were labelled disordered and abnormal. As well as addressing the emotional impacts of her experience, the counselling work involved heightening her bodily awareness in ways that were not experienced as threatening or potentially shaming.

In conclusion, we again emphasise the need for sensitivity to the possibility of shame. Given our disembodied cultures, heightening bodily awareness may make our clients feel very 'visible' in an unfamiliar and uncomfortable way. Wheeler (1996) asserts that it is impossible to work intimately with clients' longings, fears and losses without both provoking and feeling shame. Kepner's view is that shaming feelings '. . . must at least be noticed and articulated so they become part of the spoken context rather than the unspeakable ground' (1996: 42). Hence, therapists and coaches sensitively working with integrating the body can support clients to understand their creative adjustment process and help them attain a greater holistic awareness of their 'way of being' in the world.

Later, in Part III of this book, we offer some methods of Gestalt practice that support the reawakening of our whole living experience which includes our bodily presence, as well as our emotions, and thoughts.

Additional Reading

Cornell, W. (2003) 'The impassioned body: erotic vitality and disturbance in psychotherapy', *British Gestalt Journal*, 12 (2): 97–104.
Frank, R. and La Barre, F. (2011) *The First Year and the Rest of Your Life: Movement, Development and Psychotherapeutic Change*. New York: Taylor & Francis Group.

6

Wholeness: The Formation and Completion of Gestalts

Wholeness

As we said in Chapter 1, the word 'gestalt' comes from the German and translates as 'an organised whole', and the whole precedes the parts. It means that the wholeness of something – an object, an idea, a situation or a person – is not only more than the sum of its parts but also different from those parts.

As you are reading this book, you are forming gestalts or wholes. Each word is made up of letters but, unless you are just learning to read or are unfamiliar with a particular word, you will not be sounding out each letter but allowing your eyes to take in each word as a whole. It is the whole from which we make meaning. The parts, the individual letters, represent only single sounds. For example, the letters S, N, O, W taken by themselves are written symbols of particular sounds and have no meaning for us beyond that. However, if we see them together in this order *as a whole*, they instantly have meaning for us. Change the order to OWNS, and, though the parts remain the same, a new whole is formed and a totally different meaning is derived from the change in their organisation. The same is true of phrases or sentences. The parts, now the individual words, are again less than and different from the meaning of the sentence. If words are added, deleted or merely reorganised, the meaning of the whole phrase or sentence is changed. 'The snow was falling onto the house' is very different from 'the house was falling onto the snow.'

But there is a wider context, a greater whole, in the process of reading and understanding words. We may form the letters S, N, O, W into the word SNOW but, without some knowledge or experience of what snow is, we are left with a collection of sounds. We need some prior experience of a particular sound and a symbolic connection that we can make in order to make the word meaningful. If we are solely English-speaking, the French words *la neige* will have no meaning for us unless we can translate the words into our own language and have a general knowledge or experience of snow. Our understanding of the words, the whole, is dependent upon our experience.

One person's experience may be very different from another's so we cannot assume, even with words, that we are making the same meaning. Someone from the tropics whose knowledge of snow has been gained purely through descriptions and photographs will have a very different perception of snow to somebody from Alaska.

The importance of wholeness to the therapist and coach is wide. First, it has an impact on the way we approach the client. We see them 'holistically' as a complete person: body, mind and soul. We do not just look at one problematical aspect of them. We also see them within their context as a whole, taking into account the cultural and socioeconomic circumstances in which they live, and significant events which are affecting their lives. For instance, a woman comes to see a therapist because she is depressed. The therapist does not simply think, 'Here is a person who is depressing her emotions.' The whole picture is explored. Has the woman been depressed before; is it a common feeling for her? Has she recently suffered a bereavement or other major change? Has she had a baby? How is her physical health? How is her social network? And so on.

The second significant impact of wholeness is on the way we use the concept in the here-and-now meeting with the client. The way they constellate their world – the 'wholes' of meaning that they make, the gestalts they see and create in their lives – is *who they are*. The therapist's aim is to create a relationship with the client (to co-create a gestalt) in which they can become aware of how they constellate their world.

Figure and Ground

While you are reading this book, you are paying visual attention to the words on the page as well as making meaning of those words. Peripherally, you may visually perceive what is below, above and to the sides of the book: maybe the colour and pattern of your clothes below, the surface of a table to the sides and the sunlight from a window over the top of the book, depending upon the environmental context of your reading. The book is figure, the room and objects within it are ground. Momentarily, you may look up as someone passes by the window and your constellation of figure and ground changes. The person becomes figure and the book joins the other aspects in becoming ground.

Take a look at the picture in Figure 6.1. Did you see a Madonna and Child? Half close your eyes and look again at the area where the mother's left hand comes round the child's body. You may see a face which is much less appealing. You will notice that, when you see the ugly head, you cannot see the hand and the fold of cloth. The rest of the picture becomes ground. If you focus again on the mother and child, the picture resumes its beauty.

Similarly, Perls, Hefferline and Goodman (1972 [1951]), drawing upon the work of the Gestalt psychologists mentioned earlier, used a now well-known diagram (Figure 6.2) to illustrate the same point. If you see the black parts as the ground and the white as figure, you will perceive a white chalice. If you see the white part as ground and the black as figure, you will perceive the silhouettes of two faces in profile facing each other. Although it is possible to shift your attention very quickly from one

Figure 6.1   Madonna and Child

(*Source*: Nap. Thomas d'après Murillo, Imp. Par Becquet frères à Paris, Publiè par Giovanni Barducci, Florence)

to the other, you cannot see both simultaneously. As soon as you make one figure, the other becomes ground. But notice too that the figure and the ground are mutually dependent. You cannot see the chalice without the ground of the faces and vice versa. Both are necessary in order to perceive the figure within the ground. Here we can see that sense-making resides in the relation of the figure to its ground, just as we see in the interconnectedness between the chalice and the faces. Thus, as we will go on to discuss later under field theory, everything has importance and relevance: there is a connectedness within the whole.

Gestaltists use the concept of figure and ground to explain the process by which human beings organise their perceptions to form wholes in order to create meaning. As with the picture of the faces and the chalice, we cannot see the totality of ourselves and our environment simultaneously. Some things become figure, while others remain ground, depending upon our needs at the time. The figure is formed through a process of organising our perceptual and experiential context to meet a need that is important

Figure 6.2 'Visuell wahrgennommene figuren' by Edgar Rubin, Gyldendalske Boghandel, Copenhagen, 1921

for us to resolve, make complete and whole. The ground is mostly what is out of our awareness. Joel Latner (2000) describes the ground as those parts of ourselves and environment that are not in the present figure of interest which is calling for attention.

This can be illustrated with the simple example of post-boxes. In going about our everyday business, we do not usually notice post-boxes, but if we urgently need to post a letter, we start to search for one. For this short time, a post-box becomes figure against the ground of everything else. Once the letter is posted, post-boxes again recede into the ground of our perception.

We will expand upon connectedness in Chapter 7, but for the time being, as it is so intrinsic to figure and ground, this is a good place to continue using the post-box example. We can see that our need to send a letter must be connected to our knowledge and experience that letters are put into post-boxes, that post-boxes are found in certain places, that for the most part they are a certain shape and a certain colour. Hence, perhaps, our hesitation to post a letter in foreign countries, when faced with a square, yellow construction with only a letter-shaped hole to give some reassurance! The letter will need a stamp of a particular value and will be addressed to the person to whom we are sending it. All of this may seem pretty obvious to us: we have absorbed all the interconnected aspects of posting a letter into the ground of our awareness, so we need not bring them all fully into figure. Yet they are intrinsically part of the whole, leading towards the completion of that whole by the posting of the letter.

This process of figure formation and destruction will be further explored in the cycle of experience to follow. A healthy process of living is defined by our ability to form clear vibrant figures, appropriately use resources available to us to meet the need, and then re-assimilate as part of the ground upon completion. Latner (2000) suggests that it is a process of play and experiment. The figure calls for attention but without a predetermined outcome.

Completion

Not only do we have a natural tendency to see wholes, we also have an 'urge to complete'. We seek to make wholes and, therefore, meaning out of parts. Writing and reading are clearly skills which have to be learnt but they draw upon this natural human tendency towards completion. Even a child learning to read (unless they have some perceptual learning difficulties) will quite soon begin to constellate individual letters into words and make meaning of them without giving attention to the parts of which they are made up. Having read this chapter so far, it will be difficult for you to see the letters SNO without adding a W and completing the word. This natural tendency for completion and the formation of wholes was demonstrated in the 1920s and 1930s by Gestalt psychologists experimenting with principles of perception. They would show their students a series of incomplete pictures consisting of lines and shapes which the students would make sense of by seeing them as complete pictures. You have probably done this many times yourself as you notice the 'doodle' you have drawn while talking on the telephone. You perceive these accidental lines, loops and shapes as a face, a flower or some animal. You visually 'fill in the gaps' to create a whole. You may even go on to complete them on the paper. The same is true of 'cloud-watching' where, in the masses, the swirls, the light and shade of the clouds you perceive a castle, a dragon, a landscape. An example of this phenomenon is provided by Figure 6.3, where there is a small collection of lines but you have no difficulty in perceiving a face.

Figure 6.3   Completion

Our tendency to complete and create wholes applies to our everyday lives, moment by moment, as well as over time. If a conversation with a friend is interrupted in the middle of an exciting tale, we will want to return to it as soon as possible to hear the rest, to get the complete story. If we are reading a good novel, we will find it difficult to put the book down (especially nearing the end) without knowing how it ends. Novelists, playwrights and film-makers all capitalise upon our need to complete and make wholes. The daily 'soap opera' in particular is renowned for its 'cliff-hanger' endings each day which ensure a good viewing audience for the next episode.

There may be certain tasks which, if they are incomplete, are difficult to forget until they are completed. You may keep remembering the letter you need to post, the message you need to deliver, the book you need to take back to the library, and so on. You find you cannot totally put these thoughts aside until you have completed the tasks. Once they are done, your attention can be devoted to other things more clearly.

Similarly, this tendency for completion and wholeness applies to our emotional lives. Jim, for example, has not seen or heard from Stephanie for many years since she ended her relationship with him. He felt very hurt but did not let himself show it. He 'soldiered on' with his life, although feeling a frequent sense of depression. However, on meeting her again, he immediately feels all the hurt and anger he had not allowed expression at the time. He feels he cannot relate to Stephanie until he has told her about his feelings: they seem to get in the way of his renewing their friendship. Once they have been shared and expressed – in other words, once completion of that particular emotional gestalt is achieved – he can relate to Stephanie more fully in the present. Often, it is this inability to achieve satisfying completion that brings clients to therapy. Similarly, coaching provides the possibility for the unresolved interpersonal tensions emerging in organisations to be addressed, particularly at times of rapid change.

Our life experience is full of gestalts, formed, completed and then formed again. It is possible to see this process of completion and formation as a cycle.

The Cycle of Experience as a Model of Healthy Functioning

In all aspects of life there are beginnings, middles and endings which can be seen as cyclical. There is the regular rhythm of night and day, waking and sleeping, or breathing out and breathing in. There is the perpetual cycle of hunger for food and need for the satisfaction of that hunger and, of course, there is the life cycle itself from seed to birth, from early growth to maturity, from ageing to dying. In plants and animals, including human beings, the next generation continues the cycle of life. All living organisms can be seen to be moving through their life cycle and within that overall cycle through millions of sub-cycles along the way – each species at a different rate and level of complexity. In Gestalt we focus on the cycles of experience of which our lives are made.

Imagine someone is lying in bed asleep. The telephone rings. Through the mist of their dreamy sleep the sound of its bell begins to disturb them. As gradually they wake, they become aware of the insistent noise which for a few moments seemed to be part of their dream. They realise it is the telephone. For a few moments they lie still, wondering whether to answer it and, having decided to do so, they stretch their limbs before sitting up and reaching for the phone. They pick it up and say, 'Hello,' and a voice says, 'Hi, you told me to wake you at seven-fifteen.' The person thanks the caller, replaces the receiver and falls back onto the pillow. Their muscles relax again as they take some minutes to rest and gather their thoughts ready for the day.

We have just followed someone through one of the many natural cycles of which our lives are made. During the course of our lives we are subject to millions of stimuli which we automatically sort through and prioritise. These stimuli could be internal ones, such as a sensation of hunger, an emotion or a sudden idea, or they could be an external event, such as the telephone in our example, the sound of a voice, the action of another person or a change in the weather. Many of these stimuli remain part of the 'ground' and we do not make them part of our awareness. Many we notice briefly as transient 'figures'. Some we focus on and bring into our awareness as sharp 'figures'. In our example, the ringing telephone started in the ground or field of the slumbering dreamer. Gradually, it became figure and the person prepared to respond to it and take action. The phone was answered, the message received and the experience/gestalt was complete. The person was ready to focus on the new emerging figure, which was their plan for the day.

Gestalt counsellors and coaches believe that healthy functioning is this process of noticing, forming a figure, taking action, in awareness, in the present moment, and taking responsibility for the choices we make both in the selection of figure and in our response to it.

The idea that there are stages to our experience was originally expressed by Perls (1992 [1947]) and developed by Paul Goodman (Perls et al., 1972 [1951]) and called the *'process of contact'*. In many ways, it best captures the co-created and relational nature of contact. However, this process was later developed by Zinker (1977) and others as an energy cycle. We think that this focus on the individual can be extremely useful to clients and we therefore present our version here (see Figure 6.4) as a wave which you may wish to compare and contrast with others (see Clarkson and Mackewn, 1993; Zinker, 1977). We believe a wave is a useful metaphor to describe the Cycle of Experience. The beginning of a wave emerges from the depths of the ocean, it gathers energy, forms, peaks at its crest, and eventually folds and falls to return to that from which it came. Each wave is of course followed by another. Similarly, our life experiences are fluid and consist of ongoing 'organic rising and falling of the formation and destruction of a figure of interest' (Mackewn, 1997: 19). We will illustrate the cycle using our telephone example above and we also introduce an example of a senior leader involved in an organisational restructuring as part of a global change initiative.

Stage One: Sensation

The individual experiences a stimulus either from the environment or from within herself. This stage is called 'Sensation' because it involves the impact of the stimulus on our senses. For instance, something may pass across our visual field or we may begin to feel some bodily sensations. In our example above, there is the external stimulus of the ringing sound of the telephone which the sleeper begins to hear. In our second example, an organisational leader begins to notice a tension in her stomach as she hears conflicting messages from various staff members from different regions. In both examples, the 'field' (Chapter 7) is not yet differentiated into figure and ground.

Stage Two: Recognition

The sensation emerges as a more defined figure is formed, and the individual becomes aware of it, locates it and attempts to recognise it and, if possible, name it. An internal sensation of tightness in the chest may be recognised immediately as sadness by a particular person, while for another it may be recognised as the beginnings of a cold. For yet another person, the recognition may not be so easily labelled and may remain simply as an awareness of tightness. In our examples, the awakening is accompanied by the gradual identification of the sound as a telephone bell; the leader becomes aware of feeling anxious about the looming restructuring and its implications for employees, their families and the services they offer to clients.

Stage Three: Appraisal and Planning (Mobilising Energy)

At this stage, the individual begins to respond to the stimulus, make sense of it and decide what to do. The figure now has her full attention. She feels and thinks about the sensation and experiences a rise in energy as she prepares to act. Sometimes this appraisal will assist in the recognition process as the individual reacts and responds to something new and unfamiliar. Sometimes it will be an increasing awareness of the person's need or feeling as she sorts through various options and chooses her plan of action. In our examples, the awoken person, having recognised the telephone, decides to answer it and readies her muscles for action; the leader starts evaluating the current situation and makes some mental notes about how to engage others in order to ascertain the real mood of the organisation.

Stage Four: Action

Now the individual makes some movement towards achieving her goal. She may experiment with different courses of action until she finds the satisfactory one, or there may only be one direction to take. The plan is put into action. The woken person rolls over and stretches out to reach the telephone. The senior leader has conversations with a few members of staff and their clients to better understand the implications and how these compare with her currently held views.

Stage Five: Contact

Here the individual becomes fully engaged with whatever she has chosen to do. Everything else temporarily recedes into the background as the action meets the need or intention and becomes a vivid and full figure. For instance, a hungry man savours his sandwich and, in that moment, that is his only involvement; a woman focuses all her senses on the sight and sound of bees as they alight on the pale, pink flowers. And in our first example, the person lifts the receiver, hears her friend's voice and receives the message, while in the second example, the leader shuttles between appraisal and action until she is ready to work with an organisation consultant designing and delivering a large group conference that brings different roles and regions together.

Stage Six: Assimilation and Completion

If the need has been fully met with full contact, the person feels a physiological and psychological sense of completion and satisfaction. Even if the action was a painful one – for example, the expression of sadness and weeping – some sense of relief and appropriateness will be experienced. If the original sensation and aware-ness remain, the person may return to the appraisal stage to 're-appraise' and form a new plan. In this way, we see how we may shuttle back and forth between the stages as we constantly respond with awareness to inner and outer stimuli as a process of 'organismic self-regulation' or 'self-organisation'.

In our examples, the person has made complete sense of the morning's disturbance, feels her muscles relaxing and is ready to let the experience go; the leader reflects on the large group conference and integrates the main themes that emerged, including a proposal to host regional conferences. In both of these cases, the individual moves into the final stage.

Stage Seven: Withdrawal of Energy

The individual withdraws her attention from this figure which now becomes ground as it gradually loses its interest. The person replaces the receiver and rests back onto the pillows, ready to turn her attention to other things. Now, the senior leader momentar-ily retires from engaging with people. The gestalt is complete (see Figure 6.4).

The Space Between

There is a space between stages seven and one of the Gestalt cycle. It is not exactly a stage because, by definition, it is not a moving on. It is the state of being (after withdrawal but before the emergence of the next figure) during which a person is

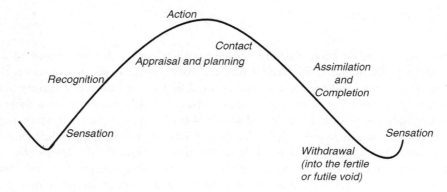

Figure 6.4

at rest. Perls referred to it as 'the fertile void' (1976: 99). Ideally, in this state, we do not hurry to the next emerging figure. We do not fill our lives with memories and plans, but we are willing to sustain the experience of directionlessness, whereby we are still in the here-and-now. Consequently we are able to respond fully and with immediacy to the moment – aware of, yet not inappropriately distracted by, the stimuli around and within us – ready to move on to the next gestalt. We can make a differentiation between the fertile void, where that experience becomes the fertile ground of growth, and the futile void, where the experience is felt as empty, meaningless or frightening and the person either lapses into despair or hurries to fill the gap with some sort of mental or physical activity. The person in our example lies relaxed and at peace with herself until the sensation of wanting to get out of bed emerges. However, the leader feels compelled to immediately take on another activity with a new group, thereby missing the opportunity for staff to become more interdependent with each other in implementing the proposed plan. She also misses the emerging figure that is calling her to take care of her own needs for a while.

We realise that a detailed account of these stages may give the impression that the cycle is a somewhat ponderous and time-consuming experience. This is certainly not necessarily the case. For instance, while writing about the cycle, one of us felt a sensation on her skin. Glancing down she saw (and recognised instantly!) that it was a wasp. Instantly, she felt a pang of fear and raised her hand to flick it off. The feeling of finger against insect, the sight of the departing wasp and the beginnings of relief and satisfaction were almost simultaneous. It took a few further moments for her fear to subside and for her to feel relaxed before the gestalt was completed. This whole cycle occurred so quickly that she could return to the task of writing with scarcely a break.

At other times, the cycle may take much longer. It can be used to describe, for example, a pianist learning a new piece of music: from the initial desire, through the learning and practising to the full contact of the performance of the finished piece, followed by the satisfaction and the eventual withdrawal of energy for that piece. This may take minutes, days or months, depending upon the standard of the pianist. The cycle of experience can also be used as a way of understanding the stages of a bereavement process or of the therapeutic journey as the client first becomes of her feelings and thoughts, then gradually begins to take charge of her life.

It is important to note that the cycle of experience involves the interacting of a whole person (thoughts, feeling, bodily sensations) with her whole environment, which includes other people and non-sentient beings. In our examples, the cycles were presented as unique, separate and not interconnected with other cycles. However, the reality of what it is to be a healthily functioning human in the world is very different. We go through multiple cycles of experience, where they are interacting with each other moment to moment, during the course of our day, or even in some cases for the duration of our lives. Relational Gestalt (Chapter 3) sees that each person is within a dialogic process of relating, both to themselves and their wants and needs, and also to others. Every person in relationship is affecting and being affected by everyone else; ideally therefore, they are not only aware of their cycle of experience but also to notice, listen to and understand the cycles of others. It is this interplay between individuals' cycles of experience that we attend to when working with families, groups and organisations. Zinker and Nevis (1981) called such a process the Gestalt Interactive Cycle. Understanding the way individuals modify their contact in their interaction with each other facilitates practitioners to be in authentic relationships with clients that support completion, integration and growth.

Disturbances in the Cycle

It is inevitable that many potential cycles are not completed. It would be impossible for us to bring every stimulus into full awareness and respond to it. There are thousands of stimuli that, by necessity, we must ignore moment by moment in order to get on with our lives. Right now, as we write this book, our senses are being assailed by a myriad of stimuli. On the inside, these may be the many and various physiological changes that our bodies go through constantly; or the memories, thoughts and feelings of all the other things in our lives not connected to writing a book. In the external world, we have before us a view of the countryside and we could stop and focus on the colours and shapes, the sounds and smells. The list would be endless, but we choose for the most part to ignore these stimuli in favour of our immediate and chosen task of engagement with writing. We bridge or make a premature ending to the potential gestalt and, in this instance, we are making a choice in focusing on our current work and we are still living in full present awareness.

However, there are also times when we may interrupt or change the flow of a gestalt cycle without awareness in a way that limits our full experience of meeting a current need in the here-and-now. Difficulties can occur in our lives when there is a disturbance at any stage in the cycle which leads to inappropriate incompletion or to the 'skewing' of the subsequent stages. A practitioner will help the client to become aware of disturbances they may have at various points, so that they can explore how and sometimes even why they have that disturbance. It may be that at some time in the past they disturbed the natural flow of their cycle in a manner and at a time when it was important for them to do so. It may have seemed vital not to

may be that the particular adjustment solved a problem at the
en thought their life was in danger. In Gestalt, this disturbance
experience is called a 'creative adjustment' to honour the fact
rst developed it was doing something creative in response to a
danger. It was something that worked at the time. The 'creative
came a habit which may not be useful in the present day. The
nces in the cycle of experience is an important feature of Gestalt

In Gestalt, we often use the term 'interruptions' to describe the active, here-and-now process by which the person disturbs the cycle's natural flow. It is particularly relevant in understanding the trauma process. However, it is important to remember that the interruption is not necessarily a simple breaking off. It is a process of self-in-relationship, by which we modify our contact as we engage with our environment.

Modifications to Contact

Sylvia Crocker (2008) says contact is meeting with another in awareness, where we mutually affect each other, yet do not merge. It is thus not only a meeting but also the process of differentiation that distinguishes what is I and Not–I.

Human beings are 'wired' for contact. We agree with Erving and Miriam Polster (1974) who believe that contact is the means for changing oneself and one's experience of the world, moment to moment, event to event and situation to situation. Healthy contact is the process of human development and growth. From our early infant years we are reaching out into the world to make contact with our caregivers to get our needs met. Gerhardt (2004) elegantly argues that as infants, our whole experience – comprising our emotional, bodily and cognitive functions – is shaped by early social interactions and contact with our primary caregivers.

There are seven processes of modification to contact – also known as resistances, disturbances, interruptions or distortions – that may occur at any point in the cycle. In other words, we may modify our experience in any of seven ways during sensation, recognition, appraisal and mobilisation, action, contact, assimilation/completion and withdrawal. When thinking of cycles of experience as being interactive, we prefer the term 'modification to contact' rather than the other terms. Like Gordon Wheeler (1991) we see all of these processes as forms of contact, albeit perhaps unhelpfully modified. They are creative adjustments, where we are organising our experiences in the best possible way given the internal and external support and resources available to us.

The seven ways we can modify our contact in the cycle of experience are: (1) desensitisation, (2) deflection, (3) introjection, (4) projection, (5) retroflection, (6) egotism and (7) confluence. For simplicity we will discuss each of these in turn before offering another elaboration on the modifications to contact at the end of this section.

Frequently, a number of these processes may combine to make a break in the natural cycle and create an alternative closure, which could be healthy or unhealthy for the person.

Desensitisation

Desensitisation is the process by which a person numbs their natural ability to sense and feel their world. This means they dull their ability to see, hear, feel, taste, smell, touch, or any combination of these. The desensitising process may also happen when a person anaesthetises their inner world of emotions at times of pain; for example, when a loved one dies. Clearly, desensitisation is most often observed at the sensation phase of the cycle of experience, where it also has the most deleterious effect. The person shuts down their sensations so they literally have no response to the many internal and external stimuli of their world. For example, as Arthur enters the consulting room, he bangs his elbow sharply on the door jamb but seems oblivious to this both then and when asked about it later in the session. Neither is he aware of any discomfort in his body as he sits awkwardly on the edge of his chair.

This helps inform the therapist that Arthur may need to focus on becoming more aware of his bodily sensations and contact functions. Desensitisation, at this point in the cycle, can range from someone who is not in touch with their own body to a full catatonic state.

Another aspect of sensitisation, apart from desensitisation, is that of oversensitisation. Here, as opposed to being numbed, the organism is overstimulated with sensation. This oversensitisation can lead to the avoidance and neglect of contact with the more appropriate stimulus which, even if painful, may need to be observed and resolved. Desensitisation and oversensitisation can be achieved with the use of certain substances such as nicotine, alcohol, drugs, caffeine, carbohydrates, sugar and so on.

Desensitisation can, of course, take place at any other phase of the cycle. For example, Ahmed had worked hard to gain approval and funding for his vulnerable older adults project. When he hears the news of his success at a directors' meeting he desensitises his full experience of satisfaction and does not hear that not only has he secured funding but he was also given extra budget and resources.

Sometimes, however, rather than impede the organism, desensitisation actually facilitates it. In the final game of an important tennis match, one of the players may choose to ignore a sharp pain in her knee in order to win the match. This raises the observable fact that in terms of self-regulation the tennis player's desensitisation interrupts the natural cycle of her care of her limbs. However, in the parallel cycle of achieving a long-worked-for recognition this desensitisation occurs at the contact phase. What differentiates a healthy from an unhealthy interruption is usually the element of awareness and choice involved. By and large, less helpful modifications to contact occur 'compulsively' and out of awareness.

You, the reader, might begin to familiarise yourself with this concept of desensitisation by identifying how it manifests in your own life, both generally and at this moment. Take your attention away from this book and notice places in your body which you may be holding in an uncomfortable way. For instance, you may be crossing your legs in such a way that the back of one knee is numb. You may be ignoring a biological need, such as hunger. Sometimes, if the mind is being nourished, the bodily needs become background. In order to reconnect with the natural sensitivity of your body, we suggest that you experiment with different positions until you find one in which you are accounting for all of your body.

In general, are there things in your life that you allow to become extreme before you take notice of them? Do you suddenly realise that you are very hungry, exhausted or stressed? Do you often find that you have eaten too much? Do you find bruises on yourself and not know how you got them? Begin to identify the areas in which you desensitise. This is the first step towards resensitisation.

Alternatively you may be oversensitised, as described earlier. Do you find yourself overwhelmed and overstimulated by the world around you? Do you have difficulty in selecting relevant data? You may wish to practise slowing down, withdrawing into yourself and deciding what you want before facing the world.

Deflection

Deflection is the process whereby we divert energy from its natural path to an alternative one. It is a way of causing some stimulus from the environment to ricochet away from making an impact upon us. This interruption may occur at any point on the cycle of experience. It is often used at the recognition phase in order to defend against some discomforting sensation. For example, Hilda looks sad when talking of her struggle to make a good relationship with her husband and, when one of her group members says how sad the situation sounds, Hilda says, 'Well, we have been married for 18 years.' When encouraged to say how she feels, Hilda then deflects again by asking, 'Well, what do you mean by "sad"?' At the action phase of the cycle of experience, deflection can be seen when Tim, who is about to tell another group member how angry he is about her repeated absences, comments on the pattern of her jersey instead.

Deflection can be very useful at times when full recognition of the situation might make it more difficult to complete. Jean is terrified of dental work and chooses to deflect from her terror by trying to remember all the verses of a song so that the dentist may complete her fillings as efficiently as possible.

You, the reader, can, if you wish, start to explore your own deflections. What are the things you do not want to think about? If you genuinely tried to answer that question, you will probably have found that you quickly distracted yourself by thinking of or doing something else. Do you know what it is that you were avoiding, what unpleasant feelings or thoughts seemed unbearable to you? As you slowly read the following list, notice which items you flinch away from: bread, books, spiders, trees, death, Mozart, cancer, sex, Hitler, lollipop sticks, dentists, Lady Gaga, caves, Twitter, birds, Harry Potter, ice, polystyrene, AIDS, starvation.

Introjection

Introjection is the process of absorbing or 'swallowing whole' some rule, message, model and so on that is presented to the organism from outside itself. This is the most pervasive of all modifications to healthy functioning. An introject is that which has in the past been accepted without discrimination and reverberates in the present. It is possible to introject at any time of life as we learn and model ourselves on people in our environment. However, most introjection is done in the early years of child-hood when we are most vulnerable and impressionable, dependent for our survival upon those powerful and loved adults whose approval we desperately need. It is from our parents (or primary caretakers) therefore that we receive and swallow most of the axioms we will continue to use in order to make meaning of life, relationships and ourselves. There are countless ways in which we introject from the world around us: the food we eat, the way we dress, the types of relationship we seek, what we deem to be well-mannered or otherwise, and so on. Advertisers depend on the phenome-non of introjection to have their products bought without careful consideration of what we are doing.

We may notice introjection at the appraisal and mobilisation phase of the gestalt cycle. Andrew seems on the verge of tears but suddenly says, 'It's too silly a thing to cry about.' Later in the therapy session he remembers that his mother often told the boys in his family not to make a fuss about silly, little things.

Celia is exploring the idea of changing her career by listing jobs that she might do. Her group soon confronts her with the realisation that her list includes only stereo-typically female options such as nurse, secretary and nursery school teacher. One of the group members says, 'You are brilliant at figures; why not include accountancy and so on?' Immediately, Celia becomes uncomfortable and anxious. After further exploration of her experience she realises that in her family of origin the men were traditionally the 'clever' ones and the females were caring and homely. A female accountant would have been seen as too unfeminine. As she begins to recall the per-vasiveness of her introject, she remembers how her mother had written in her auto-graph book, 'Be good sweet maid, and let who can be clever . . .'

Introjection can also occur at other points in the cycle and usually underpins another interruption. For instance, Hilda, who deflected from her sadness, had the injuction, 'Don't get upset', while Ahmed , who desensitised his pleasure at his suc-cess, believed that he couldn't get 'over-excited or celebratory'.

Naturally, it would be a great mistake to start to reject all that we have learned from our parents and family. Introjecting guidelines for living is part of the way in which we learn and keep ourselves safe. A beginning stage in the learning process is to copy, that is, to introject, the modeller. Later on, as our skills develop, we begin to hone our style better to suit our individual needs and talents. A child learns 'Don't run into the road,' 'Be polite to people,' 'Eat healthily,' 'This is how to read,' and so on, which are often pieces of learning vital for living in society. There are many introjects which, even when we become aware that they were our parents' opinion rather than *the truth*, we choose to retain because we find them useful and appropriate: for instance, 'It is important to be respectful to people,' 'Violence is wrong,' 'Beauty is to be treasured.' What is important is to remember that the world is changing all the time, so that the introject that was useful yesterday, may not be so today.

Another important factor in considering introjects is culture. Many of the introjects we all hold were given to us by the culture in which we live. They come via our parents, schools, friends, neighbours, religious leaders and many other sources. There will be differences in beliefs and values between people from different countries, and also between different groups in apparently the same society: Irish, Asian, West Indian, working class, middle class, Christian, Muslim, Hindu, and so on. It is important when working with clients to be aware, as far as possible, of our own cultural introjects as well as those of our clients. In that way we can try to avoid inadvertently imposing our own frame of reference on the therapy or coaching setting. We can also treat with respect the culture of our client, inviting him to be aware of the influence that his culture has had on him and allowing him to work within that frame of reference if he chooses.

We suggest you now take a moment to think about what you believe concerning asking for help. Do you, for example, say things like, 'Oh, I don't want to burden others with my problems,' or 'If you want something done well, you must do it yourself,' or 'Ask and you shall be given,' or 'I want – won't get!' or 'If you want something, you should just take it,' or other responses? Almost certainly, some of your replies will be direct introjects of parental messages and modelling.

Experiment with almost any area of your life and see how influenced you have been in your apparent personal choices. Are these beliefs about 'the way to be' still relevant or might you want to change them? If you wish to improve your discrimination and combat introjection, it can be helpful to use certain basic questions regularly – 'Do I want this?', 'Do I agree with this?', 'Does this suit me?' – and some basic self-instructions: 'Chew a while before swallowing', ' What is my own current opinion about this?'

Projection

Projection is the process of disowning some aspect of self and placing it in something outside – whether a person, animal or object. A person projects when they imagine that they know what another person is feeling or thinking or why they are doing something. Sometimes our projections are appropriately based on life experience. For instance, when Robert is scowling and answering in monosyllables, I project that he may be angry with me and I decide that this is not the moment to give him a hug. I do this without asking him and my conclusion is based on the fact that usually, when people behave like this, they are angry. I choose to interrupt the gestalt that I was forming. Equally, when a colleague approaches me smiling, with outstretched hand, I imagine that she is being friendly on the basis of my past experiences of people who have behaved in this way.

Organisational leaders use projection when developing a five-year strategy plan. Artists use a form of projection when they turn their ideas into an image on canvas, in clay, and so on. Architects use projection when planning a shopping centre in order to imagine what facilities will be needed. Or we use projection when we are packing our suitcase to go on holiday. We would be lost without projection – as, indeed, is true of all the modifications.

Projection becomes a modification to the natural cycle of experience when I do not meet another person as they are in the here and now, because I am fantasising something about their attitude and I do not check to see if my fantasy is true. I am barely aware that it is my fantasy. It feels as if it is something I 'know'.

Frequently, projections have extra dimensions. We have already talked about the powerful influence that our parents have on us when we are children. Our introjects include images of our parents and other significant figures as they responded to us, and we carry the expectation that others will respond to us in the same way. Therefore, when Andrew held back his tears, he not only activated the introject about not making a fuss, he also projected his mother's face on the therapist and thought, 'She'll think I'm silly.' Susan, whose father was stern and distant, projected her father onto any significant man who took up leadership roles and imagined that he would not be interested in her or take her seriously. In the group session, she did not offer ideas or respond to any of the men because she assumed they would not want her to. In that way, she interrupted her natural desire to reach out and get close to others.

Often, people project as a result of an injunction which forbids them to be a certain way. Using projection, a person might take that split-off part of themselves and see it in someone else, where it is more easily accepted – or even where they can criticise it with a feeling of superiority. Thus Deirdre, who must not feel anger, imagines that her therapist is angry and then feels frightened of him. John, who was bad at sports, despises Alan for being small and weak.

Besides our more negative qualities we also project positive attributes that we have not yet integrated. Jess, who had very low self-esteem, projected her intelligence and vivacity onto Judith (who, incidentally, reminded her of her younger sister – the favourite in the family) and felt both stupid and resentful. She was astounded when friends said, 'But that's exactly what we see in you.'

When projection occurs at the action stage, having mobilised their energy, a person changes their direction as a result of their fantasies and fixed gestalts. This happens particularly in the process of making contact with another person: at recognition they misinterpret the signals that the other is giving them; at appraisal they limit their options which are based on their projection; at contact they lose their true awareness of self and other as they relate to the person they imagine to be there.

A form of projection, in actuality a mixture of projection and retroflection, is named 'proflection'. Proflection is the process whereby we do for others what we hope they will do for us. Normally, people who proflect have an injunction which forbids them to have needs or ask for what they want. Out of their awareness, they have a need and they translate that into action towards another. A person is proflecting, therefore, who offers you tea when they are thirsty, strokes your back when they want attention, talks lovingly to the dog when they need to hear such kindnesses, and so forth.

In order to recognise some attribute of your own that you are projecting while you read this book, let yourself know some opinion you have had about the authors.

Is this a valid opinion based on the contents and style of what you have read or are some of those opinions disowned characteristics which belong to you?

One of the immediate ways of beginning to 're-own' what has been projected could be to allow yourself to consider some of the these questions: 'In what ways am I like this too?', 'What part am I choosing to ignore when I take an extreme stand?'. When did you last ask a colleague, friend or family member if they would like something, when in fact you really wanted that very thing? Becoming honest about your own needs and desires will prevent the use of proflection.

Retroflection

Retroflection is a process whereby energy which would naturally be directed outwards is turned inwards: a person who experiences the impulse to action in speech, gesture or deed blocks the flow of their energy and turns it back into themselves. So, retroflections are often experienced in our bodies, as in biting a lip, tightening of fist, shallowness of breath, stroking a leg. When you stop yourself yawning in the middle of a conversation, when you restrain yourself from pushing to the front of a queue, when you hold back from snapping at the traffic warden, you are retroflecting. It is easy to see how, without retroflection, society could not function harmoniously.

There are two types of retroflection. In the first, a person uses their energy on themselves instead of allowing their healthy urge to use that energy on or with another. Here I do to myself what I would naturally want to do with you. One of the most common retroflections that therapists meet is probably retroflected anger. Instead of being able to be appropriately angry with someone, a person swallows back their anger and turns it on themself, criticising themself for being stupid or blaming themself for whatever happened. Such patterns are often established in childhood when the young person turns their anger on themself, both out of fear of the parents' reprisals and also often out of a need to 'keep the parents good'. For a little child it is often frightening to believe that their parents may not always be perfect.

There are many other examples of this type of retroflection. Susan, who believed that the men in the group would not be interested in her, retroflected her want to show affection to Robert. Instead of stroking him, she began to stroke her own arm. Joe nearly shouted with surprise, then bit his lip as he remembered not to 'make a fool' of himself. In this way the retroflector is both the activator and the receiver. She puts herself in the place of the environment and relates to herself. For that reason, retroflection is most often seen at the action and contact stages of the cycle. The person holds back action, turns it on herself, and then dwells exclusively on her own feelings instead of making contact with the world around her.

The second form of retroflection occurs when a person does for themselves things that attempt to meet the need they have of the environment. The man who wants to be nurtured, but cannot ask, lights a cigarette, thereby meeting in some way his need to be 'fed'. The woman whose parents did not set appropriate limits, longs for the environment to give her clear feedback, to set boundaries for her. She sets boundaries for herself by criticising herself far more harshly than anyone else could do, and setting herself impossible tasks.

There are times when it is appropriate to learn to retroflect. Brenda had a history of losing jobs for having 'a poor attitude'. In the therapy group, she explained how yet again she had lost her temper with her new boss when he asked her to repeat a piece of work. Brenda had had an overbearing and bullying father and had a tendency to become very defensive and then to attack if she felt criticised by a man. The group helped her to understand that her angry feelings did not represent the facts and that a person who wants to keep their job sometimes needs to restrain their impulse towards an angry outburst, even in the face of real or suspected criticism.

Becoming aware how you treat yourself may well be the first step in identifying ways in which you choose to retroflect your energy rather than to propel it outwards. Do you chew your cuticles or bite your nails? Do you bite or suck your lips? Do you have regular gestures which involve some form of self-stroking?

There may be some simple actions you can take to undo your more minor retroflections. Instead of biting back your anger and clenching your fingers into your palms you could spring open your hands as though to free some trapped insect from inside them. One person, who knew it would be unwise to voice her anger in a meeting, went immediately for a walk in a wood where she could safely release angry shouts. Many retroflections, because they were developed as the best protection available at some past time, need patient and careful undoing and often require and deserve help from a therapist or coach.

Egotism

The word 'egotism' is commonly associated with selfishness or self-centredness. In this context egotism means something a little different: it is the process of 'self-monitoring' or 'spectatoring'. This prevents true involvement in any experience. Egotism can be useful for, say, the beginner learning to drive or the therapist or coach who listens to an audio tape of himself in order to self-supervise and improve his work. It can also be vital to those who need to increase awareness of self – with as many of the awareness exercises described earlier. However, it can be an incapacitating modification to contact with our internal world and the external environment.

Egotism can occur at any stage of the gestalt cycle. However, this process may especially interrupt the flow of energy at the assimilation and completion stage. Instead of being aware of the sense of completeness and satisfaction that would then naturally occur, the person stands outside himself and is aware of looking at himself to assess how he is performing or has performed. Such individuals do not refer to an inner feeling to decide the degree to which their gestalt has been completed. They become external observers who scrutinise them. For example, Sandy, after weeping copiously about the loss of a friend, finishes and sits back. Rather than be with herself and her therapist, who has shared the experience, she immediately starts to comment on and assess her work: whether it was enough; how loudly she had cried; what sort of client she had been; she had noticed that her hands had been quite childlike; she thought there was a connection to her mother; and so on.

Egotism can take the form of pride and admiration of the self or of criticism and denigration. In the latter case, the person is painfully aware of how she must be appearing to others and imagines at every step what critical thoughts they are having. Frequently, they believe that, 'If people really knew me, they would think I'm worthless,' and feel a need to hide.

It is important as practitioners to be aware that our tendency towards egotism can be increased by any theory which encourages self-analysis. Gestaltists' focus on self-awareness can lead, through egotism, to a form of self-absorbed introspection which interrupts the natural flow of the cycle of experience and loses the real, unpremeditated and unreserved contact with the environment which is the hallmark of true awareness. However, awareness is about self and other (Chapter 4). Laura Perls (1992: 110) says that 'embarrassment is the inevitable awareness of lack of support that accompanies the initial exciting contact with any new experience'. She is pointing out that, if we meet an experience freshly and openly, without controlling it in any way, we will feel unbalanced, unsettled, vulnerable. We should not avoid that experience through egotism, or any other modification to contact, but be willing to meet it fully as an aspect of growth.

In order to experience egotism you could try giving a running commentary to yourself in a given situation. For example, as you talk to a friend, you could describe to yourself everything you are doing and saying: 'I am smiling kindly and taking an interest in my friend. Now I am looking quizzical and my friend must be wondering what I'm thinking. I'm asking him to tell me more about his situation. I am listening with my head on one side.' Can you feel the way in which egotism prevents real contact with your friend?

Confluence

Confluence is the process of merging with the environment so that the awareness of separateness is lost. The negative aspect of this process is that confluence prevents differentiation and individualisation. The confluent person does not differentiate between their experience and another's. They are not in touch with their or the other's individuality. For example, Felicity and Tom have been married for nine years and have both developed the habit of using the pronoun 'we' when really talking about their individual proclivities. The practitioner and client need to be aware (and beware) that the sort of closeness, the empathic meeting and the unique quality of the relationship offered in the therapy setting may have the effect of inviting and encouraging confluence. However, meeting and merging with another can be a form of healthy confluence. For example, Ahmed and Hilda share their excitement at the launch of the recently approved project for older citizens. This enabled them to experience a quality of contact that hitherto was unknown in their working relationship.

In the 'unhealthy' confluent relationship, the individual, once merged, has difficulty in separating or letting go of an experience. This causes particular difficulties at the withdrawal stage of the cycle of experience, when we must be willing, having completed a gestalt, to let go of it and withdraw into the 'fertile void', ready to respond to the next emerging figure. Confluent clients have difficulty with endings. This can be manifested in many ways, not just in relation to unresolved bereavements, obvious losses or separations. The individual may have a great fear of being alone. They may have immense trouble choosing amongst different things because of the loss of the 'unchosen' items. They may find it hard to say 'no'. They may have difficulty in finishing generally: from leaving at the end of sessions to finishing their sentences. A client who keeps talking until you are forced to interrupt him may well have some tendency towards confluence.

Confluence can also occur at any other stage of the cycle and can result in a reluctance to let go of an idea, a feeling or a situation. For instance, Lucy, trying to generate options to solve a work problem, became confluent with one idea and seemed unable to relinquish it. The students found Ben interesting at first as he taught them about a particular trend in political history, but they started to lose interest as he clearly became confluent with his topic and lost contact with them.

Confluence is particularly relevant in relation to couples and some teams. A confluent couple or team cannot explore or experience their full individuality. Confluence precludes creative conflict within the relationship. The need to maintain homeostasis is such that there is no room for anything new, unexpected or experimental. Despite their desire for togetherness and harmony, the partners or members of the team often end up feeling bored.

However, as with all the modifications to contact, confluence has its positive aspects. We need moments of confluence in order to be empathic with one another. Hence the well known Native American Indian saying that exhorts us not to judge a man before 'walking a mile in his moccasins'. Intense intimate contact also involves moments of confluence. There is appropriate confluence between a mother and baby. Frequently, people talk of 'losing' themselves in the experience of sex. Such positive confluence, however, is followed by appropriate withdrawal.

Bob Resnick (1990) has made some important theoretical contributions with references to couples. He identifies a confluence–isolation continuum, in which people move between isolation, separation, contact, intimacy and confluence in a natural flow of meeting and parting. Figure 6.5 illustrates the continuum. This model shows how in healthy relating we need to have the capacity for both distance and closeness. It is important for us to be able to be in any of the positions.

At this moment you, the reader, could identify some examples of the way you let yourself become confluent. Let yourself think of some very close relationship you have. This may be a partner, parent, child, sibling or friend. Make a list of things you both like, starting each one with 'we'. Check with the other person its accuracy for

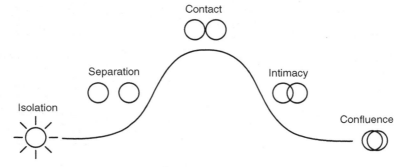

Figure 6.5   The confluence–isolation continuum

them. In order to prevent confluence you could think of another person with whom you are close and find things that you both like and dislike and things that one likes which the other does not.

Modifications to Contact: Moving between Two Poles

As highlighted by Bob Resnick, confluence is but one polarity on the modification to contact continuum, isolation being the other. Similarly, Joyce and Sills (2001, 2010) and Mackewn (1997) suggest that the original seven modifications to contact represent but one polarity in a series of continua. In our work as therapists and coaches we find it helpful to complement the seven modifications to contact with their polar opposite. We've already established that the meaning of a figure is related to the ground. Hence, if one pole of the modification to contact is figure then the other must be ground, always present should the need emerge. However, this full range is often not in clients' awareness. We have also discussed how important it is to consider the whole, where the whole is different and more than the sum of the parts. Thus, if we are to see the wholeness of the full range of modifications to contact we can view them as this series of continua. On each continuum, *both* polarities *and* all points in between are present and potentially available for persons in their contacting processes with each other (see Figure 6.6). This attitude recognises a capacity for a full range of human responses – be they 'attractive' or 'unattractive' – and allows for a fluidity of contact that presents the possibility of a person changing himself and his experience of the world in a way that is healthier and more fulfilling.

In our work we are seeking to heighten awareness of these contact styles as experienced in the here and now of the co-created relationship. We explore by inviting our clients to experiment (Chapter 12) how a movement along a continuum may be experienced, noting what changes occur and by providing sufficient support

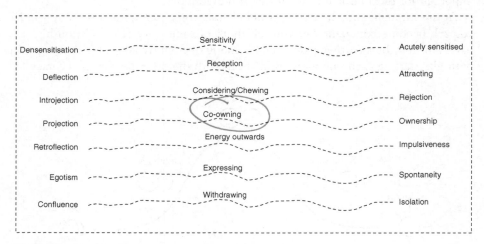

Figure 6.6   Modifications to contact: moving between poles
(Adapted from Joyce and Sills, 2010; Mackewn, 1997)

for assimilating new awareness that emerges. For example, Jacqui, a chief executive, was exploring with her coach why she always needed to carefully think through her views on issues, and decide in detail how she would communicate these at board meetings. The coach experienced her as tentative and as being preoccupied with her inner world. He informed her of what he noticed. He understood this as an egotism modification to contact – one pole of the continuum. He invited her to experiment with sharing her thoughts without censoring or thinking how she would say them. At first Jacqui was hesitant and her first attempt was whisper-like. Then, with encouragement from the coach, she tried sharing her thoughts in the here-and-now. She felt more lively and animated as she was becoming more spontaneous. On reflection she realised that accessing the spontaneous pole could also be helpful in generating ideas and engendering enthusiasm for her and the board.

Unfinished Business

Perls (1976) called interruptions to the cycle 'unfinished business'. He recognised that, until we have completed such business (closed the gestalt, made whole), we cannot be fully in the here-and-now. Our awareness of the present will be influenced by the incompleteness of our past experiences. We need to complete our experience before we can withdraw our energy from it. Of course, there will be many situations in our lives which we cannot complete at the time. We must delay the fulfilment of our needs until later and we must learn to cope with that delay. This is easier to do with some experiences than with others. You may find it easy to postpone the essay you have to write in order to chat to a friend. However, while talking, if you are waiting for news about your sister's operation you will find it difficult to give your full attention to your friend until the phone call has come through. Clearly, the level of pleasure and satisfaction attached to the need plays a part. You may happily delay visiting your dentist for weeks, but if a tooth starts aching, your need to make that visit will nag for your urgent attention until it is satisfied. Delaying the completion of a task, curbing the full expression of a feeling or halting the development of an idea all take energy. We may be able to bracket one thing off in order to deal with another, but the very act of setting and keeping it aside involves a lot of energy. Putting aside incomplete gestalts for our later attention is obviously something we do constantly in our everyday lives. It is our natural way of coping with and dealing with the many demands of living. However, there are some experiences which, for various reasons, we may bracket off and not return our attention to until much later, if at all. When we were describing the need for completion we talked about Jim and his feelings of hurt and anger at being left by Stephanie. He set aside his feelings at the time and returned to them only when meeting Stephanie again at a later stage. However, during this time of 'soldiering on', he used up a great deal of energy in not allowing himself to be aware fully of what he felt, hence his recurring 'depression'. If he could have been more attuned to himself, he could have closed the incomplete gestalt even in Stephanie's absence by sharing and expressing his feelings with a friend or counsellor.

A similar view of the way the unfinished business presses to be completed is contained in the psychoanalytic principle of the repetition compulsion – the notion that when the needs of early childhood are not adequately met, they are continuously represented in later life, albeit in a disguised form. Arthur's mother died when he was three. Ever since then, both in his childhood and also as an adult, Arthur has seemed to be searching for someone to take care of him. The women he falls for tend to be motherly types, frequently older than him, and often have an old-fashioned look to them.

There is another way in which incomplete gestalts can affect us, sometimes to our detriment. In a therapy session, Jill says she does not know what to talk about. There are so many issues that worry her – her relationships, her course work, a fight with her mother, and so on. But she says that she does not know which one to choose to talk about. The therapist asks her what seems most important – most 'foreground' – at the moment. Jill stares out of the window for a while and then says, 'I don't know. I don't know what is important. I don't know what I'm feeling. [*She laughs nervously.*] I don't think I know who I am.'

The therapist suggests that she experiment with knowing who she is now: 'What are you feeling now – in your body?'

> **JILL:** Well, I feel OK. My leg is a little stiff [*moves her leg to ease it*] and I'm aware I need to pee.
> **THERAPIST:** Do you want to do something about that need?
> **JILL:** I don't know. I don't want to waste the time – there's so many important things to look at – but OK, I will.

[*Jill gets up and goes off to the bathroom. She returns smiling.*]

> **JILL:** I understand now. I spend so much time thinking and worrying about all sorts of things that I get out of touch with me. I need to pay attention to my 'here and now' needs and wants, and act on those more – then I'll know who I am.

Fixed Gestalts

Many incomplete gestalts originate in childhood and, if we do not recognise them and pay attention to ways in which we can complete them, they will affect us throughout our adult lives. Perls used the term 'premature closure' to describe the interruption of an experience that shuts down the natural response and often replaces it with some other behaviour. This may happen in traumatic circumstances but more often happens as a result of the repetition of restrictions and injunctions from an environment which disapproves of some behaviours and encourages others. A typical example is that of Peter, who learned to interrupt his tears when he was sad, as his parents repeatedly said, 'Big boys don't cry.' They also approvingly said, 'That's my brave boy,' when he was assertive or angry. In compliance, Peter learnt to retroflect his sadness and turn it into anger. This is likely to happen again and again in the family, so the pattern of getting angry instead of sad becomes what is called a 'fixed gestalt'.

Florence was sent to her room as a child if she became upset. She was told she could come downstairs again when 'you're nice Florence again'. Alone in her room, unable to manage the distress she felt, she retroflected her feelings and deflected her energy into tidying her books and toys. As an adult, Florence used the same deflection of tidying the home when she was upset. In therapy, she realised that she was trying to 'tidy away' the parts of herself of which her parents had disapproved. The introjection of 'be a nice Florence' she interpreted to mean that strong feelings were somehow messy and should be cleaned up.

Much of the work done in Gestalt practice focuses on identifying and undoing fixed gestalts and completing these incomplete gestalts from the past so that they no longer impinge upon the client in the present. When Caroline was a child, her need of care and comfort was mostly ignored by her parents. Sometimes she would cry for their attention, sometimes she would get angry, but when all her attempts to get care and comfort were ignored, she too learnt to ignore those needs. She did, however, still have the drive to complete. Therefore she 'completed' the gestalt of these needs by telling herself she was 'too needy' and 'selfish' and must learn to put others before herself. Saying these things made some sort of sense of her experience and provided a type of closure as she found a reason to close down her feelings. This response became a pattern which continued into her adult life. Indeed, as an adult, despite her loneliness and continuous feeling of emptiness, she had postponed coming to therapy for many years. She saw it as 'self-indulgent' and many times in the initial sessions would attempt to ignore her own needs by looking after the therapist: 'How are you? You look tired' or 'Oh, you don't want to hear all about this. You must be really bored.' Over time, however, within the trust and consistency of the therapeutic relationship, she began to express her needs and more adequately complete her need for care and comfort within and outside the therapy sessions.

In this chapter, we have introduced the concept of gestalt formation and described some of its many aspects and their relevance to Gestalt therapy and coaching. Gestalt, like most psychological approaches, believes that we are greatly influenced by our past experiences. The experiences we have, the meanings we make of them and the ways in which we respond to them are often patterns of response that may start in early childhood as 'creative adjustments' to our world. However, they become fixed and so much a part of us that we become unaware of the fact that we are, in fact, *choosing* them. The Gestalt approach helps us to develop awareness of who we are, how we are living and how we are relating to the world around us. Through awareness we can begin to stand fully in the reality of the present, seeing things as they are and, in lively and exciting contact, choosing what needs to be chosen. This is a place we knew in our childhood, before we developed our habits of being, and it is a place to which in the depth of our hearts we want to return. We end this chapter with a quote from Laura Perls:

The aim of Gestalt therapy is the awareness continuum, the freely ongoing gestalt formation where what is of greatest concern and interest to the organism, the relationship, the group or society becomes Gestalt, comes into the foreground where it can be fully experienced and coped with (acknowledged, worked through, sorted out, changed, disposed of, etc.) so that then it can melt into the background (be forgotten or assimilated and integrated) and leave the foreground free for the next relevant gestalt. (L. Perls, 1992: 2)

7

Interconnectedness and the Field

Nothing exists in isolation. Everything is connected to something else. Everything has a setting, a field in which it exists. In order to perceive or understand something, we need to look at the whole context.

There was a television advertisement for a newspaper in which we are first presented with the scene of a smartly dressed businessman walking down the street carrying a briefcase. A skinhead runs up behind him, barges into him and pushes him along the pavement. We seem to be witnessing an attack. But when the scene is repeated, the camera pans back to show a heavy object falling from scaffolding above. The wider context totally alters the meaning of the scene. The younger man is in fact pushing the other man out of the way of the falling object and preventing a terrible accident. This new perspective changes our perception from the extremes of seeing the young man as an attacker to seeing him as a rescuer. The implication of the advertisement is, of course, that this newspaper will be showing events in their widest context and will thereby present us with 'the truth'. The discerning television viewer will bear in mind that there is the even wider context of this being an advertisement and, like all advertisements, it is intended to increase sales. We may appreciate the cleverness of the advertisement but we will need to read the newspaper itself and judge it in comparison with other newspapers before deciding whether we agree with its message.

Here is another example of connectedness and the need to see things in context. In a group coaching session with a community and housing services team in local government, Ahmed was speaking excitedly of a new service being launched for vulnerable elderly residents. Rita, the longest serving member of the team, seemed withdrawn and disinterested. Others were listening intently. The coach initially thought this was a recurring pattern of contact between Ahmed and Rita who were sometimes competitive with each other. However, when he inquired into what was occurring, it emerged that Rita felt sad. The new service was reminding her of the lack of support she was experiencing as she struggled to care for ageing parents in a different borough. This was not about competitive rivalry. Rita's feelings and experiences were connected with her current personal context and these were figural when she heard the outcome of Ahmed's project, of which she was actually very supportive.

You will see how these examples include wholeness, the formation of a figure, completion and also connectedness. These elements are inextricably connected. In fact, we have found it difficult to write about them individually, to write about the parts distinct from the whole, simply because of their interconnectedness. In looking at people, the Gestalt approach pays attention to the physical, emotional, psychological, social, historical and cultural environment of a person, from which they cannot be disconnected. In fact, all is interconnected where, in our ongoing multiple and varied relational interactions in various contexts, we are both forming and being formed at the same time.

Interconnectedness and Field-theory

Interconnectedness is the term we have chosen to describe what is, in effect, field-theory from a contemporary relational perspective. Kurt Lewin (1935, 1952), the creator of field-theory, saw the individual both within and in relation to the environment. How we perceive and experience the environment will be dependent on our needs at a particular moment in time, as well as our role, culture, age and so on. A change in any aspect of the field changes the whole field. The sense of all things being interconnected is further developed by Gordon Wheeler (2009). He describes people as being born into a pre-existing web of relationships where the very anticipation of our participation affects the field and the field in turn affects our self. We are constantly engaged in co-creating experiences moment to moment. More recently, complexity theory and, in particular, complex responsive processes of relating (Critchley, 2008, 2012; Stacey, 2003) suggest that we are engaged in ongoing processes of human interactions where people are forming patterns of relating while at the same time being formed by them.

There are several important consequences of this. To understand human beings, we need first to see the whole context, before attending to the parts. But the environment changes according to circumstances. The individual organises the totality of the environment according to different situations and different needs, sometimes making one particular aspect figure, sometimes another. Importantly, and with exciting implications for the therapy and coaching relationship, humans constellate the field around them so that they, in effect, create it. In any meeting a field is co-created. The practitioner and client have together a 'betweenness' in which the field is then potentially new every moment. We now introduce five principles of field-theory (see Parlett, 1991).

The Principle of Organisation

We derive meaning from perceiving the whole, the total situation. Our example of the advertisement for a newspaper illustrates how meaning is derived differently once we see the whole situation. What in one context takes on one meaning, in another means something different. A stretch of water may be a resource for quenching thirst, a means of travelling, a barrier to keep people out, a playground for windsurfers, a washing place, a source of food or a minor detail in the enormity of a landscape. The field is constellated differently according to our need and circumstances.

As Gestalt practitioners, we need to allow the field to develop in order to under-stand our clients. When Derek begins the session by saying that his father has died, the therapist does not leap in with condolences but takes time to explore the field of his experience and discover what this means for Derek. His relaxed body posture, the softness of his facial muscles, the evenness of his voice, the fact that he makes good eye contact, the words he uses and what he says with those words, once organ-ised into a whole, may make it clear that right now he is, in fact, much relieved by his father's death.

The Principle of Contemporaneity

Whatever the situation, all that is happening is happening simultaneously *now*. Only from the *present* influence of the field can we make sense of our present experience. Maybe last week you felt angry with someone who ignored you, maybe tomorrow you will feel sad because someone is going away. If you are feeling angry *now*, this can only be because of the present field of your thoughts about that person and the memories of the situation in which you were ignored. Similarly, if you are feeling sad at tomorrow's separation, it can only be that you are currently thinking about the person and imagining their absence. In the former case, the experience has happened and is in the past. In the latter case, the experience has not yet happened. Only your present field of thoughts and fantasies, based in your history of other experiences which also become part of the current field, can explain how you are feeling now.

This does not mean that Gestalt practitioners ignore a client's past or future, but that they will focus attention on the way this past or future is being experienced *now* in the current field which, of course, will include each thought, feeling and action as well as what is happening within the relationship between practitioner and client.

When Derek talks of his relief at the death of his father, the therapist will be inter-ested in the way that relief is experienced *now*, how it is currently being expressed (or avoided), how the telling affects the relationship between therapist and client at this moment, what significance the sudden twitch of the client's leg may have, how his breathing reflects his current experience, and so on. All that is happening is happening now and is part of Derek's present experience. Even when one thing is made figure, the practitioner pays attention to the simultaneously existing ground.

The Principle of Singularity

Everyone is unique. Each person's experience is unique. As you read this book you will place your own emphasis on certain ideas, make relevance of them, apply them to your experience and make connections with them which are peculiarly your own.

Your phenomenal field will influence your experience. Your emotional, mental and physical state, the context of when, where, why and how you are reading, are all part of your unique experience right now.

The focus in Gestalt is upon 'what is'. Any generalisations we make are movements away from this present experiencing, this here-and-now awareness. The Gestalt therapist does not 'treat' depression, stress, anxiety or phobias, but meets and attends to the whole person who, in the present moment, may be experiencing each or any of these generalised descriptions *in their own particular way*.

This does not mean totally ignoring any patterns or consistencies which may have relevance to a person's experience and which may, therefore, be usefully borne in mind. Rather, it places emphasis on perceiving the person's present experience as figure in the current relational field, not our preconceptions based on generalisations. In our example, the therapist may be well aware that people in all cultures, in response to the death of a person with whom they have shared some intimacy, over time move through different phases in the process of grieving. However, this experience is unique to each individual. The therapist will attend to Derek's particular process as he experiences how he is feeling, thinking and behaving *now* in response to his father's death.

The Principle of Changing Process

Nothing is static. Nothing is permanent. Life is always in process. Change is occurring all the time. Though you are still reading this book, the situation has changed and you have moved on to another experience. Even if you read this sentence again immediately, you cannot repeat your original experience of reading it. The field is newly created moment by moment.

The Gestalt approach gives emphasis to constant change, perceiving and describing experience *in process* and avoiding the temptation to use language and definitions which imply permanence. Gestaltists dislike labelling behaviour as pathology. Rather they use the term 'creative adjustment' to describe the development of some behaviour which may seem or have seemed the best alternative at the time. They also avoid words that imply a condition. There is no such thing as a shy person (implying that their behaviour is fixed for all time in all situations in shyness); rather a person is *being shy* right now in this particular situation. Similarly, to label someone as an extrovert is to imply a permanence (and, therefore, a restriction) to their behaviour. Even someone who behaves in an extrovert manner in many situations will not do so all the time in all situations. Rather they are *being extrovert* right now in this particular situation. For all we know, the person described as shy and the person described as extrovert might be one and the same, simply behaving differently according to the circumstances. It is interesting to note that Perls et al. (1972 [1951]: 373) define 'the self' as creating itself moment by moment at the contact boundary – the boundary between the person and their environment.

In the session, the therapist attends to Derek and his experience as it is right now, aware that his experience is not fixed for all time but is a flowing and ever-changing process. As he talks of his relief at his father's death, the therapist is aware that this is his experience at the moment. When later he begins to cry, she affirms his current experience. He is neither a 'relieved mourner' nor a 'sad mourner', he is a person in process, moving through the ever-changing field of his perception. When he smiles at some memory of his father he is sharing with the therapist, he is not necessarily denying his relief or his sadness. Momentarily, he is experiencing feeling warm towards his father as his own singular reality unfolds and moves on.

The Principle of Possible Relevance

Everything in the field has possible meaning. Everything is part of the total organisation. According to this principle, we cannot arbitrarily ignore the relevance of anything in the field. As Parlett writes, 'Gestalt therapists are interested in "the obvious", in rendering afresh what has become unseen and automatic, or is being taken for granted or regarded as of no relevance' (1991: 72). He uses the analogy of looking at a painting and describes how a field theorist will be cognisant not only of the picture but of the style of frame and the context of the exhibition, seeing them all as relevant to their experience of the painting.

Similarly, when working with clients, the Gestalt practitioner does not arbitrarily exclude anything as irrelevant but allows the possible relevance at each moment of, not just the content of what the client is saying, but also, for example, the clothes the person is wearing, their style of speech, their mannerisms, their bodily movements, their breathing, their eye contact, their way of relating to the therapist. As Derek clenches his fist while talking about his father's death, the therapist does not ignore this movement as irrelevant, but may choose to bring Derek's attention to it in order to explore what meaning it may have in the field of his experience. Making figure of what was previously ground, it may transpire that Derek becomes aware of his anger towards his father, of which he has previously been unaware.

Kurt Lewin informed us that there is nothing as practical as a good theory. And, we believe Field Theory indeed offers us that. Firstly, it is a way of thinking that challenges the individualistic notion of humans because it acknowledges the ongoing relational interconnectedness and interdependency we have with each other and the wider context we live in. Secondly, it provides a lens for practitioners to understand the holistic nature of human beings' experience and their context, which includes families, communities, society, the environment and planet. It is also a method that provides a way to ground our relational practice and attend to the co-creating of experiences in the relational dance between us.

Brian O Neill and Sean Gaffney (2008) identify four ways of being that are integrated into the practice of field-orientated practitioners. The first is 'being field sensitive' where the therapist or coach senses into the field and, as part of the field, trusts that meaning will emerge from the field in dialogue with a client. Here the practitioner does not seek to 'push' premature sense-making. The second is 'being field insightful' and requires the practitioner to inquire into the nature of the interconnected patterns. She explores different parts of the field, and the fields within fields (Parlett, 2005). The third is 'being field affecting' where exploratory questions are asked to understand the situation and also how the self may change as a result. The fourth is 'being field present' and it is here that the practitioner explores the co-created relationship between her and her clients in the dialogic process of relating (as described in Chapter 3). As practitioners, we are not detached observers but intricately part of the field.

In Part III of this book, we will be exploring phenomenology and dialogue in the counselling relationship and we hope to show how these concepts of interconnectedness translate into practice with our clients. Meanwhile we offer some exercises for your further exploration.

Experimental Activities

1 We each make our own connections. We have our own way of constellating and contextualising. We do not experience things in isolation. For instance, if we imagine an armchair, we may immediately picture a small, cosy room, crammed with furniture and lots of cushions. We may imagine a log-fire, a book, a cup of cocoa which might make us think of a grandparent. Then we may remember sitting on our grandmother's knee listening to a story, feeling safe and warm, and so on. See what connections you make when imagining the following objects or situations:
   - a jug of milk;
   - a tractor;
   - a walking stick;
   - two poles with a rope hung between them;
   - the smell of a bonfire;
   - the sensation of the wind against your face;
   - a pile of clothes by a river;
   - the sound of gunfire.
2 You might find it interesting to ask your friends to do the same exercise and compare their answers with yours to illustrate how different people's perceptions can be. For instance, in the example of a pile of clothes by a river, did you think of someone doing their laundry, a happy swim in the afternoon sun, or the tragic signs of a suicide? Being aware of how we perceive our world is part of self-awareness. What do you think your associations say about you at this point in time? Do any of these relate to any of your historical experience?
3 Think of a friend of yours. What is the immediate context in which you put your friend? Be aware of where you imagine them and how you imagine them. Be aware of the particular connections you make when you think of them.
4 Think of a recent work or personal situation that you were actively participating in and had importance for you. What do you most remember about this event and your part in it? What else was happening in the wider context of your organisation and your life? What other events were you aware of taking place in the wider world at that time (these may have been out of your awareness)? What connections do you make (if any) between any of the wider events, memories or experiences and your work or personal situation?

Additional Reading

Parlett, M. (2005) 'Contemporary gestalt therapy: field theory', in A.L. Woldt and S.M. Toman (eds), *Gestalt Therapy: History, Theory and Practice.* Thousand Oaks, CA: Sage. pp. 41–64.

Wheeler, G. (2009) 'New directions in gestalt theory: psychology and psychotherapy in the age of complexity', in D. Ullman and G. Wheeler (eds), *CoCreating the Field: Intention and Practice in the Age of Complexity.* Cleveland, OH: Gestalt Press. pp. 3–44.

PART III
GESTALT PRACTICE

8
Assessment and the Process of Change

Perls states: 'As soon as the structure . . . is clear to the therapist, he should plan his course of action, but remain alert and elastic during the whole treatment' (1992 [1947]). Such a simple statement belies the difficulty faced by the Gestalt practitioner with her foundation of phenomenology, holism and respect for the individual. Perls' description of 'structure' implies diagnosis, a contentious area for some Gestalt practitioners. A premature or rigidly held assessment will deaden our perception and stereotype the individual without acknowledging his uniqueness and fluidity. Consequently, many have chosen to ignore diagnosis altogether for fear of losing the quality of the here-and-now moment. However, diagnosis, as understood from its Greek roots meaning 'through *discerning*' (Staemmler, 1999), suggests that diagnosing is an ongoing process that requires care and rigour. It is an attempt to 'impose a pattern on something fundamentally unknowable' (Melnick and Nevis, 1997: 58), while remaining open to the ever-changing nature of the person. This ensures that we avoid labelling and reifying a person. As practitioners, we hold hope that people have the potential to change and develop. In practice this means we use active verbs when diagnosing or assessing. For example, Jim is obsessing about his partner rather than Jim is obsessed with his partner. Claudia is frustrating herself when she does not meet work deadlines compared to Claudia is frustrated when she does not meet work deadlines.

Most Gestalt practitioners see the value of assessing and diagnosing in order to plan for effective treatment. In a sense, we cannot *not* assess. As we saw earlier, humans are meaning-making creatures, making sense of what they notice all the time. From the moment our client comes into the consulting room we will be paying attention to him, feeling about and reacting to him. This noticing contributes to our assessment. That assessment may then be shared with the client to assist in goal setting.

Assessment in Gestalt practice is most useful if it is phenomenological (your own and your client's experience).

Phenomenological Assessment

Observable Contact Functions

1 *Movement/gestures.* How does your client move – stiffly or in a relaxed way? Does he make a lot of movements or remain still?
2 *Voice.* Loud or soft, distant or present, fluent or tentative?
3 *Seeing.* Does he make eye contact? Is his gaze steady or darting?
4 *Hearing.* Does he hear what you say easily? Does he hear correctly or appear to mishear?

Contact Boundary

1 How well does your client make contact with you?
2 What sort of contact?
3 Do you feel an immediate response from her or is she distracted and distant?
4 How and when does she modify contact?

Cycle of Experience

1 Does the client have clear sensations, which he recognises? Can he mobilise energy to respond to his needs; can he make a plan and take action? Does he complete his action satisfactorily and then withdraw?
2 What modifications to contact of the cycle do you notice?
3 What unfinished business or fixed gestalts do you notice or does the client talk about?
4 What patterns emerge from the client's account of herself with others? With you?

Self and Environmental Support

1 What is the client's breathing like? Is it deep and relaxed, trusting both in the self and in the ability of the world to offer nourishment?
2 Does she seem able to soothe and regulate her experience? Does she relax into the support of her chair?
3 Does she refuse your feedback, or is she over-dependent on it?
4 Does she report having a supportive network of family or friends?

The Field

1 What life circumstances are impinging on the client at the moment?
2 What are the cultural, social, organisational or sexual implications of his situation?

3　What feelings and images do you have in response to the client?

4　Do you like him? Why?

5　What do you notice in your body? Try to allow your observations to be tentative. To say of someone, 'He has a modification at the appraisal stage of the cycle,' has the effect of labelling a person in a fixed way. If we say, 'He appears to be modifying or interrupting,' it is an active mobile process which allows for change.

In addition to the broad assessment overview described above, there are some crucial specific questions which the practitioner needs to address. Why has the client come? What problems is she bringing and what does she want from therapy or coaching? How does what you notice in the assessment link with her areas of distress or hope? What are the ways in which she supports or impairs her contact and functioning and which of them might become the focus of your work together? There are some distinctions between therapy and coaching in the assessment phase. In the coaching relationship, clients are working on issues that are contextualised by the nature of their work within an organisation. Hence, a Gestalt coach will be interested in a client's role, current organisational field and what is happening for that organisation in the wider economic and political context. Therefore, additional questions to address here are: why now and why were you chosen as the coach? Has the client been in a coaching relationship before, and if so, what was her experience? Exploratory questions such as these can facilitate the contracting process, which we discuss later when planning the work. The coach may also pay attention to how the client makes contact when they first meet. What emerges between you and the client as you make contact? What is evoked in you? What is your embodied response? This may help to highlight implicit expectations clients may have of you as coach. It may also draw attention to some of the relational patterns that the client experiences in his organisational role that he is seeking to resolve in the coaching relationship.

In the appendices at the end of this book we have included three forms that the Gestalt therapist may find useful in helping to conduct the initial assessment. Be aware of what you notice, but do not try to make sense of it all within the session. A change in any aspect of the relational field between us changes the meaning we may make of the emerging patterns from our joint phenomenological assessment. In the co-created relationship we are mutually influencing each other and our assessment must take account of this. Assessing occurs through dialogue and contact, where both practitioner and client 'construct an intersubjective awareness regarding the nature of the situation' (Brownell, 2010: 198). What we diagnose now is what is happening here between us and not for all time. Remember, meaning is selective to the moment and it is field dependent.

Assessment should not interfere with your meeting with the client. It entails relating, for the most part, in an I–It mode, but only as a useful ground for the potential emergence of the I–Thou relationship.

Is Gestalt Suitable for this Client?

Gestalt has very powerful ways of heightening awareness, not the least of which is the work in the dialogue with its implicit demand for intimate contact. Gestalt can invite clients to be in touch with parts of themselves that they did not previously know and loosen the restrictive bonds that people place on themselves through limited knowledge, habit or fear. Gestalt is sometimes called the 'solvent' which can dissolve the old rigid patterns of living in order to open up new options.

There are some people, however, for whom the full range of Gestalt practice would not be appropriate, or, at the very least, would need to be used with caution. These include people for whom life is already too disorienting and disturbing. They often have a sense of fragmentation, of being lost or ungrounded. These people need glue, not solvent. They need to find a way of holding themselves together and taking an ordinary place in the world. This is not to say necessarily that Gestalt therapy is therefore unsuitable. Many Gestaltists work successfully with, for example, clients experiencing psychosis, basing their work on anxiety reduction, reality testing and the slow building of a relationship which encourages and supports their improving management of their lives. Awareness is increased slowly and confrontation is completely avoided. For further reading on this topic we recommend Brownell (2010), Delisle (1999), Greenberg (2003), the Spring 1979 edition of the *American Gestalt Journal* and the chapter by Harris in Nevis (1992). However, for the beginning Gestalt therapist, this specialist work should not be undertaken without careful psychiatric supervision, while a coach who considers that his client has this sort of fragile process should invite the client to seek the more regular ongoing support of therapy.

One can think about health as a continuum with perfectly healthy process in one direction and extreme disturbance in the other. We all lie somewhere along this continuum. None of us is perfectly healthy; we all have some sort of disturbances to our process at some times. A task of assessment is to find out where on the continuum a prospective client may lie, in order to be sure that they fall within the range of our competence and experience and also that they are likely to benefit from the approach we are using.

Here we offer some basic guidelines to help you decide whether the Gestalt approach is suitable.

1   If your potential client has such severely impaired contact functions that they are not able to have some real meeting with you: that is to say, if their experiences are greatly outside the range of ordinariness – for instance, if they report seeing things which are not there or hearing things which you cannot hear; if they do not answer your questions meaningfully; if their language is jumbled or strange and you cannot make sense of it – they will probably not immediately benefit from Gestalt therapy. We suggest that in this case, your job, if possible, is to facilitate this person's receiving medical help. Perhaps later, with the continued support of a psychiatrist, for example, therapy that focuses predominantly on increased self-support may be helpful.

2   If your potential client has some severe disturbance in contact functions and interruptions in the cycle of experience, yet has some meaningful contact with you and is able to think with you about the problem, it may be that medical help would still be of benefit, but this could be in conjunction with Gestalt therapy. Your supervisor will help you think how best to work with this client, and to decide whether any special measures for ensuring his safety would be relevant.

3 There is one other caveat that we would like to suggest to you. Always take your own feelings into account. For example, do not agree to work with a client if you feel frightened of them. It would not be fair on either of you. Even if you judge that your fear is a result of your own unfinished business rather than that of your client, you will still be unable to offer your best attention. Discuss with your supervisor the meaning of your fear.

Planning the Work

Once you have decided that Gestalt practice is suitable for your potential client, you are free to think about treatment direction and 'negotiating consensus' (Zinker, 1977), which means agreeing the focus of your work together. If a practitioner and a client were to make an agreement to work in a purely Gestalt way, it would be that they should bring themselves as fully as possible to the here-and-now, to meet and explore anything and everything that emerges, to achieve mutuality of contact. However, clients rarely come with this aim in mind: they come with problems and difficulties which they want the therapist or coach to help them resolve. It is the practitioner's responsibility to hold the polarity between an approach which believes that ultimately growth and health come from the relationship of two individuals meeting without preconceived expectations or desires and, at the other pole, the client's need for help with a particular problem. In other words, on the one hand there is the aim of a 'dialogic' meeting, with its natural flow between I–It and I–Thou moments; on the other, there is the necessity for a particular kind of I–It focusing on how a client may be contributing to their own difficulties.

Thus any plan for therapy cannot simply be a list of symptoms with how and in what order to treat them. It must be a subtle guide which is always available to negotiation. It is common to use the word 'journey' to describe the process of growth and change which is undertaken in the company of a therapist or coach. We prefer to see *life* as the journey and therapy or coaching as a part or stage of it. One can see planning, therefore, as being two facilitators of this part of the journey: the map and the method of travel.

The Map

It is often said that we should not confuse the map with the territory (Korzybski, 1931/1933). This is a good axiom to remember when planning a therapy or coaching direction. We must always be responsive to the actual 'territory' we encounter, being willing to take detours, make stopovers or even change the destination. The phenomenological method we describe in the next chapter will support us in staying close to the 'territory'. Clarkson (1992) said the therapist brings not a map but map-making skills to the therapeutic journey. Here, we offer an informal map of Gestalt practice. But think of it like the maps that the children in Arthur Ransome's *Swallows and Amazons* made. They explored the waterways and countryside around their home and

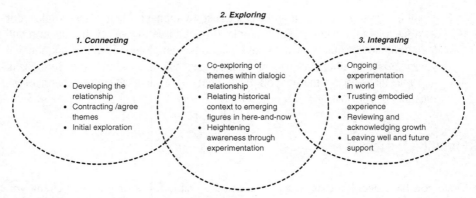

Figure 8.1   Three phases of therapeutic/coaching work

named each place in a way that was meaningful to them. They did not use someone else's map because their experience was unique and it was theirs. The same applies to your treatment plan. Take the outline and fill it in with the unique details of the journey with your client. Use it to plot your adventure, rather than dictate it. Our map is simple. It contains three phases that support the process of change and growth within the co-created relationship (see Figure 8.1). The length of the phases varies depending on the client's personality, history, phenomenology; the issues they are seeking to address; and whether it is short- or long-term therapy.

The First Phase: Connecting

Arguably, the most important task of the first phase of therapy and coaching is the building of a relationship of sufficient trust and commitment that the client can feel safe and supported. This is establishing our working alliance, where we are paying attention to the relationship, agreeing how we work together and identifying the issues that a client is seeking to address. The boundaries of time, place, fees and confidentiality are agreed as part of the administrative contract. The work begins with an agreed focus knowing that this may change and evolve over time. Clients soon realise that they are expected to pay attention to themselves and respect themselves and the task of heightening awareness through co-inquiry. It is to be hoped that they also feel attended to, heard and understood.

The client's task is to find out 'Who am I? How am I in the world?' Normally, it is not a phase concerned with change – unless there is an immediate crisis or problem that needs action – but with being oneself and expressing oneself. It is also concerned with developing enough 'self-support' to go on to a deeper exploration and the possible challenging of old ways of being. Themes and patterns of thinking, feeling and behaving begin to emerge and are brought to awareness. Another important feature is that disowned parts of the person may be recognised, struggled with and integrated.

For some clients, this initial phase may be quite short, particularly in coaching, when our clients are usually robust and have sufficient support. If the client makes good contact and is familiar with the notion of heightening awareness, he may move on swiftly. For some, however, it will take longer: weeks, months, or years. If a client habitually modifies contact by projecting danger, he may take a considerable time to build a relationship in which he can trust the practitioner. If he often desensitises at the sensation and recognition stages of the cycle, the process of heightening awareness will be slow.

The length of this phase will also depend on whether the client and practitioner have agreed a long- or short-term contract. Sometimes a client may choose to leave at the end of this phase. It may be that they came wanting to understand themselves better, to get help in making a decision or to mourn a bereavement. In this case, their work will be completed. Indeed, at a suitable point in any stage of therapy, a client may choose to continue their journey without the therapist as companion. At some future time they may decide to re-enter therapy for another stage.

The Second Phase: Exploring

In the second phase of therapy and coaching, the task is to explore the themes that have emerged within the co-created relationship in more depth. Sometimes this may involve identifying and resolving unfinished business from the past. Gestalt practice emphasises the here-and-now. However, the aim of Gestalt is not just to make today's figure lively: it is also to discover how yesterday's figures – our history (what Gordon Wheeler, 1991, calls 'structure of the ground') – are still affecting our present, and to look to the potential figures of our desired future and to grow towards them. Clients may discover and challenge core beliefs about themselves, others and the world which underlie their disturbances in process. They may experiment with new options of behaviour. Continuing our analogy of the map, this stage involves going further into uncharted waters. Another metaphor of Gordon Wheeler's is relevant here. He describes feelings as the 'compass' . . . 'they serve to *orient* us, to point us where we want to go (or away from where we don't want to go)' (1994: 16).

The second phase of therapy or coaching may also vary in length. The practitioner must be aware of whatever difficulties the client brought initially and ensure that the focus of the work addresses them. For the coach this means periodically referring back to the focus for the work agreed in the first phase. Together, therapist/coach and client metaphorically explore the outline map they made and this provides the structure to the journey. The practitioner does not push the client to get an ocean-going boat and sail out to sea. If you have read *Swallows and Amazons*, you will know how singularly inappropriate and irrelevant that would be.

The Final Phase: Integrating

This phase of the journey involves integration and the practising of new ways of being and behaving. Some of the work done will need to be repeated or consolidated. The relationship between therapist and client is characterised by an increase in authentic dialogue as both see the other as they really are, and can meet with mutuality of contact. There is an awareness that each person is changing in the presence of the other.

Clients increasingly trust their embodied experience, and become more 'choiceful' in the multiple and varied encounters of their lived lives both inside and outside the therapy or coaching relationship.

Gradually, issues of ending begin to be addressed. Client and practitioner sit down with the map and review where they have been. Sometimes it is necessary to revisit some parts of it. There is sadness at the ending of this particular part of life's journey as well as excitement at making plans for the future. For clients who experienced difficulties towards the end of the cycle experience – completion and withdrawal – this is a particularly important time and much vital work can be done. They are given the opportunity to do their ending differently, neither clinging on to the contact, nor breaking it off precipitately in an avoidance of the pain of separation. Ideally, they can reflect on what they have learned and achieved and name any regrets they may be leaving with. Hopefully, with the support of the practitioner they can acknowledge the difference in themselves, express their feelings and prepare to leave. The practitioner will do the same. Then they say goodbye.

The Method of Travel

The second facilitator of the journey is the method of travel used. The Swallows and Amazons used a combination of walking and small boats, sometimes with oars, sometimes with sails. The method chosen was of course relevant to the particular activity of the day, the weather, the depth of water, the task at hand. In Gestalt therapy and coaching the method of travel is an approach which also, broadly speaking, has two elements or domains.

The first domain involves using the phenomenological method in order to increase awareness and the ability to relate in the here and now, within the dialogic relationship. It also involves supporting healthy functioning (as described above and in Chapter 11) and the development of self-support. These are approaches that you will use with all your clients, regardless of their particular problems and needs.

The second domain involves the use of specific interventions designed to assist the client to achieve better understanding and awareness of herself, learning about or developing new opinions and exploring previously hidden parts of herself. Some of this overlaps with the first band, as these interventions will also, for example, increase self-support. These interventions are grouped under the heading of 'experiments'. This word is chosen because it underlines the philosophy that the Gestalt practitioner does not set out to *change* the client, but to meet her where she is and invite her to push the boundaries of her habitual ways of being by experimenting. Experiments pay specific attention to interruptions to healthy functioning: fixed gestalts, unsatisfying completions, absences or difficulties in contact functions, and indeed any aspect of the client's functioning. The practitioner notices the figures and how they are related to the client's presenting problem. She may then choose from a number of Gestalt techniques in order to address the particular area – techniques which may be either to promote healthy functioning or to undo some pattern of living which is limiting the client. The choice of experiments will depend on the particular needs of the client, and their effectiveness will be linked to a number of variables, including timing, appropriateness and so on.

As you may imagine, the difference between the two domains is subtle and we have had to be quite arbitrary in our categorisation. In practice, the Gestalt practitioner flows easily between the two domains as she follows the pace and the energy of the client: phenomenological exploring develops smoothly into an experiment as the work progresses. However, it is useful to consider them separately in order to become more aware of what the therapist and coach does. In the next five chapters, we will describe these two domains in depth and use a coaching example to bring these to life for you.

With the Gestalt Coach

John, a coach, is approached by Lisa, the Human Resources Director (HRD) of an innovative furnishing company 'Home for You' which was building a brand presence across Europe for its niche products through on-line sales. It was known not only for its creative designers but also its commitment to the environment and it had pioneered several important sustainable sourcing and manufacturing processes for their products. Also, it had a remarkably inclusive attitude to its employees, all of whom were share-holders in the business. During their initial phone contact, Lisa said a little more about what she wanted from coaching. She had been sitting on the board of 'Home for You' for the past year and was finding it difficult to 'have a strong voice' there. She was having trouble with some dominating members of the board and she thought that she needed to be more strategic – and perhaps more assertive. She clarified that 'Home for You' was paying for the coaching and she had the support of her MD and Non-Executive Board Members. Given her role as a board member no one else was required to be part of the coaching contract. John said he would be delighted to meet her and told her his fees, which she agreed. He suggested that they have an initial meeting to 'get to know each other a little' and see whether they thought this was something he could help with.

Connecting Phase

John had offered Lisa the choice of his visiting her office or her coming to his consulting room. Lisa chose to come to him, believing it would be easier to stay focused away from the work-place. She arrived for the appointment exactly on time. While John fetched some coffee, she looked at his bookshelf and was clearly delighted with his section on ecology and sustainability in organisations. John noticed that her face, which had seemed rather wary and serious as she arrived, softened and relaxed as she sat down and launched into her story. He was a bit surprised that she didn't seem to need to know anything else about him, but he supposed that she had heard enough from the person who gave her his name.

(Continued)

(Continued)

Lisa started by telling John the situation. As he knew, the company was founded in the North of England and had a richly multi-cultural workforce. It had always had a strong commitment to maintaining a culture which respected and honoured its people, their communities, and the environment, as well as being committed to generating profit. Three years ago, 'Home for You' had acquired and integrated another retailer. Like many acquisitions, this integration of two businesses was a mixture of excitement and pain for many colleagues, particularly those from the acquired retailer. The current work-force consisted of people from both organisations at all levels. Following an organisational restructuring and rationalisation of systems and processes, attention was now being placed on the development of the people and the organisational culture they were creating. Right now, it was an exciting time as they were market leaders and experiencing year-on-year growth in the demand for their services.

As HR Director, Lisa had been sitting on the board for the past year. She strongly felt that the new integrated company still had work to do to successfully establish and maintain the sort of culture that they wanted – and for which they were known. She believed that a stretching and innovative leadership development programme for the top 25 in the organisation would be enormously helpful in this and the leaders themselves were in agreement. However, it had become clear that the Finance Director and the Sales and Marketing Director did not share her commitment. The Marketing Director had been a powerful figure in the retailer that 'Home for You' had acquired, and Lisa felt that he was determinedly protective of his status. Although the CEO, a long-time friend of Lisa and her husband, was totally committed to the development project, he seemed not to be willing to support her at the board. It was this struggle that had brought Lisa to coaching. She felt frustrated and powerless to influence these two key stakeholders.

As John listened and took in the story, he also used his own here-and-now awareness to assess the woman in front of him.

Observable contact functions. Lisa was a striking woman in her mid-40s. She was clearly of Indian descent and, when he later asked, described herself as a 'modern Indian woman'. Her voice was clear and firm, she looked him straight in the eye as she talked and she sounded passionate as she described the proposed leadership development. As she talked, she leant slightly forward and held out her hands as if reaching for something. When John interjected a question or comment, she responded appropriately.

Contact boundary and cycle of experience. As she talked, John soon felt as if she desperately wanted to persuade him of something. He felt drawn to nod and demonstrate that she was coming across 'loud and clear'. It was interesting, therefore, to note that as she reached the core of her argument – that the programme should take place – her eyes dropped and her voice fell. She looked for a moment as if she was in class and had forgotten the words of the poem she had learned.

Support – self and environment. Clearly, Lisa was well supported in her private life. She spoke warmly of her husband – a white Englishman, whom she had met when she worked for the charity he ran – and her school-age children. At work, she felt the care and support of her deputy, Maria, an Irish woman whom she had recruited some years before. And yet there was a way that her most passionate concerns were not received and heard by anyone. John was still aware that she hadn't really taken much time to get to know him and he wondered if that left her feeling subtly unsupported. What is more, when John questioned her about some of the things she said, she sometimes seemed to lose confidence in herself, and asked him if she had got it wrong. John wondered whether Lisa's self-support was less strong than it might seem.

Coach's response. John noticed his urge to help Lisa. He liked her and admired her passion for what she believed to be right. She was clearly a capable woman to have risen so high within this successful organisation. And still there was something that was making him feel protective of her and nurturing. John was slightly amused to notice this – it was something of a pattern of his to rescue 'damsels in distress'. He wondered what they might be co-creating. However, he didn't allow it to interfere with making some 'test interventions' to see if Gestalt coaching was suitable for Lisa. A couple of times, he drew attention to her body language and inquired into her feelings. On each occasion she seemed curious and was interested in exploring her responses.

By the end of their discussion, they had agreed that they were keen to work together, and agreed an initial three sessions, with an option for another three. The sessions would be 90 minutes and take place, at least at first, in John's office. It was clear that Lisa was well able to make use of John's Gestalt approach. They had begun to identify some strategic conversations that Lisa needed to have, and some actions in her position of HRD. Importantly, they had also begun to identify that some of the ways that Lisa was behaving, some of her patterns of relating, might be interfering with her ability to be potent at the board, and perhaps elsewhere. These became the subject of their first contract for the coaching.

Additional Reading

Brownell, P. (2010) 'Assessment in gestalt therapy', in *A Guide to Contemporary Practice: Gestalt Therapy*. New York: Springer Publishing. pp. 189–212.

Delisle, G. (1999) 'A protocol for the initial interview', in *Personality Disorders*. Quebec: Les Editions du Reflet. pp. 141–51.

Greenberg, E. (2003) 'Love, admiration or safety: a system of gestalt diagnosis of borderline, narcissistic, and schizoid adaptations that focuses on what is figure for the client', *Gestalt!*, 6 (3) (accessed 20 May 2011 from: www.g-gej.org/6-3/diagnosis.html).

Joyce, P. and Sills, C. (2010) *Skills in Gestalt Counselling and Psychotherapy* (2nd edn). London: Sage. Chapters 5, 6 and 18.

9
Phenomenology and Awareness

In this chapter, we look at the way phenomenology translates into practice through the phenomenological method. Remember that we described phenomenology as the subjective experience of 'what is'. It is the study of the client's feelings, somatic sensations, meaning-making and truth without interpretation. Here's an exercise: Look at the picture of the man in Figure 9.1 . Write down at least eight things that come into your mind as you look at him. Do not stop to examine your responses, simply list them as they occur to you. How many of them are pure description? For instance, you may have noticed that he is grey-haired, clean-shaven and so on. Probably many of your responses, however, involve some interpretation on your part. You may have described him as grumpy, thoughtful, severe, peaceful, friendly-looking. You may have noticed that he seems not to be meeting your gaze, or something about the way he dresses. You might be interested to ask a friend or colleague to do the same exercise. Do they notice the same things or do they notice different ones? Are their focuses, perceptions and experiences the same as yours? Probably not.

What do you notice about your responses to the picture? Do they confirm or reveal anything about you? For instance, do you have biases in your expectations of people

Figure 9.1   The thoughtful man

relating to gender, age and social status? Are you the sort of person who describes someone but does not 'get a feel' of them? Are you, on the contrary, someone who quickly thinks about someone in relational terms – how they might behave to you and you to them?

The exercise illustrates very simply some of the concepts we have written about in Part II of this book. We have our individual ways of noticing and of interpreting what we notice. They are based on individual, social and cultural learning experiences of which we are only partly aware, as well as on situational factors and the mood we are in. As Spinelli puts it:

> far from being objective, our perceptions of others typically contain variables which more correctly define and describe psychological factors in the make-up of the perceiver rather than point out accurate, universally shared 'facts' about the perceived. (1989: 67)

This concurs with the much earlier assertion from the Talmud that, 'We do not see things as they are, we see things as we are'.

The phenomenology of our clients is the way *they* see themselves, other people and the world and our first job as therapist or coach is to help them become aware of this. Carl Rogers (1951) pointed out that a person cannot move psychologically from their position until they have been fully accepted in that position. The truth of this is easy to confirm. Think of a time when you had a fierce argument with someone. Chances are you had different viewpoints and that what you felt most angry and frustrated about is that your view was not being taken seriously. Normally, we do not need the other person to *agree* with us (though that is nice too!) – we need to be *heard*. When someone sees our point of view and can say, 'I see, so the way you feel is this . . .' or 'So what you experienced is that . . .', we immediately become calmer. We feel understood, confirmed in the fullness of our experience, and we are more ready to hear another point of view. Clients need us to listen and to understand; they need to listen and to understand themselves. They become aware of who they are. Then paradoxically they will be open to growth and change (Beisser, 1970). We, as practitioners, must put aside our own perceptions, biases, interpretations and value judgements in order to be fully open to the client's true experience. In this way, we can invite our clients to raise their awareness in a spirit of interested and genuine inquiry rather than one of labelling and judgement. The phenomenological method enables us to support heightening awareness. In order to follow the phenomenological method, the practitioner attempts to follow three distinctive yet interrelated elements.

Epoche or Bracketing

Epoche is a Greek word meaning a stop, check or pause. It comes from *ep-echein*, 'to have or to hold'. In therapy and coaching terms this means that we are willing temporarily to hold to one side all our own values, prejudices, understandings and priorities – in short, everything that colours our experience – in order to be able to meet the client's experience 'without memory and without desire' (Bion, 1967). Later we may choose to share something we have held aside, if the time seems right. Spinelli (2011, personal communication) uses the analogy of the 'bracket' in a mathematical equation, alerting us to the fact that what we put in brackets is still an important part of the equation (the relational field), whether we share it or not.

In any case, in practice, it would be impossible to bracket off all our perceptions and judgements. They are too much a part of us. But, as Gestalt practitioners, this is what we aim to do: we try to put to one side all our 'everyday' expectations and assumptions so that we can listen to what is arising for our clients and also for us, as the session unfolds. When our client says, 'I am expecting a baby,' we do not automatically assume that this is a happy event; we may say, 'How do you feel about that?' Our client may be scared, shocked, angry or excited. Similarly, when our coaching client says, 'My boss shouted at me in the corridor,' we do not assume that she feels upset in the way that we might. She may have felt invigorated because her boss showed some interest in the project. We wait to see what emerges, noting simultaneously, and with curiosity, the assumptions we have bracketed and what part they may be playing in the relational field. What part may my assumption of a birth being a happy event be playing? How might my assumption of my client's being upset by her boss be part of our relational encounter? (See Horizontalism below.)

Thus the Gestaltist's exploration should not be interpretation or association. It is not asking the question: 'Why?' or 'What for?' It is asking questions like: 'What are you doing now?', 'How are you holding your body?', 'What are you feeling?', 'What are you saying to yourself as you do that?', 'What does that do for you?', 'What happens next?', 'What else could you do?' It is also paying attention to feelings, sensations, thoughts and images that arise for the practitioner as she sits with her client.

The following is an example of a therapist practising bracketing. Emily says that her boss is abusing her. The therapist has an immediate picture of a tyrannical, balding man – somewhat like his own father – and feels angrily sympathetic. However, he brackets off his reaction.

THERAPIST: What's that like for you?
EMILY: It's funny really, because she is in a wheelchair and couldn't hit me, but I feel terribly scared?
THERAPIST: So you think it's strange of you to be scared.
EMILY: I suppose I do. But she shouts and screams so.
THERAPIST: And what are you frightened of?
EMILY: Well, I'm frightened . . . Actually, I'm frightened that she will die, like my grandmother did when she was shouting one day. [*Pause*] I never realised until now that it was Grandma she reminded me of.

Every one of the therapist's interventions involved some bracketing. There was his initial reaction when he imagined his father, then his own view that shouting in any form is unpleasant. Then he bracketed his assumption that Emily was frightened for her own safety. He did not bracket, however, his sense that Emily's fear was very real and important. By phenomenological enquiry, he was able to facilitate Emily's understanding of a deeper cause of her fear.

Description

The second rule of the phenomenological method is to describe rather than explain or interpret. Having bracketed our assumptions and values, we are then faced with another tendency, vital to human living, yet restricting in this context. It is the tendency to make meaning and explain what is happening rather than simply to experience it. An example is that of a woman sitting in a deckchair, full in the sun. She is squinting up her eyes. A description is simply that: she is squinting up her eyes. An explanation is that she is protecting them from the glare. However, if we release ourselves from the limitations of our first perceptions (remember the figures in Chapter 6) there are many possible explanations for her behaviour. She may be involved in thinking about a puzzling dilemma; she may be experimenting to see what the trees look like through half-closed eyes; she may be exercising her face muscles.

Following the rule of description we avoid putting any interpretation on things and allow the client to explore their own phenomenology. We may draw their attention to what we notice about them and invite them to notice themselves in the same way and find out what is *their* explanation. And we do not look for the obscure or subtle; we look at the obvious. Clarkson and Mackewn (1993: 93) quote Perls as saying, 'I have frequently discovered that the obvious has been taken for granted not only by the patient, but by the therapist as well.'

Gestalt therapists are aware that fixed gestalts, though originally formed as 'creative adjustments' to situations in the past, are no longer in the past. They are in the present. By noticing, naming and exploring 'the obvious', we help people become aware of those fixed gestalts and restore the ability to respond creatively and flexibly to life's experience. Sometimes, of course, it will be necessary for the client to talk about the past and even relive parts of it in order to complete unfinished business. However, often the therapist's approach will be to bring these old patterns of behaving, thinking and feeling into the foreground where they can be experienced in the present as conscious activities for which the client can take responsibility. Erving Polster's (1991) tight sequencing can be useful to the client here. This is a process where the practitioner is tracking the moment-to-moment unfolding sequence of contacting by noticing and inquiring. This is done by noticing a tone of voice or gesture, a facial expression, the use of a word, a choice of clothes or job or car and so on, and commenting and inviting awareness through questions such as: 'what is happening now?', 'what are you feeling?', 'where in your body?', 'how are you doing that?' . Polster observes, 'Without detail, the "understanding" provided by abstraction is like substituting a title for a story. It is surprising how often therapist and patient settle for titles' (1991: 176). This process presents opportunities to amplify here-and-now experiences, unmet there-and-then needs being experienced in the present, or the co-created encounter, in order to heighten awareness. All these descriptive interventions allow the client to explore himself fully and honour the detail of his living story in the present.

Horizontalism

This means that everything in your client's context (including you and your relationship with your client) is given the same importance as everything else. It is also known as equalisation. In a way, it is a form of bracketing, as it involves the practitioner suspending her powers of prioritising and selection. The client's experience is approached as if it were a jigsaw puzzle. Each piece is equally important in making the whole, even though it may be 'just' a piece of sky rather than part of a person's face.

The value of horizontalism in therapy and coaching is that it allows both practitioner and client to look at the whole. Everything is relevant, from the client's tiny finger movements as she talks, to something in the wider field, like the fact that she has bought a new pair of gloves, to what you both are thinking or feeling in the relationship, including those thoughts or feelings you may have bracketed. Also important may be the parts that the client does not mention; for instance, what she was doing for the hour before her mother came to visit, or how she felt as she prepared to make a difficult telephone call to a colleague. A client's concern in making a telephone call is seen differently in the context of her call focused on sharing the success of a recent project, or having to inform her colleague that redundancies will be required.

For some weeks, Betty has been talking about her lack of confidence. Today she seems listless and unable to focus on anything.

THERAPIST: I notice you are wearing a red sweater today. I have never seen you in red before.
BETTY: Oh, I never wear it. It was because everything else was in the wash.
THERAPIST: You looked quite lively as you said that.
BETTY: Well, I guess . . . actually, you know, I had just received that letter from my mother. And I thought, 'Mum would hate this, she'd say it was too loud,' and I put it on.
THERAPIST: So the choice is significant.
BETTY: [*Giggles*] I think it is. I think I wanted to defy her. I like red and I like wearing it.

Betty goes on to talk animatedly about wanting to stand up to her mother.

Examples of the Phenomenological Method

In practice the three domains of the phenomenological method are interdependent. In the following examples the Gestalt practitioner uses bracketing, description, horizontalism and also her own phenomenology to heighten the client's awareness.

The client is talking about differences in her marriage.

JEAN: The more I think about him the sadder I feel. I keep wishing I hadn't said what I did and I just want to cry all the time.
THERAPIST: You tell me you are sad, then you look at me and smile.

JEAN:	Do I?
THERAPIST:	Weren't you aware of it?
JEAN:	No I wasn't, you see I . . . there, I just did it then – I smiled at you as I started to speak.
THERAPIST:	What are you aware of as you smile?
JEAN:	I'm thinking that I don't want to upset you . . . umm . . . I think I want to reassure you that I'm all right really.
THERAPIST:	I notice you tensing your face and your breathing seems shallow.
JEAN:	Yes, I feel anxious. It's silly but I'm afraid you might get depressed . . . like my mother . . . if ever I had a problem, she became deeply depressed. I learned to pretend that everything was fine. Pretend and pretend. And you know what? I do the same with Rick.
THERAPIST:	And I notice as you talk to me now you've stopped making those little smiles.

In this example, the client realised how she projected her mother onto the therapist and, with a combination of introjection and retroflection, modified her relational contact.

In the following example, therapist and client explore Bill's lack of energy at the appraisal and mobilisation stage of the gestalt cycle.

BILL:	I'm not getting what I want out of this group.
THERAPIST:	What is it that you want?
BILL:	Well that's it . . . I don't know what I want . . . I want the group to help me.
THERAPIST:	I notice the position you are lying in right now. How is that for you?
BILL:	Well, I'm almost lying flat with just my head propped on the cushion. I guess I'm 'slumped'.
THERAPIST:	Take your time. Very slowly allow yourself to be aware of what arises in you as you focus your awareness on your slumping.
BILL:	Well . . . I feel heavy . . . and there is a pulling sensation in my back.
THERAPIST:	I notice you are breathing shallowly.
BILL:	That's true. It's hard to breathe deeply in this position. I feel like a walrus on a beach.
THERAPIST:	You look sad at the idea of being a walrus on a beach.
BILL:	I feel scared when you say that. That would mean I couldn't move easily. I'd be waiting for the tide to come in before I could have my freedom.
THERAPIST:	Freedom?
BILL:	To move . . . to be what I want to be. [*Bill looks thoughtful*] But even walruses move on their own. They can get down to the sea . . . I need to go down to the sea . . . to go where I want and do what I want.
THERAPIST:	And, as you say that, you have started to sit up and gesture with your arms. What is going on for you now?
BILL:	I want to stand up and walk around.

In the final example, Dave, an IT Director, is interrupting the cycle at the sensation-recognition stage as he arrives for his coaching session.

DAVE: I don't know what to talk about. I feel flat and low today.
COACH: Your voice sounds low and flat. Your body looks quite tense and restless. How do you feel in your body?
DAVE: Yes, I feel restless. I don't know why. I feel restless and agitated.
COACH: Now you're frowning and your voice sounds quite angry.
DAVE: You're right. I do feel angry. Actually, I think I've been feeling angry ever since yesterday when my director ticked me off for something that was nothing to do with me.
COACH: You are very energised now. The whole atmosphere in the room has changed.
DAVE: I do feel angry. I think I'll go and speak with him tomorrow and explain.

Adopting the Phenomenological Method: Support for Therapist and Coach

Gestaltists believe in the innate potential of all human beings to grow, develop and live fulfilling lives. This trust in the capacity of the person leads to methodological principles that are fundamental to the approach. The central one is that it is through heightening awareness that change occurs. Increased awareness of 'what is' supports clients in having a wider variety of options from which to choose how they make contact and live in relationship with others.

As we have seen, adopting the phenomenological method supports this awareness-raising and requires therapists and coaches to stay close to the unfolding experiences in the co-created relationship. This can be challenging for practitioners. Understanding the paradoxical theory of change as described in Chapter 4 can be of support, as can understanding the co-transferring relationship.

The Co-transferring Relationship

Knowing which experiences to share in the therapy or coaching relationship requires care. Practitioners have a responsibility to be discerning when informing clients of their own experiences or when inviting clients to attend to their phenomenology. As we have seen above, clients can transfer historic figures or events onto the practitioner and relate 'as if' it is the historic person with whom they are in contact. Equally, they might import patterns of relating from the past into the present. This is known as 'transference'. Of course, out of awareness, this can also happen to practitioners. Hence the importance of supervision. It can be helpful for therapists and coaches to understand their transference and counter-transference 'profile' so they can differentiate between participating responsively in the real here-and-now relationship or the transferential there-and-then as re-enacted in the here-and-now. In Gestalt, the transferential relationship is more appropriately understood as the 'co-transferring relationship' as therapists and coaches are in a relationship of reciprocal mutual influence with clients. If understood through the phenomenological method, it may illuminate

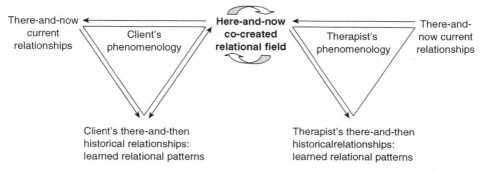

Figure 9.2 The co-transferential encounter

how a client (and therapist) habitually organises himself and the environment – a re-enactment of a fixed gestalt. Heightening awareness of this process with care, may facilitate healing and growth for our clients (and, concomitantly and unavoidably, for the therapist too). Figure 9.2 adapts Chinnock's (2011) development of Menninger's (1958) 'triangle of insight', and demonstrates graphically how both participants are shaped by their own experiences – back there-and-then in the historical field, out there-and-now' with current relationships and in the 'here and now' of the engagement. The potential exists both to recreate old patterns and also to create a new and unique encounter.

There are ways the therapist can recognise the co-transferring relational process and his part in it, involving re-enacting his or her previous experience in the here and now with clients. To explore your transference profile you may reflect on the relationships in your life. Take a moment with pen and paper and write your first responses to the following questions:

- What are your particular prevalent patterns of relating with friends?
- Do you challenge figures of authority or tend to appease them?
- Are you likely to be proactive and nurturing in your relationships or more reactive and tentative?
- What is your relationship with people of the same or opposite gender and how does this resonate with relationships in your family of origin?
- Do any of your answers to the above questions relate to some of your historical experiences that may be fixed gestalts or unfinished business?
- When you look at some of your responses, do any of these patterns relate to how you are with some clients?

A good indication of a co-transferring relationship is when you notice yourself responding in a way with a particular client that is very different from other clients. For example, the therapist noticed it was difficult to finish a session on time with Hannah, a widow. On reflection, the therapist became aware that Hannah reminded her of her own mother who regularly suggested that she did not get enough time with her daughter. This is an example of the therapist 'transferring' her own mother onto the client and, out of awareness, offering to the client what she did not provide in her own daughter–mother relationship. This example also illustrates the importance of self–reflection and supervision for therapists and coaches both in the work and post hoc.

Melnick (2003) provides five indicators of counter-transference for the therapist and coach. The first indicator is *content*. Sometimes we may find ourselves inquiring into the detail of an event when this is no longer of interest for the client or figural in the work. The second indicator is *self-disclosure*. For example, Ahmed is struggling to challenge the chief executive. Here the coach feels the desire to share his experience of challenging an autocratic leader in his previous role as a social worker. The third is *story telling*. At the stage before assimilation and completion the coach feels compelled to tell a story. Here, he is trying to prematurely move the client to learning more quickly when he may still be at the contact stage on the interactive cycle of experience. The fourth indicator is the *giving of advice*. Sometimes advice-giving is appropriate, as part of our role is to 'educate'. However, it may sometimes be more about inviting the client to move out of a place of uncertainty when the coach or therapist is feeling uncomfortable in it. The final indicator occurs when the practitioner is *wanting more* for the client even when the client is satisfied with what they have achieved.

The therapist's or coach's lack of awareness of their historical events and patterns may impede the emergence of new ways of relating for the client. Thus, awareness of the transference and counter-transference profile supports practitioners in being more attentive to their phenomenology and that of their clients in the here-and-now relationship.

With the Gestalt Coach

Exploration Phase. John and Lisa had scheduled the second session for only two weeks after the first because Lisa felt that time was running out to garner support for her leadership development intervention and budgets were being finalised for the coming financial year. John was looking forward to the session. Lisa had described the leadership development programme that she was putting forward and had already drafted a proposal for a creative leadership development intervention that was highly experiential, grounded in their current and anticipated leadership practice and supported by individual coaching and group coaching. John felt fully supportive of her.

Lisa reported feeling excited since the last session. She had been reflecting on the way she became collapsed and disappointed when she did not receive support from her board colleagues. It had reminded her of when she was a small child – the youngest in her family and teased for her passionate approach to life. John felt rather angry as he listened to her and he was left feeling puzzled. He was aware of clenching his teeth, tensing his jaw, drawing his stomach inwards and making himself smaller. This figure receded into the ground, and he made a note to bring it to supervision.

Lisa began to talk again about the leadership development project. John followed his normal approach in a second session, and continued the exploration they had started at their previous meeting. Using the phenomenological method, he bracketed his previous assumptions and opinions about Lisa and her project, in order to simply remain faithful to raising awareness in the session itself. He was struck by the strength of her feelings as he enquired with genuine curiosity about why she thought a leadership development project of this type would be useful. She gave several reasons, all of which sounded compelling. In the here-and-now John practised description, observing, 'I notice you are leaning forward, your eyes are wide, you appear to be speaking very quickly and your tone of voice drops off.' Lisa looked surprised at his comment and seemed interested, then answered slowly, 'I think it's because I so want you to understand. I feel rather desperate and I notice my energy level dropping.' John then inquired into her loss of energy, perceiving her modifying the interactive cycle of experience at the contact stage. She said, 'You know, it's sort of embarrassing – it's almost humiliating – to get knocked back at the board like that, and I was afraid you were going to disagree with me too.' John shared that he had picked up her potential to feel easily crushed by rejection. He owned his tendency to 'rescue' and commented that the danger of that was that he might avoid challenging or disagreeing with her, in case even a small disagreement made her feel put down. Here, John was in the connecting phase of the coaching work as he was seeking to enhance the quality of their co-created relationship. At that, Lisa immediately became thoughtful and wondered aloud whether this happened at work. She left aware that she needed to support herself by breathing deeply and grounding herself before engaging on this issue at the board, so as not to feel crushed. In the coaching work she also realised that she needed to make contact with the board members separately outside the meeting and informed John that she would meet all board members – the supportive *and* the sceptical.

In supervision John began to understand his angry experience at the beginning of the coaching session as a co-transferring process where he may have been enacting a particular sort of transference, that of resonating with a disowned part of the other person. Had he been experiencing how Lisa really felt towards the board members but 'crushed' her anger instead? He was curious to discover if this was a fixed gestalt – a pattern of relating that became habituated for Lisa, and, thus, made her less influential with board members. He decided to keep this in mind for his next session.

Experiential Activities

Surfacing assumptions

Return to Figure 9.1 on page 92. Imagine that the man's name is Augustus Bennet-French. What new or altered assumptions do you make about him?

Now imagine that he is a doctor; a dustman; an accountant; a Gestalt practitioner. What effect does this have on your interpretation of this picture?

With a partner, take it in turns to talk about something that is interesting or worrying you. The listener limits any interventions to clarifying the belief system of the talker. Use phrases like 'So you believe that . . .' , 'It sounds as if you feel . . .', 'It's important to you that . . .' , and so on. This is not an exercise in phenomenology but in heightening your awareness of the number of assumptions and values that are embedded in everything we say. Here is an example to demonstrate the exercise.

> **JO:** So I was driving along at between 35 and 40 miles per hour.
> **JIM:** It sounds as if accuracy is important to you.
> **JO:** Yes, it is. And there was this stupid man tearing along in the outside lane doing at least 80.
> **JIM:** You thought he was wrong to go that fast.
> **JO:** Well, it was faster than the speed limit.
> **JIM:** Your belief about what is wrong is justified by the law. So you think that breaking the law is wrong?
> **JO:** On the roads, I do.
> **JIM:** So you think some laws are OK to break and some aren't?
> **JO:** I guess so. And there were children in the car.
> **JIM:** So it sounds as if you think that the safety of children is more important than that of adults.
> **JO:** Well, yes. They can't take care of themselves, can they? They rely on grown-ups.
> **JIM:** So if a person can't take care of themselves, then their safety becomes more important.
> **JO:** I guess I've always believed that the needs of the vulnerable were more important.

And so on. Play with this exercise and see what you discover about yourselves. With clients, of course, it is not appropriate to interrupt at every turn in order to clarify their beliefs. Sometimes you will need to make provisional assumptions which you will change or confirm at some future point.

Description

Stay sitting as you are, reading this book. Now describe yourself as you might be seen by someone else. Take care not to explain or interpret.

Do the same exercise with a figure on television, the man opposite you on the bus, and so on.

With a partner, practise reflective listening as they talk, confining your description to the content of what they say and of what you see or hear.

Horizontalism

What is the most significant thing about you that you are aware of at this moment? Now focus on your left arm. How does it feel? What position is it in? Imagine that your left arm is the most significant part of you right now. What are you telling yourself with your arm?

With a partner, take it in turns to talk and listen, commenting on anything you notice, whether it seems relevant or not. Give feedback as the speaker about how you experience the exercise.

Combining the Elements

With a partner or with clients, practise all three elements of the phenomenological method. Pay attention to what your client is bringing but also specifically try to bracket your assumptions and open your awareness to the variety and richness of their present experience.

As you practise, you will find that your attention is drawn this way and that until some compelling figure emerges from the ground. You and your client explore it. Your attention rests with that figure: is it vivid and new, is it completed in a satisfying way or is it fixed or interrupted? What does the client reveal to you and himself in relation to the figure? Now withdraw your attention from that figure and again be open to the next compelling emergent figure.

Additional Reading

Clarkson, P. (2003) 'The transference/countertransference relationship', in *The Therapeutic Relationship* (2nd edn). London: Whurr Publishers. pp. 67–122.

Staemmler, F.M. (2009) 'The willingness to be uncertain: preliminary thoughts about interpretation and understanding in gestalt therapy', in L. Jacobs and R. Hycner (eds), *Relational Approaches in Gestalt Therapy*. New York: Routledge, Taylor & Francis.

Yontef, G. (1993) 'Gestalt therapy: clinical phenomenology', in *Awareness, Dialogue and Process: Essays on Gestalt Therapy*. Highland, NY: Gestalt Press. Chapter 6, pp. 177–98.

10
Working in the Dialogic Relationship

Yontef and Simkin (1989) say, 'Awareness and dialogue are the two primary therapeutic tools in Gestalt.' The 'dialogic' or 'dialogical relationship' indicates a particular form of encounter that seems to differ from the phenomenological method in that it requires the therapist and coach to bring their whole self to the relational contact with a genuine desire to meet the other person, knowing that both will change in the meeting. Hycner and Jacobs (1995, 2008) and others, have developed Buber's (1958 [1923]) work on the 'I–Thou dialogue', identifying the qualities, which, ideally, practitioners will bring to the therapy and coaching relationship. This form of relating is in contrast to the 'I–It' relationship, seeing the other person objectively in order to understand them or interact with them to best advantage.

Hycner says the dialogical is not something that '. . . occurs *within* a person but rather is that mysterious experience that occurs in the realm *between* one person and another provided both are open to it' (1991: 54; emphasis in original). It is the essence of this *between* that we will expand upon below as we introduce the three essential elements of an I–Thou dialogue, as an aspect of the dialogical relationship.

But first, a qualification. It is not the practitioner's goal to be in an I–Thou meeting all the time. It would not be possible. As Hycner (1990) says, 'To try and "force" an I–Thou relationship is to be guilty of a modern "hubris".' Indeed, Staemmler (2009: 305–34) offers the concept of 'I–Thou–It', pointing out that even the purest I–Thou encounter takes place in a context of the real world. He challenges the focus on process without content that Perls and the early Gestaltists claimed to espouse, saying that on the contrary, the 'It' of the client's material, and the words he uses to describe it, are deeply important. Further, the 'It' in the therapeutic or coaching work can be what is often referred to as the 'analytic third position' whereby the practitioner invites the client into awareness of and reflection on himself and his patterns, almost as an 'other'.

With this proviso, we now go on to focus on the I–Thou intention using the work of Jacobs in Hycner and Jacobs (1995), as the means to co-creating a real and authentic meeting with our clients.

Presence

As the name implies, presence means being fully in the here-and-now, ready to be alive to every facet of the moment. In relation to dialogue, this involves the willingness to meet the client honestly, to be aware of our thoughts, feelings and behaviours in response to them and to the relationship we are developing. The emphasis is upon being authentic rather than assuming a caring role or attempting to be neutral. We respect our own selves as well as our clients and are ready to know ourselves. The openness and acceptance that we demonstrate invite a similar openness in our clients. We aim to be present and available throughout the session.

John walks into the therapy room and sits down. The therapist sits and focuses herself on the two of them sitting together. She is aware of her feelings of warmth for John, whom she has known for some time. She is aware of the peacefulness of the room, and the comfortable feel of the chair in which she sits. She looks at John. His face looks drawn and sad to her. She feels concern for him. She waits for him to speak.

Inclusion

This means that the therapist, being present, attempts to enter the phenomenological world of the client, to see it through the client's eyes and then offer *confirmation* that the client has been 'apprehended and acknowledged' in their whole being (Buber, 1965a). The act of confirmation is more than an acceptance. We confirm their current existence *and* we also remain open to all that they may become. We try to experience what it is like to be that person, with all their thoughts, feelings and attitudes. Some experiences, such as loss or loneliness, are common to everyone. We can resonate with such experiences, easily and immediately, even if the circumstances are very different. This helps us to momentarily step inside our client's world. However, the cautious practitioner remembers to check the accuracy of their resonance with the client, as different people have very different responses to the same event. Sometimes the client's situation is so different from our own life experience that we have no match. However, human feelings are universal and there are always some aspects of a situation that we can imagine and with which we can identify as we pay close attention to the client's account and see the world through his eyes. Indeed, neuroscientific evidence suggests that a 'right brain to right brain' resonance allows us to attune automatically to the feelings of another (Schore, 2003).

Inclusion does not mean total immersion in the experience of the client. While meeting them with deep empathy, we retain a sense of our self as a separate person and do not become confluent with our client. We remain aware of self as well as other. In other words, we allow ourselves to be affected by the client while remaining aware that we are the Thou or It to our client's I, as well as vice versa. We are willing to put aside our own values and prejudices in order fully to respect the truth of the other. We cannot feel our clients' feelings for them or think their thoughts for them but we can empathise with their experience. It is as if we move briefly into their experiential world – enough to understand it cognitively, emotionally and somatically – and then step back into ourselves. This process of connection and separation can be so fast as to seem simultaneous.

Looking at the floor and speaking in a low voice, John starts to talk about his loneliness. His wife died three months ago and, although he is coping with the day-to-day tasks of living, they seem to have no meaning for him. He says that he either feels deeply sad or completely empty. He finds it hard to see other people going on with their lives as usual. It is odd to him that for the rest of the world nothing has changed. The therapist feels great sadness as she responds to his experience of loss and alienation. She can imagine what it might be like to be in John's shoes. She has the sense that John is a long way away from her. She expresses her empathy for John and how moved she feels. Then she says, 'It sounds as if you don't feel as if you belong in the world any more.' Tears come to John's eyes and he looks at the therapist for the first time. 'That's exactly how I feel.' They look at each other for a moment and for that moment John's sadness is shared.

Genuine Communication

Being present and inclusive, we then experience a response to our clients that is immediate and based in our own phenomenology. The sharing of this experience becomes an open and honest communication with our clients. We must be willing to communicate some of our thoughts and feelings, even when they may not imme-diately seem to be sympathetic. In this way we are in a real relationship with another person: we are not just a mirror or an interpreter.

This does not mean that we will necessarily say everything of which we become aware. Self-disclosure must be carefully considered and only done in the service of our clients and our relationship with them. For instance, if we notice something about our clients before they do, it may be appropriate to allow the client to bring this to their own awareness at their own pace. Nor would we interrupt our client to share every response when this would mean getting in the way of their unfolding process. We aim not only to further the genuineness of the meeting but also to raise the client's awareness of 'himself-in-relationship'. What patterns of relating might he be repeating with us? And of course, the subtlety is increased because we know that our relational patterns are also shaping the encounter. This dimension, too, will be open for exploration.

Being present and genuinely communicating our experience may mean reporting our feeling of irritation or telling a client that we have been distracted from their story by a particular mannerism. It may mean sharing the fact that we have started to feel unaccountably sad while our client was talking, even though we do not know why or how this is relevant. We are willing to take the risk of putting our experience into the 'between' of the relationship (Hycner, 1990, talks of 'submitting to the between') without controlling the outcome, but being open to meeting and being met. We move towards the client and invite the client to move towards us in a spirit of genuine and open exploration. We accept what *is* rather than what we may think *should* be. This is an example of the paradoxical theory of change (see Chapter 4) at work in the dialogical relationship. The client and therapist meet each other as they are in the here and now of their unfolding relationship.

Later in the session, as John describes his wife's funeral, the therapist becomes aware that she has noticed John pulling at the neck of his sweater several times. She begins to feel constricted and finds herself hoping that the session is nearly over.

THERAPIST: This may be quite unconnected to your experience, but I notice that, for some reason, I keep thinking about getting away.

JOHN: I wanted to get away from the church. Isn't that terrible? But I did. I wanted to shout out, 'Let's get it over with.'

The Dialogical Relationship in Process

We flow between these three interdependent elements in a constantly moving process as we attend to our clients and their story. We let ourselves be aware of our response and find a way of sharing that usefully.

Counsellors honour and enter the client's subjective world, accepting and confirming them as they currently are. At the same time [they] are trained to stay in touch with themselves sufficiently to *know and judiciously show* themselves, rather than act 'as if' they were something else. (Mackewn, 1994: 106; emphasis added)

The following illustrations of working in the dialogue demonstrate that flow.

Mary starts to describe how unconfident she feels most of the time and how anxious she is about 'doing the wrong thing' with anybody she sees as in authority. The therapist asks who she sees as being 'in authority' and Mary answers with a little laugh, 'Almost anybody, really. I'm afraid they're going to criticise me.'

THERAPIST: Do you see me as someone who will criticise you?

MARY: Yes, I do.

THERAPIST: How do you feel with me right now?

MARY: I feel anxious – my stomach is all knotted up and I'm thinking, 'She thinks I'm silly, I'm so stupid . . .'

THERAPIST: I have a suggestion. Are you willing to say that to me?

MARY: You think I'm stupid. [*She looks away*] It's hard to look at you and say that.

THERAPIST: You find it difficult to look at me?

MARY: Yes, I'm frightened of seeing your criticism in your face.

THERAPIST: How are you imagining my face at this moment?

MARY: Angry and cold, with your eyebrows in a frown and your mouth hard as if you were getting ready to shout at me.

THERAPIST: That *does* sound frightening.

(The therapist resonates with Mary's feeling of anxiety and simultaneously is aware of feeling uncomfortable and trapped in the powerful position Mary perceives her to be in.)

THERAPIST: There are two things going on for me now. You fear that I am critical, and I can see how frightening that is for you. But at the same time, while you stay feeling frightened, you break contact with me by looking away, and you won't find out if what you believe is true or not.

MARY: Find out? . . . Oh yes, I see, I am frightening myself with what I imagine you are looking like and what you are thinking. I could check. [*Looks at therapist*]

THERAPIST: What are you seeing?

MARY: Your face. It isn't as I thought [*Smiles*] . . . what *are* you thinking of me?

THERAPIST: At this moment I am thinking how much more confident you look. Your body seemed to relax as you looked at me.

MARY: I don't feel frightened now. I am pleased that I risked looking at you.

In this example, Mary starts off by relating in the I–It mode, not seeing the therapist as another whole person. This is often the case with our clients, who may be very involved with the problems they are bringing and not free to make contact with us. Here, the therapist remains present with her in an I–Thou attitude. She practises inclusion by allowing herself to understand Mary's experience; then, by judiciously sharing some of her own responses and thoughts, she offers the opportunity for contact which Mary is willing to take.

In another example, Michael's manner seemed to the coach to be rather arrogant and domineering, and although she surmised that he might also be nervous, she had difficulty in holding on to that understanding as time after time he responded to her comments with a dismissive glance and continued his monologue. She tried to find ways of telling him how she was experiencing him but failed to get beyond a few words. Frustrated, she began to interrupt with 'I–It' observations like 'You seem to use "one" rather than "I" a lot of the time' and invited him to experiment with 'I' statements – to no avail.

Things changed only when the coach stopped competing for control. Michael was talking about how he tried to do things properly, how he always noticed the details that were not perfect. He said with a laugh, 'You could say I'm pretty hard on myself.' Suddenly, the coach saw the tension in his body and heard the anxiety in his voice. She understood how much he feared disapproval – including, she realised, *her* disapproval. She felt a wave of warmth for the stressed person before her. Gently, but from her heart, she said, 'Yes, you really are hard on yourself.' Michael stopped and looked at her directly for what seemed like the first time. He said, 'Thank you,' and his eyes filled with tears.

Their relationship deepened from that moment. The coach realised how, in focusing on the fact that Michael dismissed her, she had managed to do the same to him. She had been relating from an I–It position, failing to see and hear his experience and trying to get him to be something other than who he was. It must have felt to

Michael like yet another person who wanted him to 'do better'. No wonder he did not want to listen. Her moment of inclusion was a moment of I–Thou meeting.

Deepening the Dialogical Relationship

The dialogic attitude facilitates the growth and learning of a client and requires the therapist or coach to appreciate the other in dialogue without the expectation of mutuality.

You may notice, as you put this approach into practice, that there are differences in the way your clients relate to you. Some may talk easily about themselves, not appearing to need any response from you. Some seem to crave understanding or empathy but do not respond to other interventions. Others, on the contrary, seem to be more interested in hearing your comments. Regardless of how the client makes contact, the dialogic attitude is one where the therapist and coach are open to meeting the other in the fullness of their humanity, knowing that they too will be changed in the dialogue.

In this book we have been describing the importance of contact and asking you to notice the ways that your client may modify their experience and their contact with you. Bringing this to the attention of your client is part of a practitioner's job. You ask yourself certain questions. Is the client who talks without wanting your response avoiding connection with you and indeed with himself? Or does he think he is alone in the world? Is the client who desperately needs you to understand her showing an inability to trust her own feelings or perhaps an unwillingness to deal with difference? Is the client who wants your opinion avoiding thinking for himself about what he wants or believes, and trying to shift responsibility for his actions onto you? It may well be that the manner of making contact reveals much.

However, it may also be that these phenomena reflect a valid and healthy need and that at various stages of the therapy or coaching process your client may have different needs of your attention. Hence, the practitioner needs to attend not only to a client's phenomenology but also his own. As he '. . . becomes a resonating chamber for what is going on between [them] . . . he receives and reverberates to what happens in this interaction and amplifies it to so it becomes part of the dynamic' (Polster and Polster, 1974: 18). The client and coach are part of an intersubjective field. Hycner and Jacobs (1995) argue whatever emerges in this field is a function of *both* therapist *and* client, not one or the other. Through dialogue, meaning arises from the *between* of the relationship.

Some people find it useful to think about child developmental stages and needs in relation to such issues. One of the developmental models congruent with Gestalt and the dialogical relationship is the work of Daniel Stern (1985). He identifies four domains of relatedness: the domain of emergent relatedness; the domain of core relatedness; the domain of intersubjective relatedness; and finally, the domain of verbal relatedness. Stern stresses that all domains remain active and relevant 'as distinct forms of experiencing social life and self' (1985: 32) in the lives of adults. However, we may hypothesise that, if, at a particular stage in their growth, the client did not receive the appropriate relationship or received it inadequately, there may be a particular developmental need of that form of relating that is part of the unfinished business that they bring. This need may lie at the heart of the client's relational style in the consulting room. It may be the need to be met emotionally – to receive the 'affective attunement' as Stern (1985) and others describe it, that is linked to 'emerging into the world' as an infant, and accompanies the beginnings of self-disclosure to a therapist or coach. It may be a way to complete the unfinished business of the pre-verbal child, perhaps in the domain of core relatedness. Alternatively, it may be the need for help in naming and verbalising experiences, or thinking about them and planning for what they want in the domain of intersubjective relatedness. Or it may be the client's need to 'do it myself', which in the therapy room may translate as working it out for themselves, with minimal intervention, in order to achieve a sense of power in their own lives. Again, it may be an echo of the three- or four-year-old – chattering excitedly about themselves and what they have done, figuratively trying on different identities as they explore themselves to find out who they are and who they want to be. In this case, the therapist would be working in the domain of verbal relatedness, where the client would need nothing but interested appreciation from the therapist, who will be careful not to limit them with 'guiding' comments. And so on. The Gestalt practitioner might lightly hold the notion of these types of unfinished business as he or she sits with the client.

There is an implication of this framework for the dialogue. It requires the therapist and coach to consider carefully before self-disclosing, ensuring it is orientated towards the healing, learning and growth of clients. Before commenting on a client's seeming lack of interest in your responses, reflect whether perhaps your *presence* as an interested witness is all that is needed. When they are struggling for words, it may be that emotional *inclusion* is sufficient and that cognitive understanding misses them, precisely because there are no words for the experience. At other times quiet, affective attunement would be irrelevant because your clients need you to name what you are hearing in order for them to understand themselves, or need you to interrupt them in order to feel the containment of your presence. There are times when *communication*, however genuine, could have the effect of interrupting the client's need to explore on their own, or simply to tell you their story. And then there are times when great excitement will come from exploring together in the give and take of the dialogue. As you offer yourself to the meeting, be aware that *confirmation* is a vital part of what a therapist offers. We are confirming the client's wholeness and that confirmation may be of different aspects of the individual at different times. Importantly, confirmation is also holding the possibility of what may emerge, as 'in the present lies what can *become*' (Friedman, 1985: 135).

The reader who is interested in these ideas about developmental stages may read more about them in, for example, Erikson (1950), Gerhardt (2004), Mahler et al. (1975) or Stern (1985). However, a detailed knowledge is not necessary if you are working fully in the dialogue. If you give your complete and respectful attention to the client, if you are willing to respond to her, and then notice whether your responses were helpful, you will be able to discover what your client needs from you at a particular time. And of course, if you are not sure what you are doing is useful to your client, you can ask. This is also an aspect of the dialogical relationship.

Finally, you may have noticed that while, in some respects, the phenomenological method (Chapter 9) and dialogue overlap, such as in the bracketing of assumptions and opinions, in other ways they are apparently different. The phenomenological method requires the practitioner to take a faithful interest in the client's experience and their world, while the dialogical encounter offers the chance simply to be with another, to be open to being deeply affected and changed in the mutuality of the relational encounter. However, if the practitioner aims to offer an I–Thou attitude and pays attention to what emerges, he/she will move naturally between the more I–It relating of the phenomenological method of exploring what is and the relational resonance of the dialogue.

With the Gestalt Coach

Four weeks later John and Lisa met for their third session. John was mindful that it was time to review their work and determine whether the coaching contract would be renewed or terminated as agreed at the first session. He wondered if Lisa had remembered this too. He was feeling a little annoyed with Lisa as he approached the session as she had postponed on two previous occasions due to 'urgent budget meetings'. He wondered if this pattern of commitment to the task taking precedence over people and relationships also happened for others in 'Home for You'. He knew from the email exchanges with Lisa that she had had some success with most board members as she had adapted her way of relating to each of them. She had now secured funding for the leadership development intervention but still did not have agreement with all board members on its primary focus and the overall design principles. Lisa felt satisfied that her increased awareness from the last session had helped her build more support for the initiative. Yet, a key issue with the Sales and Marketing Manager remained.

Exploring Phase/Integrating Phase

Lisa arrived for the session, rushed into the room and sat on the chair with a thud. Her face seemed tense as her eyes darted about the room. John, holding an I–Thou intention, took a deeper breath and noticed his embodied experience in the here-and-now with Lisa. He became aware of a knot in his stomach and an uncomfortable sensation across his shoulders. He was feeling apprehensive. He did not self-disclose as he was not sure this would be in the service of the work at this point in time, as they had yet to contract for the session. Lisa informed him she wanted to explore her relationship with the Sales and Marketing Director, Marek. It seemed to John that Lisa had a pattern of not holding some commitments in mind so he reminded her that they had agreed to review their work together at this third session.

Lisa told John that she had a difficult meeting with Marek and their relationship was becoming increasingly tense. She was worried, not least because Sales and Marketing support for the leadership development programme was critical. Over half of the potential participants would come from Marek's directorate.

(Continued)

(Continued)

John moved between I–Thou and I–It modes of relating in the here-and-now work with Lisa. In the I–It mode, he sought to understand the interpersonal dynamics between Lisa and Marek and the wider organisational field within which this relationship was embedded. Lisa informed him that sales were lower than expectations this financial quarter. John inquired which part of 'Home for You' was underperforming and learnt that it was the company that had been most recently acquired by 'Home for You', which Marek had come from. Lisa had not considered this as something that could be contributing to the tense relationship with Marek. She told John how she was wary of Marek and did not trust him. As she talked, John noticed how Lisa seemed to withdraw as she averted eye contact, and diminish in size as she hunched down into her chair. John practised inclusion, and cognitively, emotionally and somatically attuned to Lisa's experience in the here-and-now, while remaining aware of his own experience. As he briefly moved into her experiential world, he felt apprehensive and noticed that he felt smaller in physical stature. He imagined that Lisa might be frightened. He wondered if this was also happening between Lisa and him when she modified contact by withdrawing. He was also curious to explore if this pattern was related in some way to her recent session postponements.

John decided to self-disclose, genuinely communicating his phenomenology, and wondering aloud if she might be a little fearful of him. Lisa was moved and became tearful. John felt caring towards her but did not feel the urge to 'rescue a damsel in distress', his familiar pattern. Lisa acknowledged that she recognised John's experience and that this was how she often felt around men whom she saw as having greater expertise than her. John invited Lisa to reflect on this awareness (an I–It mode of relating from the 'analytic third position'). Lisa realised that this pattern of relating was an early cultural value that she had introjected at school and at home. She was told to always 'respect and accept' the views of people (particularly men) who held positions of expertise: doctors, teachers, and so on. When she did challenge, she was often reprimanded and recalled feeling frightened. Linking this awareness to her relationship with Marek, it emerged that he had worked for many years as a management consultant specialising in the development of leaders in senior marketing roles. So, she perceived him as an expert.

John and Lisa spent time exploring her introject and Lisa became aware that she feared being reprimanded if she was to challenge Marek. Her contact style was impulsive when she met with him and she had not considered the pressure he may be under to improve sales.

Recognising that these contact styles of apprehension and impulsiveness were also part of their co-created coaching relationship (she had postponed two sessions at the last minute and she did not remember their agreement to review), John invited Lisa to stay with her feeling of fear and apprehension in the here-and-now. He also invited a discussion about their differences – a young Indian woman and a middle-aged white Englishman. They shared some of their projectionsand expectations and talked a little about how their cultural histories might play out in the here-and-now. Lisa recognised that she was vulnerable to deferring inappropriately to men who were not only experts in her eyes, but also part of the dominant culture within the country. John wondered aloud whether the difference in their ages, gender and race was contributing to his tendency to 'nurture'.

Then John invited Lisa to critique and review (working in the intersubjective domain of relatedness) their co-created coaching relationship over the past three sessions. Lisa found that by carefully thinking through what she wanted to say (her egotism modification to contact) she could then express her points clearly and still maintain contact and not withdraw if there was difference. She also learned that by explicitly checking for understanding and maintaining contact rather than averting her eyes and imagining John was annoyed or disapproving, she could see her challenge was met with interest rather than disapproval. Lisa recognised that she could critique and explore what was working well and less well for her with John, who she had seen as an 'expert'. Lisa took her newfound awareness into her meetings with Marek. They also agreed to three further coaching sessions.

Experiential Activities

For Yourself

Presence

Next time you are talking with a friend, let yourself take a moment to be aware of where you are. Put other thoughts out of your mind, whether they are things from the past with which you are still preoccupied or plans or worries about the future. Allow yourself to bring all your awareness into the now. Notice your body position and your breathing. You may want to shift your position so that you feel well supported. Notice any sensations within your body. Now look at your friend. (Although this has taken several lines to write, it need only take a second or two.) Notice any changes in your attitude to the encounter with your friend.

Inclusion

When listening to someone telling their story let yourself fully imagine what it might be like to be that person in the situation they are describing. How does your experience alter? Now let yourself live for a few moments as if you were in the shoes of that person without any comment or opinions coming from your own experience.

Ask someone you trust to engage with you in an exercise. Ask them to tell you about something that has happened recently in their lives.

Practise checking in a variety of ways that you understand their experience. For example:

(a) by summarising the salient facts of the situation that you have heard. When your friend says, 'My boss said that I could take my holiday from Friday but now he's asked me to go to a meeting on Monday and I don't know if I should say something about it,' you might respond with 'You don't know whether to confront your boss or not';

(b) by reflecting your friend's feelings with: 'It sounds as if you're anxious about the idea of confronting your boss';

(c) by commenting on the values or beliefs inherent in your friend's statement with 'I get the impression that you think people should keep the agreements they make,' or, 'It sounds as though you don't want to believe that your boss might have made a mistake.'

Allow yourself to resonate with your friend's experience and then notice how you feel in response to them.

Genuine Communication

Again ask the help of someone you trust. Listen to an account of their experience. Notice your emotions, thoughts and sensations as they talk, and share them regularly without stopping to analyse or inhibit them: for instance, 'I feel excited as you say that ... I feel rather sad now ... I feel less engaged with you now ... I feel a bit scared in response to that.' Notice the movements, gestures and language in the story and comment on that also.

Experiment with noticing and then letting go of your passing thoughts or responses, sharing only those which recur or remain in your awareness. For instance, you may notice that you feel irritated with your friend's hesitation, then, having let go of this, begin to empathise with his dilemma. Later, you become aware that you are experiencing some anxiety. You continue to feel slightly anxious in spite of attempting to let go of this, so you share your feeling.

With Clients

Developing these aspects of the therapy and coaching relationship with your clients clearly cannot be done in the form of an exercise but only within the genuine face-to-face encounter. For this reason we suggest that the practice of the above exercises with trusted others be carried out extensively prior to working with clients until you feel that you have a real sense of what the dialogue involves. When working with clients, offering them your full presence and inclusion will probably be the greatest gift you can give them. As for what you communicate of your own experience, remember to check before you speak that you are doing so from a respectful position and that the expression of your thoughts or feelings is in the service of the client and with 'dialogic intention', and not for relief of your own unfinished business. Checking with your client that they are willing to hear your communication and that it is not an unwanted intrusion into their process – and being prepared to let go of it – encourages a therapeutically collaborative and respectful relationship.

Additional Reading

Clarkson, P. (2003) 'The person to person, or dialogic relationship', in *The Therapeutic Relatonship* (2nd edn). London: Whurr Publishers. Chapter 5.

11

Promoting Healthy Process

The Gestalt practitioner aims to work with 'creative indifference' – in other words without any opinions about what outcome would be 'better' for the client. However, as we have said before, we see the Gestalt approach as implicitly holding very clear assumptions about what constitutes healthy functioning. Therefore we believe that the Gestaltist, in dialogue with the client, has certain responsibilities to encourage and nurture specific aspects of the client's functioning in order for a client to develop a wider repertoire of choices in living and being. We offer six areas in which this is the case.

Integrating Mind and Body

We have seen in Chapter 5 that human experiences are embodied. Perls et al. (1972 [1951]) recognised that people are 'unified organisms', part of and in relation with their environments. He believed that the 'mental–physical' or 'mind–body' split is a completely artificial one, and asserted that to concentrate on either term in this false dichotomy would reinforce people's difficulties, not cure them (Perls, 1976). The body holds 'memories' and is a part of the 'I', not something separate. Kepner states that 'experience of our body is experience of our self, just as our thinking, imagery, and ideas are part of our self' (1993: 10). The Gestalt practitioner helps clients to reclaim and reunify the conceptual separations they may have made both in their view of themselves and in relation to their environmental field. They encourage clients, stuck in the habit of 'thinking about' or analysing situations, to refocus on their bodies and emotions in order to integrate them as natural parts of healthy living. Even as we wrote the previous sentence, we were aware how the very phrases are suggesting a dichotomy between mind, body and feelings. It is almost impossible not to. Despite this paradox, we invite you to lean towards the notion of unity. This Gestalt approach has been fully endorsed by neuroscientific findings (see e.g. Schore, 2003; Siegel, 2010) which emphasise the importance of the integration of all these aspects of self-experience as vital to healing and growth.

Humans sense, feel and think, as well as perceive their world, at the same time. Attention to all of them is necessary in order to be a wholly integrated person. We cannot, of course, be fully aware of all of them simultaneously. However, we can learn to flow between them in a rich and flexible way. The practitioner invites the client to have more awareness of all of themselves and to learn to move that awareness to the different aspects with easy and natural familiarity. This requires a client to have the necessary support to move fluidly and seamlessly between inner, middle, outer and co-created zones of awareness, discussed in Chapter 4.

Everybody has a preferred mode of experiencing. For some it is intellectual, for some emotional and for some physical. This leads to a preferred mode of expression and communication.

The therapist notices that Dorian reports on his thoughts to the exclusion of emotions and sensations. She gently invites him to focus on his body and notice what messages he is getting from his muscle tension, or what emotion he is feeling. Jill, who focuses chiefly on her bodily sensations – her headaches, the tensions in her body, and so on – may need help translating these feelings into emotions, naming them and thinking about them. Salia is mainly aware of her senses in relation to the outside world – what she is seeing or hearing around her. For her, the area of growth is to refer inward rather than outward. Equally, Carlo, who is strongly emotional, is asked by his therapist to think about how he is understanding something: what sense he makes, what he thinks will happen, what he wants to do.

Facilitating Healthy 'Aggression'

Perls et al. (1972 [1951]) use the word 'aggression' to mean the proactive, self-fulfilling movement outwards towards the world and the environment. It is 'a force, life energy, without positive or negative moral overtones' (Yontef, 1993: 179). It manifests in the person where there is sufficient support for such excitement with awareness. We all sometimes suppress this excitement for lots of reasons, some healthy, some not. We may quite properly hold back from running across the busy road to catch the bus, but we may unnecessarily hold back giving a compliment or making a complaint to a friend.

We have said that at the heart of Gestalt practice is the relationship. It is in the relationship that practitioner and client make the contact through which a person experiences the excitement which can lead to healthy 'aggressing' on the world. The Gestaltist's job is to help the client become aware of the way they make contact in the sessions and to allow that contact to become as vibrant as possible. The therapist or coach is attending to the way *both* her client is modifying contact *and* also her own part in this co-created contacting process. The practitioner asks: Am I in contact with the client? What is the contact like? When does the client break the contact? How? What happens then? The practitioner reflects to the client what she has noticed, so that he begins to be aware of what modifications to contact or fixed gestalts are suppressing his natural excitement and his natural drive to reach out and 'aggress' into the world.

Strengthening Support

Support means the awareness of, and the ability to use, all internal and external resources and options. Support is a field phenomenon and emerges from within the person and the inter-relationships between the person and his environment. It means doing whatever we need to do in order to feel confident enough to meet whatever situation arises in the best way we can.

A person who does not have sufficient self-support is likely to withdraw from their full experience of themselves in any moment of stress, reducing here-and-now contact and falling back on fixed gestalts. This can also be the process of shaming. Shame occurs due to a lack of both self and environmental support. It is a fundamental cause of a person's creative adjustment. The person diminishes his presence in order to survive, as his whole experience is not confirmed and may in fact be refuted. Thus, facilitating our clients to achieve support is important for healthy contact. There are several ways to achieve support.

Physical Support

A self-supported person breathes evenly and at a depth which is both nourishing and comfortable. Their body posture is relaxed and evenly balanced so that their energy is contained and yet also accessible. They do not sit collapsed or crushed; they do not unsettle themselves by twisting limbs in awkward angles. Try an experiment yourself: sit on the edge of your chair and then slump back, relying on the chair-back for support. Put your head on one side and lower your chin so that your breathing becomes shallower. How do you feel?

Now settle yourself comfortably on the seat with your weight evenly distributed. Straighten your head and relax your shoulders. Breathe deeply but comfortably. Let yourself be aware of the sensations in your arms and legs; be aware of the solid weight of your body as you sit. How do you feel now? It makes a surprising difference, doesn't it?

Contact Functions

Another important source of self-support is the ability and confidence to use all our contact functions. This can be done in many ways and will increase awareness. (Examples can be found in Chapter 4.) As the client is encouraged to focus on and trust their senses, and be aware of what they are seeing, hearing, touching and so on, they experience an enhanced excitement and a fuller quality of contact with themselves and the environment.

Being Present

Being fully self-supported includes being fully in the present, being aware of our senses, our sensations, our bodies, thoughts and feelings. It does not mean that the past and future do not exist for us at that moment as we will also be aware of what we are imagining or remembering. We have the ability to plan for the future and to keep our past experience available as a creative resource. The essence of being present is to bring our full conscious awareness to all of this – even to the part of us that is being aware!

Using the Environment

People sometimes assume that being self-supported is the same as being self-sufficient. We believe that health is interdependence and that real self-support is having the ability to trust and use the environment for support when it is needed. We do not need a perfect environment for growth, only one that is 'good enough' (as Winnicott, 1965 famously said). A self-supporting person knows the right time to call on the environment and the right person or persons to call upon.

Identifying with the Experience

Bob and Rita Resnick (Resnick, 1990) say self-support is identifying with, or 'owning' your experience. Under stress, we frequently retreat from our uncomfortable feelings precisely because they *are* uncomfortable or because they do not fit the image we have of ourselves. We distance ourselves from our anxiety while repressing part of our experience. Acknowledging and naming what is going on inside us can do much to free us, so that we can think about what we need and plan a way forward. This is true in traumatic situations such as bereavement, when we need to allow ourselves to recognise our feelings and responses, and it can also be true in more trivial situations such as feeling embarrassed if someone points out a mistake we have made.

Increasing Self-responsibility

The notion of self-responsibility is contained in the existential beliefs that we are fundamentally alone and create our own meaning. Our task is to accept that we are fully responsible for our experience because we create and therefore, in a sense, choose it. Self-responsibility is a central principle of Gestalt practice, which is part of why it is considered to be a humanistic approach to therapy and coaching. Of course, this does not mean that we are responsible for everything that happens to us, or for the unpredictable events of life. We can, however, be responsible for how we *are* within all that. As we become more aware of ourselves in our context, we increase our knowledge and understanding of our needs and how we attempt to meet them as well as the ways in which we respond to people and events in our lives. We recognise that we have the ability to respond (response-ability). We can choose our responses and we know that there are other ways in which we could choose to act, think or feel.

Here is an important implication for therapy and coaching. A client who has little self-awareness is unlikely to believe that they are responsible for their own experience. As they become more self-aware they become more capable of understanding how they create their own experience and can therefore start to feel more in charge of it. The considerate practitioner proceeds at the client's pace towards self-responsibility through growing awareness.

This process of increasing self-responsibility is in itself a powerful support for change. Harris (1989), presents a simple model of change based on three stages of increasing awareness and self-responsibility.

Stage One: 'This is how I am'

The first step towards change is to accept fully and without judgement the existence of all our feelings, thoughts and behaviour, even those which previously we have preferred not to notice. For instance, Alex complained that nobody liked her. The therapist invited her to look at her own behaviour. She realised that she treated her friends in a surly and critical way. At first she felt embarrassed about this but then, encouraged by her therapist, she put aside her moral condemnation and 'owned' her surly behaviour. When we use the word 'owned' we do not mean 'owned up to', as in making a confession of a misdeed, we mean 'ownership'. She was able to say, 'This behaviour is mine.'

Stage Two: 'I Am This Way Because I Choose to Be'

Having accepted ourselves as we are, the next stage is to recognise that, moment by moment, we are choosing how we respond to the world. At first this may seem hard, for often we feel as if we 'can't help it' or we say 'it' (or he or she or they) made me feel this way. Gradually, we begin to realise that there are other options. We may be acting according to choices made long ago that were 'creative adjustments' to our environment at the time but are now habitual and out of awareness. The important question is how are we stopping ourselves from making different choices in the present? Alex realised that, because she was expecting rebuffs from others, she approached them with suspicion and anger. At first it seemed impossible to her that she could choose to be different. How else could she respond? Her therapist invited her to become more aware of how she made her meaning. She allowed herself to contact a level of real anxiety and sadness and she realised that she stopped herself from welcoming her friends through fear of rejection. She protected herself by being the first to reject.

Stage Three: 'If I Choose, I Can Be Different'

In this stage of self-responsibility, we take charge of our lives. We can choose to experiment with different ways of thinking and behaving. Sometimes this really can be as simple as it sounds. Sometimes the very act of becoming fully aware of who we are and how we keep ourselves that way can be enough for us to facilitate change in ourselves. Sometimes it can seem more difficult. It can involve taking a risk. After all, the familiar may be painful, but at least it is predictable. We human beings have a need for some structure and certainty; newness involves the unexpected, which can be exciting but can also be frightening. However, Gestalt practitioners believe that, if we let ourselves become aware of our needs and wants, our natural drive for health and growth will emerge.

In our example, we left Alex beginning to recognise the possibility that she could respond differently to her friends. She began to see the many ways in which she could treat them warmly. First, she experimented (see Chapter 12) with her therapist, for, as you might expect, she had treated him with surliness and suspicion too. Letting herself be aware of her true feelings, she started to notice and comment on things that she liked about him. She became aware of the fact that she felt scared that he would not like her, and she shared that with him – and that she wanted him to like her. Then she tried behaving differently with people she met in the world, commenting on the things she liked instead of criticising, asking them about themselves with interest and telling them about herself. Quite quickly she began to report that she was having very different relationships with her friends and family.

In the list of Gestalt principles (Chapter 2) we pointed out that a human being cannot exist apart from his environment. We are all part of a system of interaction and interdependence. Our example shows how a change in ourselves can have a marked impact on our environment (and vice versa). Taking responsibility for ourselves means also taking account of the consequences of our actions.

One last point about self-responsibility. We are implying here that we have total choice about how we are in the world. Of course this is not always the case. It would be rather pointless to discuss whether or not we can be 'made' to feel something if we are defenceless children, for instance, or if we are starving or being tortured. What is more, there is much evidence to show that we are emotionally shaping each other all the time (Philippson, 2009). However, as we mentioned earlier, while we cannot be responsible for everything that happens to us, we can be responsible for our reactions and the meaning we make. Social deprivation or psychological abuse can make it hard for us to feel as if we have any choice in our responses. Nevertheless, even in extreme circumstances people have been known to show astonishing and moving strength in continuing to be responsible for how they feel, think and behave. Examples of this kind are described most beautifully in *Man's Search for Meaning*, by Victor Frankl (1964), which concerns experiences in a concentration camp; in Bruno Bettelheim's *The Informed Heart* (1986 [1960]), which treats the same subject; Brian Keenan's account of his years as a hostage, *An Evil Cradling* (1992) and the remarkable account of Nelson Mandela's life in *Long Walk to Freedom* (1995).

Educating

There is a sense in which Gestalt therapists and coaches are educating their clients from the moment they arrive with us. We are educating them to pay attention to themselves and to become aware of who they are. Within the dialogical relationship (see Chapter 10), we are nurturing a collaborative learning space. Together, the client and practitioner explore how the client configures his relationship to himself, others and the wider environment. However, there are occasions when a therapist may educate by actually giving information.

Normally a Gestaltist does not teach a client. This would imply imposing one's own values on the client, which would go completely against Gestalt philosophy. However, there are times when it can be appropriate and useful to 'teach' a client – when we believe that they lack information about something. It may be non-directive to allow a person to struggle with a problem but when we know some important information which may help, it may sometimes be disrespectful and even unethical not to share solutions.

Ruth was complaining about how tense and agitated she always seemed to be. She said that she was 'in a constant state of mild anxiety. I don't know why.' Discovering that Ruth drank at least one or two cups of tea or coffee an hour at work, the therapist checked whether she knew about the stimulating effects of caffeine and she did not. She decided to give up caffeine for a while and see what happened.

It can sometimes be helpful to give clients a brief explanation of healthy process as we see it, telling them about contact and interruptions, about unfinished business or self-responsibility. Many people enjoy and benefit from being given the theoretical model so that they can apply it to themselves. This sort of information helps them to feel competent and hopeful. It may be more ethical for a therapist to share their frame of reference. Instead of its being an unspoken influence on the client, it is clearly offered as an approach and the client is free to take or leave it as they choose. Indeed, there is extensive research evidence (e.g. Asay and Lambert, 1999) to say that a shared agreement about what client and practitioner are doing and how they will work together is an important contributor to effective therapy. We believe that, while some clients intuitively sense the benefit of developing full, here-and-now awareness (also proved by research to be powerful in facilitating change, see Siegel, 2010), others might need to have it explained, so that they commit themselves wholeheartedly to the process.

Another example of therapist educating client is found in the area of relationships. Many people lack information about social skills: safer sex, self-expression – what Steiner (1984) called 'emotional literacy' – and so on. It can be helpful if the practitioner is able to address the deficits in the client's education. There are also times when a client may need additional support outside of the therapy relationship. In such instances, this may involve referring a client to an appropriate agency or self-help group.

The rule of thumb in this area, as in all therapy, is that educating needs to take place within the framework created by the phenomenological method, the dialogue and the relational field, so that the therapist is responding to a clear gestalt of the client's emerging need in the context of their life.

Working through Rupture–Repair Cycles

Ongoing support is important, and so too, is challenge, which from a dialogical stance can be offered as an invitation to awareness. Inviting clients into such a process as part of the dialogical relationship may feel uncomfortable. A client may be faced with re-assessing the 'ideal self' image nurtured over time. Such work may mean that ruptures occur in the therapy or coaching relationship itself as the client yearns to be fully accepted for who they are yet fears the reverse. Often, shame may be evoked as the work unfolds. Facilitating the repair of such ruptures requires practitioners to track the client's quality of contact and be available to meet him in the here-and-now, to support what is yearned for. This involves appropriate self-disclosure from the therapist in order to be experienced as fully there. The experience of being received and known is the antidote to the felt sense of disconnection a client experiences at times of shame (Simon and Geib, 1996). Shame cannot be avoided. In fact attempting to avoid shame is itself shaming. However, working sensitively through cycles of rupture and repair associated with a shaming process helps build a client's resilience and facilitates a renewed and potentially enlivened awareness of oneself as a person.

James, a busy executive, came to brief counselling seeking greater autonomy. He rejected the possibility of being dependent on others. When the counsellor challenged James about his regular late arrivals, inviting him to explore how often he arrived late, James got angry.

JAMES: I can't believe you are asking me this! What relevance has this to our work here? You are a phony!

COUNSELLOR: When you say that, I feel pushed away and a little confused, not knowing whether you want to have some distance or you want to be closer right now.

JAMES: Huh! It's difficult knowing that we'll be finishing in two weeks. [*Pause*] I don't want to get closer as you may let me down.

COUNSELLOR: I feel sad as you say that. I am here and not going anywhere. I wonder if you'd like to consider revising our contract once our brief work is finished.

Here James had felt shamed as he was challenged about his lateness. This evoked a sense of his longing for male friendships that he failed to make as he felt unsafe. He was argumentative and pushed people away to avoid the risk of closeness and being let down. The counsellor disclosed his phenomenology to maintain contact with James and engaged James in a conversation about their relationship.

With the Gestalt Coach

Six weeks had passed since their last session, at the end of which, despite their rewarding work together, John noticed a heavy feeling in the pit of his stomach, his body ached and he felt a sense of loss and emptiness. This experience prevailed when he reflected on his coaching relationship at the next session with Monika his supervisor. John was reminded by her that all aspects of the relational field are relevant. She quoted Parlett (1991: 73) who said that '. . . no part of the total field can be excluded in advance as inherently irrelevant'. John found this supportive and held this awareness in mind for the next coaching session with Lisa.

(Continued)

(Continued)

Lisa arrived on time and looked composed. She informed John that while her relationship with Marek was not always comfortable, she felt progress had been made as there was greater 'buy in' from him. This was exemplified in the increased financial budget she secured for the leadership development programme and the growing interest board members expressed in aspects of the development process. Lisa said she now needed to explore how to engage potential participants in the leadership development programme. John remembered from the previous sessions that Lisa's support was not always as strong as it first seemed and he held this in mind as the session started.

Exploring Phase/Integrating Phase

John invited Lisa to outline the various business divisions, teams and roles that potential participants for the leadership development programme would come from. She was clear, articulate, energetic, and demonstrated 'healthy aggression' when she spoke passionately of the benefits of this programme for potential participants and the whole organisation. However, John once again noticed the feelings of loss emerging in him. He decided to tell Lisa about his experience. She paused, looked thoughtful and then seemed to withdraw. John invited her to describe what she was experiencing. Lisa said, 'My chest is heavy, I feel sad. I'm now wondering if I haven't inquired sufficiently with potential participants to fully understand their hopes and concerns about this opportunity.' She commented on how she was now able to stay in the conversation with John, as she had trusted her embodied experience. Previously she would have withdrawn more or moved the conversation in a different direction.

Next, John and Lisa explored the current organisational context as he wondered if the feeling of loss and sadness resonated with anything else occurring in the organisation. Lisa quickly jumped in and said 'Oh my! Yes! We have recently acquired some more new companies in 'Home for You'; some people have left and others have been made redundant but we haven't really addressed the impact this may be having on those staying.' Lisa became aware that she attempted to take on all the responsibility as HR director and did not seek support from others in her team who could engage with staff to understand what they were thinking and feeling about the impact of these changes. She realised that to be successful and effective she needed to reach to others around her, otherwise there was a significant risk that she would be perceived as someone who spoke about the importance of trusting others to deliver yet, did not, as she said, '. . . walk the talk'. She also told John that she found loss painful and usually buried it by becoming busy with work project activities. John noted this but, as their contract was to explore how to engage others, rather than explore her personal history, he decided now was an opportunity to talk to Lisa about the process of loss in organisations at times of change. He explained the potential damaging impact, that when associated feelings of loss such as denial, anger, confusion, grief, sadness or relief were not attended to, people often found it more difficult to stay focused on their daily activities and had little energy or genuine enthusiasm for new exciting projects. Lisa now realised that she needed to pay attention to others' feelings. She left the session knowing she would engage her own team more widely and trust them to initiate 'conversation groups' to inquire into how potential participants were really feeling about this leadership development opportunity at this time. John felt excited for her as they ended the meeting. He also wondered whether he had deflected away from exploring the loss, using as an excuse their contract for the session. He was aware that the conversation had also evoked strong feelings of anger in him at that moment. On reflection, he attributed this to a recent assignment where another organisation client terminated his contract without any explanation. He decided to bring this to his next supervision session with Monika, as it was unfinished business for him.

Experiential Activities

1 (a) What is your major channel of expression – feeling, thinking, sensing or action? Make a point of practising referring to all your functions regularly so that you expand your experience of yourself. You may find that you are most comfortable taking them in a particular order. Some people prefer sensing, then thinking, then feeling; while others prefer feeling, thinking, sensing, then acting; and so on. Experiment with them all and see if you can find your preferred path.

(b) Start to notice the preferred channels of your clients and respectfully invite them to extend their awareness of themselves.

2 (a) Go through the list of methods of self-support. Let yourself be aware of which of these are areas of strength for you. What can you do about the other areas?

(b) With clients, notice the moment when they lose self-support. One way you may see it is in the way they interrupt contact with you. Explore with them how they have done this. It may be that they have lost touch with themselves or are repressing some feeling of discomfort. It may be that they are interrupting through projection or retroflection and so on. Explore the interruption and invite your client to think about what methods of self-support have worked for them in the past and whether they could be used again. Offer support as they regain their balance and make contact with you once more.

3 Think of an incident in which you were involved that you felt annoyed about. Recount it to a partner in a way which takes no responsibility for it. Now tell the story again, this time using the language of self-responsibility, particularly using 'I'. You will notice a profound difference in the two ways of telling the story.

Additional Reading

Jacobs, L. (1996) 'Shame in the therapeutic dialogue', in R.G. Lee and G. Wheeler (eds), *The Voice of Shame.* Cambridge, MA: Gestalt Press. pp. 297–315.

Melnick, J. (2007) 'Managing differences: a gestalt approach to dealing with conflict', *Gestalt Review*, 11 (3): 165–9.

Starrs, B. (2008) 'Working with adolescents from a Catholic background in Northern Ireland: a generation's long accumulation of shame', *British Gestalt Journal*, 17 (1): 5–14.

12
Experiments

What is an Experiment?

Experimentation is another major pillar of Gestalt practice. In an experiment, the client literally experiments or 'tries on' a new way of being or behaving so that, as Mackewn (1994: 106) says, he 'tries out new behaviours, and *sees what happens*' (emphasis in original). The function of experiments in Gestalt practice is to offer new potential figures to the client. But the best experiments are not engineered. They emerge from the process of the session, and neither therapist nor client should constrain themselves by becoming attached to a particular desired outcome. As Yontef says, 'The combining of dialogue and phenomenological experimentation is one of the valuable and unique contributions of Gestalt therapy' (1991: 114).

The experiment should be an adventure of discovery to 'explore what is going on' in the here-and-now (Wollants, 2012: 113). Adopting an attitude of creative indifference (Friedlander, 1918; Perls, 1992 [1947]; Perls et al., 1972 [1951]) is an important element, so that the practitioner is genuinely engaged with the whole of the client, 'while not being *invested*' in any particular outcome (Mackewn, 1997: 66; emphasis in original).

Experiments typically place emphasis on attending to our imagination, bodily feelings and expressive acts – often associated with more right-brain functioning rather than our logical, rational left-brain hemisphere. Like any new experience, this can often feel frightening or strange, so while they may sometimes take place outside the session (as 'homework') it is often preferable that such experiential learning happens first in the safe container of the therapy or coaching situation. Perls et al. (1972 [1951]: 320) called this contained procedure the 'safe emergency'. It is an interesting use of the word 'emergency' to imply both risk and the emerging figure.

Zinker writes, 'Most experiments have one quality in common – they ask the client to express something behaviourally, rather than to merely cognise an experience internally' (1977: 124). For example, Christina, in a flat and formal way, tells her action learning group about the successful completion of a challenging piece of work. When she is asked if she wants anything from the group, she says, again in rather a prim way, that she would like people to acknowledge how well she has done. The facilitator notices that, as she is talking, Christina has her arms firmly folded across her chest. She invites Christina to stand up, hold her arms out and shout, 'I've finished my work. And I was brilliant!' Christina does so and the group sees her come alive as she 'owns' her excitement and pleasure in herself.

Charles is recounting a story about how badly he has been treated by his car mechanic. The therapist observes that as he complains, he is jiggling his foot. She invites him to become aware of his foot and to exaggerate the movement. As he does so, he begins a kicking movement and very quickly connects with his retroflected anger. This he releases by kicking a cushion around the room. He sits down feeling lighter.

The Phases of an Experiment

The experiment emerges from the dialogical relationship while client and practitioner are attending to the client's phenomenology. An experiment must be 'field sensitive' – mindful of a client's wider relational field and life context. It is not a 'technology' or set of 'techniques' employed by the practitioner. This does not mean that the client is involved in every aspect of the design, as they may not have the resources to do so. It does mean that the choice to engage with the experiment and/or adapt it rests with the client. Building an experiment follows certain phases, which we illustrate using the stages of the cycle of experience. They are not followed rigidly: the therapist/ coach and client move through them fluidly, shuttling between them as the process unfolds (see Table 12.1).

Phase One: Sensation

In this phase, the practitioner's task is to be in a dialogue with her client, using the phenomenological method and inviting awareness of emerging figures.

Phase Two: Recognition

Therapist and client recognise the theme or themes which start to unfold from the ground of the client's thoughts, feelings and behaviour, noticing which figures carry the most energy, which contain important themes, and which perhaps

Table 12.1 Phases of an experiment

Phase of experiment	Stages of cycle of experience (that each phase is attending to)	Therapist's/coach's/client's task and focus
Phase One	Sensation	Noticing the figure forming process and emerging theme
Phase Two	Recognition	Recognising and sharpening the emerging theme
Phase Three	Appraisal and planning	Attending to the timing Choosing level of risk Choosing format/procedure Negotiating, collaborating, adapting and accepting
Phase Four	Action	Initial executing and adapting as process is unfolding
Phase Five	Contact	Full, vibrant contact with the experience
Phase Six	Assimilation and completion	Completing the experience Integrating and making sense
Phase Seven	Withdrawal (fertile void)	Withdrawing of energy and interest

contain gaps in the story or an incongruence between content, process and the emerging figures.

For example, Bob is talking a great deal about his mother. Now and again he refers to her cruel criticism. As he does so, he has his eyes lowered to the floor, rarely looking at the therapist. With this information at her disposal, as well as the knowledge she has from previous sessions of Bob's low sense of self-worth and his sexual abuse, the therapist is considering which theme to follow. The possible themes could include exploring Bob's introjection of his verbally and physically abusing mother; his projection of his mother onto others; his self-criticism; his low self-worth and his lack of eye contact. She is aware that criticism is a thread which runs through the figures. Also it seems to be currently carrying most energy for Bob. She waits to allow other shifts of energy which may validate her observation.

As Mackewn says, 'Gestalt counselling is a co-created experience. It is experimental from moment to moment, in the sense that neither counsellor nor client can predict the unfolding process of the session' (1994: 106).

Phase Three: Appraisal and Planning

Practitioner and client will take all aspects into account in order to co-create an experiment that contains enough challenge and novelty to 'loosen' the client's habitual patterns while allowing him to stay centred and comfortable enough in himself for integration to take place.

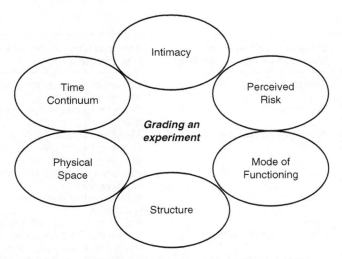

Figure 12.1   Factors to be considered when grading an experiment

Timing

In some of the videos of Fritz Perls' work, he moves into experiments with his clients within minutes of meeting them. This is sometimes a powerful and expedient form of intervention. On the other hand, its very speed may undermine the trust between client and therapist or may focus attention on something that was just a 'warming-up' to the more important issue for the client. For example, inviting Steve to experiment with completing the sentence, 'I want to miss . . .' when he arrives five minutes late for a session may be irrelevant or even abusive if this is his first time of being late, whereas it may be a potent intervention if he has a history of arriving late. Furthermore, if powerful experiments are used within a single session, enough time must be allowed for their integration before the client leaves the safety of the consulting room.

Focus and Level of Experiments

Some experiments are deep and/or complex. They move to areas which may have been out of the client's awareness for many years, challenging core beliefs and ways of being. These experiments are appropriate for clients who have already established a trusting alliance with their therapist over a period of time. Even with this connection there may be occasions when the use of deep experiments is not appropriate, even with a very experienced client, for instance, during a time of difficult life circumstances.

For example, when working with Mike at a time when his wife is seriously ill in hospital, the therapist avoids pitching experiments at a level which could leave Mike more fragile than usual and in greater need of support from those close to him.

It can be useful to calibrate challenge in some areas and safety in others; for example, by using the *mode of functioning* (thinking, feeling, sensing or behaving) that is the client's preferred channel of expression, or by very gradually increasing the degree of *perceived risk* (see Joyce and Sills, 2010, for more on this topic).

Factors you may consider when grading an experiment are pictured in Figure 12.1.

Choosing Formats and Procedures for Experiments

There are innumerable formats for experiments which include self-sensitisation, role-play and enactment, empty-chair work, guided fantasy, creative expression using various media, dream-work, encounter with another or others and experiments for the client to do between sessions.

There are examples of these types of experiment throughout the book, so we offer just a brief vignette of some of them, while including a more detailed account here of two of the more unusual experiments.

Self-sensitisation/Amplification
Muriel exaggerates the stroking of her top lip with her thumb and then notices how she feels and what thoughts arise. Deborah is slouched and experiments with slouching even more, while paying attention to her sensations, then putting words to the slouching aspect of her experience.

Role-play and Enactment
In order to discover unknown parts of himself, Peter asks members of his group to role play his team and give him feedback about his marketing presentation.

Empty-chair Work
Beatrice is invited to imagine her depression in the empty chair and to begin a dialogue with that externalised part of her.

Guided Fantasy
John is extremely tense and nervous about his forthcoming driving test. He requests a guided fantasy from the therapist which will assist him in being relaxed and successful. His therapist asks him to find a relaxed position in the room. She chooses a tape of soothing and unobtrusive music which helps John to move away from the over-structured left hemisphere of his brain, and connect with his more creative right hemisphere. She then suggests that he find a time in his life when he had achieved something he wanted and was feeling good. She takes time to guide him through the details of the scene as though it were happening in the present. She alerts his awareness to all his senses, asking him to notice what he can see, smell, hear and feel,

how his body is positioned, who else is there, and so on. She particularly invites him to focus on whatever he is feeling at that moment of triumph. Then, as a way of linking this past success to his future ambition, she invites him to choose, in his imagination, something from the scene, a totem or talisman, which he can bring back as a support for himself. She next asks him to project himself forward to the time of his driving test, to allow himself to imagine having his chosen totem in the car with him and to vividly imagine a successful test. She closes by reminding him that he will be relaxed yet alert on returning from the fantasy. She then instructs him to come out of the fantasy and be fully aware of the present moment, making contact with her and the room around him.

The example illustrates the use of various hypnotic induction techniques such as relaxation, the use of unusual juxtapositions of images, the lulling of the left brain and the invitation to the imagination of the right. It is important to remember that some people respond very powerfully to these techniques. Do not use this type of fantasy with someone that you do not know well unless you are sure that their usual grasp on reality is very strong. Someone who finds life disorienting already will not be helped by such an experience. Also, pay careful attention to safety procedures. It is helpful to say at an early stage, 'If I use an image which is not useful or relevant to you, simply ignore it.' At the end, you must give as much attention to the 'coming out' of the fantasy as to the going in, naming all the stages of returning to the here-and-now.

Creative Expression Using Various Media

Jean cannot connect with a childhood experience, remaining detached and 'grown-up' as she talks about a very important time when she had not felt in control of her life. The therapist gives her paper and pencils and suggests she write her name in childish handwriting, using her non-dominant left hand rather than her dominant right hand. Jean at first giggles as she wrestles with the task, and then spontaneously connects with the unexpressed feelings from that incident in her childhood.

Dreamwork

Many Gestalt practitioners hold the belief that all aspects of a dream are projections of some aspect of the dreamer themselves. Dreams may be connected with everyday issues in the present or be resolving the past in the present or preparing for the future; a dream may provide missing developmental links, integrate traumatic experiences or 'own' disowned aspects of oneself. Dreams may be communal or shared; spiritual or supernatural.

Perls perceived each aspect of the dream as a part of the dreamer's personality. Thus, working with the dream involves re-owning and reclaiming those parts of the dreamer which have been projected away from themselves onto characters and objects contained within their dream-story. In this way, a dreamer dreaming of a car journey might usefully explore being the car, the road, the destination, the scenery, the speed and so on. For example, 'I am driving from London to Glasgow.

I am in a blue car. I cannot find the main road but I cannot stop. I am tired. I now see a road sign,' and so on. Having recounted the whole dream in the present tense, the dreamer then recounts the dream from the point of view of various aspects of the dream – 'I am a blue car. I am being driven by a scatter-brained young woman who is trying to take me to Scotland.' In this example, when the dreamer mentioned being 'blue', she began to cry as she realised she was depressed and the way she stopped herself knowing this was to 'drive' herself incessantly to work hard and to keep going.

Negotiating, Adapting and Accepting the Experiment

Although the practitioner may suggest an experiment to a client, they will co-design it together. Deborah has been working on her inability to stand by her own opinions in the face of loud opposition. Remembering some details of her family of origin, the therapist asks Deborah if she would be willing to do an experiment, role-playing a family meal with others in the therapy group represent-ing the members of her original family. Deborah thinks about this, agrees, and then decides who in the group represents her family, saying that Sunday lunch would be the most appropriate meal for the experiment, where she could take the opportunity of standing up to her family.

Phase Four: Action

As the client puts the experiment into its initial execution further adaptation may be necessary, so that the client is 'neither blasted into experiences that are too threatening or allowed to stay in safe but infertile territory' (Polster and Polster, 1990: 104). While recounting her traumatic assault, Margaret begins to go pale and her words dry up. Her therapist realises that she is becoming over-aroused and is at risk of disappearing into the emotional world of the memory. She invites her to speed up her account to the time when it was all over, so that she experiences time passing rather than being locked in terrified feelings.

Sometimes to support change, clients need also to experiment outside the session. Kate, Dean of Humanities, explains to her coach Michaela that she becomes inundated with requests from her team and can't seem to say 'no'. Michaela invites Kate to finish the sentence 'I won't say no because . . .'. Kate realises from her responses that she fears letting her team down and holds a core belief that she 'should' always be available. Kate decides to experiment at work with placing a 'boundary' around some time for herself. Kate first experiments with working from home one morning a week, then discovers that one morning a week does not work and instead she allocates an hour at the beginning and end of each working day.

Phase Five: Contact

The stage of full contact is usually a short one and it belongs entirely to the client as they immerse themselves completely in the experience. In the example given above, Kate notices how she feels less pressured and stressed when she holds uninterrupted time to work on her own tasks.

Phase Six: Assimilation and Completion

Once an experiment is completed, time is needed for the client to make sense of their new experience and integrate it. The amount of time required may vary from seconds to minutes or longer.

During Deborah's psychodrama of Sunday lunch, she eventually stands up at the table and tells her domineering brothers to shut up. This gives her immediate relief and pleasure. During the assimilation and completion phase, she shares with the other group members how different she felt during the experiment and thinks about other situations in which she can, and will, be more assertive. Group members who participated in the experiment are also invited to share their experience and reflections.

Phase Seven: Withdrawal

At this important stage the client withdraws energy from the experiment and allows it to fade into the ground of his awareness. It is probably important not to talk a lot about the experiment and divert energy too quickly back into some aspect of it. For the moment, the client is at rest before a new sensation arises. Often, during this withdrawal, the client continues to make sense of his experience. The effects of it may emerge gradually in the ensuing days or weeks as he goes about his daily life.

For example, in the following illustration, the transcript of the therapy work is annotated in a different typeface to indicate the phases of the experiment. Remember, the phases are overlapping. The therapist and client are moving between them as the process unfolds.

Simon

Simon is talking about preparations for his final examination.

Phases One and Two: Sensation and Recognition of an Emerging Figure

SIMON: Several of my friends are taking the exam in July. I know I could too. I want to take it. My tutors and supervisor say I'm ready, but somehow I'm too scared. Maybe I'm not really ready. I just don't know what's best to do. This has happened to me before. Whenever I have to face some big test I get really anxious and don't know what to do.

THERAPIST: So this seems to be a pattern for you, that when you are under stress you get tense and anxious and don't know what to do.

SIMON: Yes, absolutely.

THERAPIST: I'm aware that your breathing is very shallow and that your body seems tense and constricted.

SIMON: Yes I feel like a piano wire ready to snap.

Phase Three: Appraisal and Planning

Sharpening the Figure

THERAPIST: I suggest you stay with your awareness and see if you can really feel the tension in your body.

SIMON: OK. It feels like it's getting stronger as I'm more aware of it, it's as if . . . I really want to do something, I've got all this energy . . .

Offering the Experiment

THERAPIST: And as you say that, you are sitting completely still. I have a suggestion, if you're interested.

SIMON: Yes, what?

THERAPIST: Get up out of your seat and start to walk up and down.

Phase Four: Action

[*Simon starts pacing up and down briskly. The therapist also stands and walks beside him.*]

THERAPIST: How do you feel now?

SIMON: I feel stronger somehow, as if I am more in control.

THERAPIST: OK. Keep moving, and tell me what you are thinking now.

SIMON: That I don't want this exam to lick me, that I want to be in control.

THERAPIST: Your voice sounds strong and convincing as you say that. 'I want to be in control.'

SIMON: Does it?

THERAPIST: Yes. You sound surprised.

SIMON: I don't see myself as strong or in control.

THERAPIST: How come?

SIMON: I always thought my father knew best when I was a child and I was never allowed to argue with him. He was always in control.

THERAPIST: Was he in control about exams?

SIMON: Oh yes. I remember, when I was taking my 'A' levels, he told me I had to get better grades than my brother. That scared me as I wasn't very good at some of the subjects and I felt this enormous pressure to try and do better than I thought I was capable of. I got more and more scared and I couldn't seem to get on with my work.

THERAPIST: What would you want to say to your father if you could go back and speak to him?

Phase Five: Contact

SIMON: [*Stops pacing and clenches his fists*] Leave me alone. Let me do the exams my way. I can only do my best. [*Looks at therapist*] Yes, I really wanted to say that to him. I can picture his face now. He wouldn't like to hear that, but I don't care.

THERAPIST: How are you feeling now you've said that?

Phase Six: Assimilation and Completion

SIMON: I feel much clearer. I don't feel so tense. And I've just realised something. The reason I'm so anxious about this exam is that my friends are taking it and I feel as if I've got to compete against them to see if I can do better than them.

THERAPIST: Is that really important to you?

SIMON: I can see now that I don't need to; it doesn't matter who is better. I want to just do my best – for me . . . [*pauses*] I feel so much better now. A weight has been lifted off my shoulders. I could almost see me enjoying taking the exam!

THERAPIST: You look pleased and excited now.

SIMON: Yes. I will take that exam in July.

Phase Seven: Withdrawal

THERAPIST: Is there anything more you need about that now?

SIMON: No. I feel finished.

The Experimental Field

In a sense, the experiment is an energiser which may mobilise the client to follow their own direction – sometimes to a completely unexpected outcome. However, there are times when a practitioner (or indeed the client) might suggest an experiment with a particular intention, if not investment in outcome. For the sake of simplicity we have categorised experiments into three general, major areas: (1) heightening awareness; (2) restoring healthy self-regulation; and (3) exploring and developing new behaviour and skills. Many areas, of course, are not discrete and there is much overlapping and interweaving. However, we will look at each category separately, offering some examples of experiments in each. You will notice that some of the interventions in this part of the book have been described or implied in previous chapters. Many of the routes for heightening awareness or restoring self-regulation would arise automatically out of the phenomenological method. In that case, the phases of building an experiment we have just described would not be necessary as the interventions are a natural part of your dialogue with the client. This chapter looks at times when a more intentional experiment is appropriate.

Heightening Awareness

Sharpening the Figure

Much of what the practitioner does in terms of interventions will fall into the category of sharpening the figure. The aim for the client is to have as full an experience of her thoughts, feelings and actions as possible. This can be facilitated in a number of ways. The practitioner chooses to focus on aspects of the client and her story, in detail, aware that anything and everything may be relevant. Thus comments such as, 'You sighed as you said that,' 'Notice what your hand is doing,' 'What does that word mean to you?', 'What sense are you making of that?' or 'Where in your body are you feeling that?' and so on, are all ways of sharpening the figure.

Polster (1987, 1991) talks about what he calls 'psychological slippage', by which he means a looseness of direction, an unconnectedness of ideas in a client's discourse. He offers a method of 'tightening the sequences' whereby the practitioner aims to guide the client to 'follow the natural directions of his words and actions, one after another, with a minimum of circumlocution, qualification, allusion, illogicality, self-suppression' (1991: 65). The client can then be swept into a stream of 'continuing nextness', the natural flow of which both limits the sense of fear because of its 'rightness' and enhances the vibrancy of the figure. For example, if you are dimly aware that you are sad, you may do nothing but complain. But if you become fully aware of your feeling, you may connect it to its natural expression, crying, or to a memory or to a desire or a decision. And so on.

Polster offers us three dimensions which are relevant to tight sequences. The first is the relationship *between real contact and transference*. Tight sequencing means that either one or the other should be done fully – not, as usually happens, a mixture of both. So the practitioner may help the client to 'unhook' the transference, for instance, by suggesting direct eye contact; or alternatively she may invite the client to go more fully into the transference projection by making the connection with a memory of a father or mother.

The second dimension is the *relationship between awareness and action*. Awareness on its own, says Polster, can lead to compacted energy, 'implosiveness' or dreaminess. Equally, action without awareness is mechanical, purposeless and unrewarding. A practitioner helps a client to make a connection between what he is aware of and the actions that might accompany the experience. Thus it could be the awareness of a feeling and its expression, as in the example of sadness above. Alternatively, the practitioner could invite the client to link what they are talking about to an apparently incongruent or unconnected action.

For example, Joan is talking about a difficulty with her husband, who is often wanting to have sex when she would rather not. Her voice is quite calm and reasonable as she explores the issue, taking great care to see it from both sides. The therapist notices that she is continuously brushing her skirt as she speaks and asks the woman to exaggerate it very slightly. Immediately, she becomes aware of a feeling of anger as she firmly brushes something away from her. Raising her voice she says, 'Get off me!' and uses both hands to brush her skirt with a pushing motion. This action stimulates another thread of awareness as she remembers being trapped and molested by a group of boys at her school. Her anger turns to rage as she verbally and physically defends herself in a way she could not do at the time.

The example shows how cognitive awareness became linked, first, to unaware action, then to aware action, which led to a deeper awareness, and so on. Later in this chapter you will find many experiments which aim to tighten the connection between awareness and action.

Polster's third dimension is the *relationship between abstraction and detail*. Basically, abstracting means the generalising of details into a summarising statement. Detailing means describing the specific elements of an experience, situation or event. Polster makes the analogy of the difference between a chapter and its title. He stresses that we cannot do therapy with just headlines. Using generalisations, a client and therapist may discuss something together on an abstract basis, 'settling for . . . empty and distorted understandings that many generalizations offer' (1991: 67) and making assumptions that they each know what the other means. Inviting a client to be specific – saying, for instance, to John: 'You say your dad comes and shits on you. What exactly does that mean, how does he shit on you?' – invites him away from complaining in an 'Isn't it awful' way into telling *his true story*, the one that happened to *him*, the one which carries his real feelings and thoughts. If you wish to read more about Polster's ideas on bringing the client's story to life, you can find them in *Every Person's Life is Worth a Novel* (1987).

What is fascinating to remember, however, is that the reverse is sometimes true. Sometimes a client can get lost in a mire of rambling detail which drains them and their therapist of energy. This is the 'can't see the wood for the trees' syndrome. In that case it is useful if the therapist can facilitate an abstraction. For instance, Brian, also talking about an abusive father, had just such a tendency to deflect from feeling and action by over detailing. The therapist first asked him to imagine his father sitting in the room with them, then suggested, 'Imagine your father sitting in front of you and tell him what he has done to you – in one sentence.' Brian paused for a moment and then let out a despairing cry: 'YOU HURT ME!'

Intensifying an Experience or Enhancing Vitality

It is important to remember that, every time you suggest something to your client, it is, in a sense, a confrontation – an interruption to their process and an invitation to become aware, or more aware, of their experience. This is true whenever you choose to focus on a word or phrase, whenever you notice a movement or comment on a theme. As soon as you suggest that they do something differently it is an invitation to an experiment.

Thus intensifiers or 'heighteners' can be quite small suggestions to experiment. These would include inviting a client to:

- say it again and be aware of what you're saying;
- follow that movement through;
- slow down and say that again, noticing what happens in your body;
- breathe and say that/do that;
- say that imagining him (her, them, mother, father) standing in front of you;
- stand up and say that;
- can you look at me while you say that?

Do not forget that these are powerful interventions and should be delivered with sensitivity as the possibility of shaming may be heightened when clients are invited into such experiments. Thus it is important the practitioner pays attention to the client's support (see Chapter 11) as the experiment unfolds.

Focusing on an Aspect of the Present – the Here and Now

Experiments are used to focus on some aspect of the client's present behaviour in order to enhance their contact with the world.

While Malcolm talks about how he is feeling he keeps staring at the floor. Experiments to increase his contact may include asking him to look at the therapist without talking; suggesting that he turns his back on the therapist while continuing his conversation; requesting that he continues while increasing his eye contact with the therapist; inquiring of Malcolm what it is he is seeing on the floor; playing with trying to get in front of his gaze and so on. Whatever the experiment, it is important for both therapist and Malcolm to carefully track his response both to the idea and also his feelings as he engages with the experiments. Doing something even slightly new will create new experiences and awareness of them is vital.

Focusing on an Aspect of the Relationship between Client and Practitioner

At different times the practitioner represents, for the client, people from the client's past and present life. Furthermore, the ways in which the client relates to the practitioner may well be indicative of the way he relates to members of his family, work colleagues and the society in which he lives. This works both ways and the practitioner will also need to be aware of those times she may be 'projecting' onto her client, and consider if and how this might be relevant to their work. It may be appropriate at times to focus on aspects of the client–practitioner relationship in order to increase the contact between them or to become aware of ways in which past or present patterns and relationships are being co-created and repeated in the consulting room.

Paul is listing ways in which he feels let down by his friends and in particular his colleagues at work. So often, it seems, he feels disappointed, but he does not say so. The coach asks him to think of ways in which he feels let down by the coach herself and to share them with her. At first Paul says, 'Oh, I couldn't do that,' and looks horrified. The coach invites him to experiment. Paul says, quietly at first and then more strongly, 'You have let me down. It's important that you remember what I tell you, and sometimes you forget.' Back at work, Paul begins to challenge colleagues when he feels his point of view is not being heard. In her next supervision session, the coach explored who Paul may represent for her and realised there were aspects of Paul that reminded her of her self-effacing brother to whom she tended not to give her full attention.

Bringing the Past or the Future into the Present – the Then and Now

Latner says that the Gestaltist is interested in 'the experience and awareness of remembering' (1992: 17), rather than what is remembered. If some of our energy is preoccupied with experiences from our history or anticipated future, it is not available as a resource for our experience of the present. This not only means that we have historical problems but, inevitably, risks creating a sort of vicious cycle: with diminished energy or awareness available now, we may well be creating another area which will require retrospective energy later. Contradictory as it may seem, the experiments we describe here are to bring fuller energy into past or future concerns, in order to bring about completion and integration so that they will no longer impinge on the present.

When Betty's grandmother died, Betty, aged eight, was not allowed to go to the funeral. One of the experiments used with Betty was to recreate the service in the therapy session giving Betty the opportunity to express her grief and say goodbye.

Fred told his therapist that he had had several sleepless nights, feeling anxious about a forthcoming speech he was to deliver. He experimented with exploring both his most catastrophic and his most successful expectations in the therapy group. The group agreed to support him in his experiment. First, he stood awkwardly in front of the group and allowed himself to spout gobbledygook, to insult his audience and to pretend to drop his papers and spill his water. He and the group roared with laughter. Then he started again. He breathed slowly and deeply as he took his stance facing the group. He made eye contact with them and began to talk clearly and enthusiastically about his topic. The group applauded.

Restoring Healthy Self-Regulation

Focusing on Self-responsibility

One of the major ways in which we perpetuate unhealthy patterns of living is by denying our power to change our lives. We wait for someone or something to do the changing for us. The language we choose to use confirms and supports either our freedom or our self-restriction. Words such as 'one' instead of 'I', 'never', 'can't', 'have to', 'should', 'must' and so on maintain our passive position.

Ruth is describing the parting from her son as he left for boarding school for the first time. When she says, 'At such times one feels so sad,' the counsellor suggests that she say 'I' instead of 'one', and notice if she feels differently. Ruth does so and at first feels uncomfortable at the shift in focus. Then she begins to 'own' her thoughts, feelings and actions and to take responsibility for them, including her decision to choose boarding school for her son.

Resolving Interruptions and Modifications in the Cycle of Experience

Fundamentally, all experiments aim ultimately to improve contact and healthy functioning in some way or another. Sometimes it is appropriate to focus specifically on the modification that accompanies the client's difficulty. Different types of experiment are relevant when dealing with the seven different modifications to contact (see Chapter 6). We offer some examples here. However, they come with a caveat. Do not rush to offer experiments to eliminate interruptions or change modifications before you and your client have explored them. Of course, in some ways you will be testing and challenging modifications right from your first session: you invite your client to feel and to be aware; you reflect her thinking back to her; you describe her behaviour and sometimes share your own responses; you invite her into contact; you ask her to assimilate, and learn from her experiences; you expect her to support herself as a separate human being. In these ways, and others, you may be offering challenging experiments to your client and you will notice if she finds these challenges difficult. If she does, it may be tempting to offer an experiment with the express aim of resolving the modification at once. Modifications to contact were once 'chosen' because they were the best way of managing at the time. They will certainly be accompanied by introjects which provide the reason for the person's way of being. A careful exploration of the modification, starting with, for instance, 'I noticed your energy drop then . . . what happened?' will lead to an awareness of the underlying core beliefs. Awareness and understanding are not only more respectful of the person and how they are, but are also safer. It may be that the client would find that there are dire consequences for some core belief if full here-and-now awareness were not achieved before a major change is made.

For example, Paul discovered that, when he was a little boy, he believed that he would be abandoned if he did not keep his mother happy by being constantly loving and helpful. As an adult, when as a result of therapy he started to be assertive about his own needs, he became depressed and withdrawn from the world. Careful exploration revealed that he still carried the belief that he would be abandoned for being 'self-willed' and was, in a sense, bringing this about by his withdrawal.

Having invited caution, we now urge you to enjoy and invite your clients to enjoy the excitement of using what is happening *now* between you to invent and undertake experiments which will restore their healthy, vibrant functioning.

Jake dismisses a burn on the back of his hand with 'Oh, that's nothing much.' The therapist, to challenge his *desensitisation*, invites Jake to 'become' his hand and allow it to express feelings.

Sarah, in the middle of recounting a nightmare to her therapist, suddenly remarks on a new ornament on the bookcase. The therapist, to confront her *deflection*, suggests as an experiment that Sarah, as the ornament, comment on her nightmare.

George is thinking of treating himself to his first new car but keeps remonstrating with himself for being so extravagant and selfish. The therapist, knowing that, though George is very generous to others he seldom indulges himself, asks him to explore this internal tension. George chooses to create a dialogue between himself and the *introject* of his mean and miserly father. George imagines his father in the room and talks to him.

Connie tells the therapist that she knows he is impatient with her slow progress. Knowing as he does that he does not feel at all impatient with her, and to help her to reclaim her *projection*, he invites her to sit in his chair and talk to the self-doubtful Connie, so that she begins to realise that the criticism comes from a part of herself.

Robert bites his bottom lip as he talks about his parents. The therapist, to enhance his awareness of what he is 'biting back', suggests that he allow his lips to 'blow raspberries' at the imagined pair. In this way, Robert undoes a physical element of the *retroflection*.

Penny is constantly referring to how she sees herself and how others might see her. She is in a state of self-conscious self-monitoring. The therapist surprises her into participating in a playful pillow-fight, during which her *egotism* is replaced by spontaneous delight.

Elizabeth often talks about her interests using the pronoun 'we' – referring to her husband and herself. She is encouraged to 'own' her independent personal preferences by enumerating some of the things that she likes which her husband does not, hence needing to use the word 'I' and diminishing the negative aspects of her *confluence* with him.

Through contact, awareness and experimentation, Gestalt therapy and coaching can transform:

- desensitisation through resensitisation;
- deflection through reception;
- introjection through regurgitation and selective assimilation;
- projection through reclamation and co-ownership;
- retroflection through proactivity;
- egotism through involvement and expression;
- confluence through differentiation.

To reiterate, we see a modification to contact as one pole of a continuum and suggest that healthy process is having all the positions on the continuum available to us.

'Owning' Polarities

There might also be experiments explicitly designed both to explore a client's avoidance of a particular polarity and to enable him to achieve a point of creative indifference, the mid-point between polarities where he is open to possibilities, without pre-judging, in relation to the issues he is bringing to his sessions.

Warren says he does not enjoy being close to people. He would always prefer to be on his own. The therapist suggests that he explore this polarity by exaggerating it. Warren begins, 'I like being on my own, I'm perfectly happy away from other people. I don't ever want to be close to anyone. I will always be by myself. I won't love anybody and nobody will love me.' Suddenly he stops and turns pale. 'That's not true. I'm lonely.' He begins to cry.

One of the most famous early concepts in Gestalt is that of the polarised parts of us referred to as the 'topdog' and the 'underdog'. This describes an intrapsychic conflict and also, as our field theoretical approach (Chapter 7) indicates, potentially an experience in the wider field. The topdog part of us, as implied by its name, is often those introjected voices in our heads that are critical, admonishing, punishing, moralistic, prescriptive and prejudicial. They can bombard us with rules and regulations, injunctions and prohibitions. The underdog, as the recipient of these messages, is that part of us which, while yearning for spontaneity and natural expression, unquestioningly complies or rebels in the face (teeth) of the topdog. Experimentally creating a dialogue between these two parts brings into awareness both the process of the inhibitions and the point of impasse. This often brings about the shift of energy necessary to break through the impasse.

While preparing for an important presentation to the board, Brenda easily loses her concentration and complains to her coach that it is useless for her to try to present. The coach suggests that she uses the word 'I' instead of 'it' and from Brenda's reactions to hearing herself saying 'I'm useless,' develops a topdog–underdog dialogue. After a while, the coach invites her to say 'you are . . .' while in the topdog position, rather than 'I'. She begins to hear and identify the topdog as the imagined voice of her highly critical father. This enables Brenda to move to a position of realistic self-assessment in which she realises she is not useless and can quite competently present her important project to the board members.

Exploring and Developing new Behaviour and Skills

Joseph Zinker describes the Gestalt approach as an integration of phenomenology and behaviourism. He says, 'a unique quality of Gestalt therapy is its emphasis on modifying a person's behaviour in the therapy situation itself. This systematic behaviour modification, when it grows out of the experience of the client, is called an experiment' (1977: 123). While the Gestalt approach has changed a lot in the last 30 years, we believe that it is important not to discard this powerful aspect of it. A practitioner's task is to support the next small step a client may make in the here-and-now of their relationship.

Resolving Internal and External Conflicts

Many clients bring conflict issues to the therapy or coaching situation. The impasses in which they live can be between internal and/or external polarities, as mentioned earlier. Their thoughts, feelings and desires may be in conflict with each other or with the thoughts, feelings and desires of other people. Experiments within this range of problems are designed to bring about conflict resolution.

Steve says he does not have time to play the sports he loves. He spends much of his time trying to respond to the demands of his wife. When asked about his own needs, he says that he 'wouldn't think of' putting himself first; his wife has their baby to look after and is tired and needs him. The therapist invites him into a dialogue with his wife, being first himself, talking to his wife whom he imagines sitting opposite him, then switching seats and becoming his wife. He tells his wife that he 'wouldn't think' of his own needs and wants. The therapist invites him to exaggerate a little: 'I would *never* put myself first.' As he begins to speak as his wife, Steve realises how nervous she feels about his selflessness, and how much she expects to be 'punished' later by his martyrdom. Ruefully, he becomes aware of the potential truth of this and resolves to negotiate for himself more fairly in the future, rather than become the martyr.

Occasionally the resolution of an impasse is acceptance of uncertainty, however uncomfortable this may feel.

Michael is faced with the decision of leaving his wife or losing his lover. In the course of his exploration of this dilemma, the therapist suggests that within the therapy room he enacts walking along a path that eventually forks, the one to life with his lover, the other to a continued life with his wife. She suggests that he spend some time down each path and report his imagined experiences there.

Completing Unfinished Business

As we have described earlier, there may be many situations in the past that require completion before we can totally devote our energy to the present. Using experiments with the guidance of a therapist is one of the most likely means by which a person can achieve congruent completion and closure.

Sharon regrets not telling her mother both positive and negative things before she died. The therapist invites her to imagine her mother on her deathbed and to share fully with her all that was left unexpressed at the time.

Restoring Developmental Deficits

As children growing up, we are often required by the adults in our environment either to rush through or hold back from achieving our natural developmental milestones. This can result in areas of deficit which impede our adult life and the awareness required to navigate our adult developmental stages. Therapists ideally have some training and understanding of childhood stages and the developmental needs of each stage. They will recognise and identify areas of deficit and design experiments accordingly.

Adrian spent much of his toddler time restrained in a plaster cast to counteract his hip disorder. He is aware in his adulthood of restraining his curiosity about aspects of others and the world. He is invited to ask members of his therapy group whatever questions he wants and allow himself to re-invoke the curiosity of a robust four-year-old.

Summary

In this chapter we have offered an overview of experiments. You, the practitioner, can gradually introduce and co-create experiments with your clients, checking with them to make sure that your suggestions are appropriate, co-tailoring them to suit the client. You will find, as you become familiar with working like this, that some experiments flow quickly and easily and the clients' awareness and options are immediately and irrevocably expanded. Sometimes, however, a piece of behaviour or a habit of feeling and thinking is so deeply entrenched that an experiment, while apparently successful, seems to have no effect and the client goes back to 'square one'. It is important that neither client nor practitioner be discouraged at this. It does not mean that the therapist or coach was poor or that the client is not trying hard enough. Some of our most ingrained disturbances take slow and careful work; old patterns are sometimes inextricably bound to the client's sense of who he is. Exploration to increase awareness takes time and experiments will need to be repeated in many forms before the client is finally freed to be what he wants to be. Whatever emerges from an experiment should not be judged right or wrong, but simply *interesting*. It is what it is. The client is who he is. That is part of the fascination of therapy and coaching from a Gestalt orientation.

With the Gestalt Coach

Eight weeks later, John and Lisa were in their fifth coaching session. Lisa updated John on the progress she and her team had made with potential participants following their 'conversation group' meetings. These conversations revealed different leadership development needs for potential participants which Lisa and other board members had not previously identified. This required a renegotiation with the board, as some of the core principles for the leadership development intervention, for which significant financial funding was granted, had changed. However, as she spoke about engaging the board in a renegotiation, Lisa's tone of voice dropped, she appeared tentative and seemed to be choosing her words carefully. Her facial skin tone became flushed and her body seemed tense. John wondered if Lisa was modifying her contact by retroflecting and thinking 'egotistically' (see modifications to contact Chapter 6) as the theme of renegotiating with the board became figural. He asked what she was experiencing in the here-and-now. Lisa responded, 'I feel rigid, as if I am unable to move. I'm not sure what to say and I feel stuck.' John told her he had a suggestion and checked whether Lisa was interested. She nodded, and said, 'Phew, for a moment I thought I was all alone in this situation – I'm glad to hear you have a suggestion.' John recognised from her comment and phenomenology that additional support was required. He asked her if she was willing to imagine each of the five board members in the room and 'rehearse' what she could say to them. She agreed and was about to eagerly launch into the experiment. He invited her to slow down and to first write each board member's name on a separate piece of paper and then locate each name to a position in the room. She arranged the board members in a circle. John then asked her to describe how she felt towards each one and to notice what she was thinking, feeling and sensing. He asked where she would like to sit in relation to the board and noticed that she put herself outside the circle. He invited her to tell them what she seemed to have been rehearsing in her head earlier in the session when she appeared tentative. She clearly outlined why changes were required and the key issues from the conversation groups that shaped this, and then explained why the leadership development intervention needed altering. Her voice was low and while her speech was more fluid she seemed anxious. John asked her to describe how she felt and also to notice where she was sitting in relation to the board. She said she felt a little more comfortable but still disconnected. This was a familiar experience for Lisa in her relationship with board members. She imagined that they had heard her but were not really engaged. John commented that she did not take up her position (physically in the experiment) as an equal; after all Lisa was also a board member. He invited her to remember previous successful discussions with board members (which she seemed to have pushed out of awareness), for example, when she had initially secured 'buy in' for this project. He then said to Lisa, 'I invite you to move your chair slowly, paying attention to your breathing as a support while doing so, and join the circle with your peers. Notice what you are thinking, feeling and sensing as you do this and also look at your peers.' Lisa reported feeling more robust, her chest and abdomen seemed full, and she realised that her peers were probably not as scary or disapproving as she had imagined. She then rehearsed briefing the board, outlining not only what she unveiled from the conversation groups but also sharing her own experience and feelings from these conversations. John was impressed! Lisa seemed to have really stepped into her role as a board member with confidence.

When Lisa had said all she wanted to say, John started to close the experiment. He knew that an experiment like this one relies on the willingness of a person to suspend their reality and move into what is, effectively, an altered state of consciousness. It was important, therefore, to ground them both back into reality. John asked Lisa to think about where each board member might actually be located, at that moment, in the 'Home for You' organisation. Once that was done he checked what she wanted to do with the named papers, and she decided to keep them for now as a reminder that she was one of the board members. Indeed, she also wrote one with her own name on it! Then, John invited her to reflect on the experience. Lisa recognised that one of the key issues that undermined her confidence was that until now she had felt unworthy of being a board member and was hesitant in taking this role up fully. Now, she realised that she *could* do this as she had much support (which she now recognised she had pushed from awareness) for the work she was doing. She also realised that her own experience, including thoughts and feelings from the conversation groups, made her argument for changing the core principles much more compelling. Lisa left feeling quietly confident that renegotiating the principles was appropriate to ensure 'Home for You' resources were used wisely and ethically. She also recognised that she needed to be more aware of her role and responsibility in taking up the formal role as board member in addition to her more familiar role of HR Director. Lisa left the coaching session, saying her PA would be in touch to arrange her next coaching session with him, which she looked forward to. John had noticed that previously, she had personally managed all the administrative contact with him. He smiled and felt a delight in hearing and seeing her take up her role, as she was immediately engaging her executive assistant to support her.

John was reflecting on his work with Lisa in preparation for their forthcoming sixth and final coaching session. He recalled from their fourth session that Lisa experienced endings as difficult and sometimes painful. He also noted that her relationship with the CEO never became figural in their work. He became curious about his part in that; how had he contributed to 'forgetting' the CEO. He wondered what was calling for attention within this figure of 'forgetting', an aspect of the field as yet unattended to. He acknowledged to himself that they had co-created

(Continued)

(Continued)

a solid working relationship to explore relevant challenging issues for Lisa. This had heightened her awareness and provided a sufficient level of support for her to take action. He also noted that Lisa had become much more confident in her role as board member and this had resulted in a considerable redesign of her leadership development programme. This programme was now perceived as radical, innovative, exciting and integral to shaping the emerging culture of the highly staff-participative 'Home for You'. John thought it was important to facilitate Lisa in assimilating and integrating her whole learning experience from the coaching relationship, and to check what support she could put in place to maintain her effective and developing reflective leadership practice.

Integrating Phase

At the outset of the final coaching session, John and Lisa had agreed to spend the time reflecting on their coaching relationship as well as Lisa's learning – including achievements, regrets, disappointments and future support. Lisa seemed 'edgy'; she moved about in her chair and her eyes darted around the room. Just as they were about to start the review, she changed the subject saying, 'I'd like to update you on the leadership development programme.' John suddenly had a strong feeling of wanting to leave the room and wondered if this was also Lisa's experience. He decided to share what he was feeling and thinking. Lisa responded by saying, 'I feel awkward sitting here today. I felt I wanted the session to end as soon as we started.' John asked whether she was willing to explore what happened between them. Lisa agreed.

They jointly inquired into her experience and discovered that she had modified her contact with John by deflecting when she heard John's invitation to review their work and acknowledge regrets and disappointments. It turned out that she also felt a little awkward about not having addressed the issue of her relationship with the CEO. John owned his responsibility in this as he realised that he too had 'forgotten'. He then inquired if this was a familiar process to forget important people in her life, particularly if she had an issue to resolve with them.

Lisa recalled that her mother, who was a refugee, never spoke about the close friends and family she had left behind in Pakistan. With tears in her eyes, Lisa told John that in her family, endings and goodbyes were avoided, even when she left for college, and on the occasions she went home to visit. Lisa became aware that she seemed to have introjected these beliefs and generalised this way of relating in all her relationships, personally and professionally. Endings in her family were always abrupt, leaving her with the unfinished business of unexpressed disappointment or regret. She saw how this had manifested in her relationships with some colleagues, including the CEO, with whom she was avoiding sharing her disappointment. She also connected to a recent experience at the end of the successful leadership development launch when she immediately left once the event had finished. She realised that her behaviour may adversely impact her credibility as a leader who advocated care and compassion as well as commerciality. In these encounters she 'forgot' to attend to acknowledging the moment of completion and left feeling unsatisfied only to become busy with activities again, rarely allowing space to enter the creative fertile void.

John invited Lisa to experiment, as he hoped that by slowing down the ending process in their work together, they could provide Lisa with a different experience of ending. He encouraged her to acknowledge and share what she felt as they ended each phase of the review process in the session. After reflecting on her achievements and learning, John invited her to spontaneously finish the following sentence: 'I am now ending this phase of my work with you and I feel . . .'. She then repeated this process, changing the sentence to reflect her own experience. Lisa became aware that when she allowed herself to stay in contact with John and acknowledge the ending, she had a range of experiences – a mixture of delight, pride, relief, sadness, satisfaction. John imagined that, in future, she would feel more self-supported and be more effective in her HR leadership and board membership roles when working with endings as well as new beginnings in a rapidly changing environment. As they said their final goodbye Lisa looked at John, thanked him and acknowledged her feeling of hope and confidence as a result of their work together. John felt proud of her, acknowledged his sense of satisfaction to have accompanied her at this time and wished her well for the future.

Experiential Activities

Inevitably, it is difficult to suggest exercises in creating experiments, because they normally emerge naturally from the field. However, here are a few suggestions for you to play with:

1 Watch a film or play on TV or the internet, and let yourself notice when a person is blocking their healthy process with a modification to contact, a fixed gestalt, and so on. Halt the film on 'Pause' and take your time to imagine what experiments you would design for that person.
2 Enlist the support of a colleague and take it in turns to talk and listen. Identify moments of high energy. Then discuss what experiment may be suitable. As you become more confident, allow your hunches and intuition to come to the fore. Remember to practise the phenomenological method, so that you will be open to a wide range of options as you flow with the emerging figures.

Lastly, try two experiments with your own boundaries and options.

1 What is going on inside you now? Did you answer with a feeling, a thought, a sensation or an action? Experiment with giving answers with the other three.
2 You are now finishing this chapter. What would be a typical thing for you to do now? Experiment with doing something very different!

Additional Reading

Gestalt Review (2009) 13 (2) – All articles in this edition of the journal focus on creativity.

Joyce, P. and Sills, C. (2010) *Skills in Gestalt Counselling and Psychotherapy* (2nd edn). London: Sage. Chapter 8.

Yontef, G. (2005) 'Gestalt therapy theory of change', in A.L. Woldt and S.M. Toman (eds), *Gestalt Therapy: History, Theory and Practice.* Thousand Oaks, CA: Sage. pp. 81–100.

13

With the Gestalt Therapist: A Case Example

Janice Scott

The Setting and the Client

The therapist worked at a local authority service which offered short-term bereavement therapy. The client, Alice, was a 58-year-old married woman, who worked part-time as an occupational therapist. In her spare time she worked as a volunteer driver for 'Meals on Wheels'. She had two children – a married son of 35, Michael, and a daughter, Fiona, who had died nearly a year earlier at the age of 32. Fiona had had epilepsy since childhood and had died of a seizure while in the bath and alone in her flat.

Alice was the youngest of four children, two of whom were the offspring of her father and his first wife. Alice and her brother were the children of the second marriage. Her mother took her and her brother away from her father when Alice was about four years old. Initially, she had no memory of that experience. Her mother told her that her father had died. It was only years later that Alice discovered that he had not died then, but later. As she told the therapist this, she said that she could have seen him again, if she had known that he was alive. Her mother had died 18 years previously, following a stroke.

Alice had no previous psychiatric or therapy history. She was seeking help from the bereavement therapy service as she had been experiencing despair, depression and an inability to be involved in her work. She thought that this was due to grief following her daughter's death and that she had not mourned sufficiently. She had had a medical check-up and was physically healthy, although very tired.

The therapist now takes up the account in her own words.

Assessment Interview

Alice was a well-dressed woman, stocky and squarely built, with upright posture. Her face was a little lined and, at times, her eyes looked puffy and swollen.

She sat back in the chair with her legs crossed and appeared to relax during the assessment meeting. Her hand movements held no specific repetitive gestures. However, she did have a mannerism of rubbing her eyes, in a particular, almost circular motion. I had the sense that it was as if to reassure herself in some way. She had a clear voice but it was thin and sounded very much younger than her age would indicate.

Her level of support was low. Her breathing was shallow and when she was distressed she held her breath. She neither asked for nor received support from her environment. (I found it interesting that in this and future sessions Alice would bring and use her own tissues, rather than use the tissues freely available in my office. It seemed symbolic of the level of her 'self-sufficiency'.) When asked what support was available to her, Alice talked of her husband Bob, who sounded somewhat withdrawn. Alice said that he 'takes good care of himself' following a heart attack three years earlier. She also mentioned her son who lived abroad, and just one good friend, who was experiencing difficulties herself, so that Alice did not wish to burden her by asking for support.

Alice was in contact with her distress and was finding life very difficult, as she did not feel able to control the expression of her grief. She was able to make contact with me, including meeting my eyes, and was articulate in describing her life as she felt and experienced it. Alice appeared to hear me well, rarely mishearing. She did not make a move to shake hands or in any way to have physical contact with me.

My Responses and Thoughts about our Relationship

My response to Alice was positive. I was interested in her and felt empathic towards her. I was aware of our age difference and wondered if she would be inhibited by the fact that I was much younger than her, although I did not experience it as a difficulty for me.

In relation to co-transferring processes, I was aware that her daughter and I were of similar age. I thought that this might become important in the course of the sessions, in that I imagined that I might represent Fiona, her daughter, in transferential terms. I also wondered whether the ending of therapy might mirror the way in which she last had contact with her daughter. That is, might Alice leave without saying goodbye or end abruptly? Or would I, in a co-transferring process, somehow leave suddenly and unexpectedly? I resolved to pay particular attention to that.

The Issues

It seemed that Alice was presenting with an unfinished gestalt. She was in the process of grieving for the daughter of 32, who had died less than a year before. While the event had been traumatic enough to justify her intense pain, Alice herself believed that she had somehow got 'stuck'. She could not come to terms with the fact that Fiona was dead and she volunteered that, irrationally, she knew that she hoped her daughter would come back because 'I've been good.'

I talked with Alice about whether the loss of Fiona had re-stimulated her feelings of loss in relation to events and memories of her childhood, such as the separation from her father and family life. Fixed gestalts of her childhood had suddenly begun to move into Alice's awareness as she felt the grief of her daughter's death, and this made sense of her rather child-like introject about 'being good'.

Agreement

Alice was highly motivated, had some insight into her difficulties and was willing and able to enter a relationship with me. We both believed that she would be able to make effective use of Gestalt therapy as she seemed ready and willing both to share her experiences and to reflect on them. Because of the specific focus of the work, I thought that short-term therapy would be appropriate.

We agreed to meet for 12 one-hour sessions. She identified her wants as follows:

1 To function better at work. By this she meant that she wanted to work with her patients without feeling so anxious about the possibility of being upset by them.
2 To feel and talk about her daughter without being overwhelmed or incapacitated.

Discussion of the Gestalt Assessment

When she felt stressed, Alice demonstrated a number of interruptions and modifications to contact, which I believed to be signposts showing how, during her childhood, she had learnt to be in the world.

Desensitisation and Deflection

Alice remembered, as a child, looking at other children and seeing that they were smiling – and realising that she never smiled or felt happy. She noticed that children got a response from adults if they smiled, and began to practise smiling. She had little memory of feeling happy and no memory at all of the six months after she was taken away from her father. We agreed that this might be an area to explore at some time.

Alice's language included a high level of deflection when she talked about herself, with the use, for example, of 'one', 'you' or 'it' rather than 'I'. My response was to feel slightly pushed away, but I made the decision not to address this clearly deeply ingrained pattern by continually inviting her to use 'I'. I felt that such a repeated intervention could be perceived as criticism, and might in itself be a deflection from her work. What I did was hear and respond to her, as if she had said 'I'.

In the second session, Alice said, 'As a small child you have enough pain and you can't cope anymore.'

I believed that Alice had adjusted to her environment, in the best way she could, by modifying contact with her experience through desensitisation and deflection. It seemed to me that the only way to help her re-engage with her experience was for me to attempt to attune to her with an I–Thou attitude.

Retroflection

The most destructive act of retroflection is suicide. Indeed, Perls states, 'Suicide is a substitute for homicide or murder' (1992 [1947]: 139). Suicide was an option that Alice talked about in the second session. She imagined being on a mountain and yelling, 'I hate this bloody world, I want out.' I said that I realised that she was in a great deal of pain. I also noticed that she had sounded very angry when she talked about hating the world. As part of my assessment process I explored whether she had actually made any real plans to take her own life. She replied that she hadn't. I also asked her to commit herself to keeping alive for the duration of our work together, and she agreed. I suggested that, if, in the future, she thought about suicide, she might find it useful to think about who or what else she might be angry with. In the event, although she talked about suicide in the beginning and during the middle sessions, she said in one of the later sessions that the frequency of her suicidal thoughts had diminished markedly and that she knew that she wasn't going to kill herself.

Another way in which Alice retroflected habitually was in her inability to express her feelings freely and openly: 'I've got very weepy eyes, tears are very close to the surface.' At first, when she cried it was quiet and restrained, the tears barely welling up before she blotted them away with her handkerchief. She sniffed a lot as if to hold in the enormity of her feeling.

Introjection

Alice manifested many introjects when she was feeling sad and vulnerable: for example, 'I'm wasting your time, wallowing, embarrassed. I shouldn't be doing this.' She also had rigid introjects about 'being a good girl', caring for others and doing the 'right thing' (we began to refer to these as 'got to's'). Her mother had told her that she 'should go out to work; take care of people; be a nurse; a teacher'. Alice herself had never wanted to be an occupational therapist. She had allowed her mother's injunctions to be so powerful that they had directed her choice of career as well as strongly underpinning her retroflection.

Projection and Proflection

In the early sessions, Alice would project her need for care onto others. She would begin by talking about a patient with whom she had been working who was experiencing a bereavement. She seemed able to give to others care which she herself found very difficult to receive.

Confluence

The relationship that Alice had had with her daughter seemed strongly confluent. They talked together every day: Fiona lived five minutes' drive away from her. She would bring her washing to Alice's home, to use the washing machine. Looking to the other polarity, Alice made decisions as a child which were relevant to the position of isolation, and indeed that was the position that, at first, she held in her relationship with me.

She had been a child in Belfast during the troubles and remembered that at age 11, she thought a lot about dying. She decided that the painful aspect of dying would be the leaving of things and people, such as her doll's pram and her mother. In the therapy she remembered she had made the decision, 'Don't love anyone or anything,' so that dying would not be so painful.

The Therapy

First Session

'Can I just talk and cry?' Alice very clearly stated what she wanted for this session. I assured her that the time was for her to use as she wished, and began to listen to her unfolding story (phenomenological inquiry). She described the last phone call with her daughter, where Fiona kept apologising to her with 'I'm sorry, mum, I'm sorry' and Alice in the end said, 'If you don't stop saying I'm sorry I'm never going to talk to you again.' Her daughter apologised again, and Alice put the phone down. That was the last time that Alice spoke to her daughter. She began to repeat to me the questions she had been asking herself since her daughter's death: 'I don't know how upset she was, I don't know whether she needed me . . . I don't know why she should have died, she'd had loads of fits . . . I feel guilty about everything that happened to my daughter, and I think it was my fault.' Alice had put together the pieces of Fiona's childhood and her history of illness and decided that she was responsible for her daughter's epilepsy. I said little as I resonated with Alice's feelings of grief and guilt and I felt relief as she allowed herself to really sob as she let go of some of the horror.

Alice also described how her 'got to's' were being shaken, and did not seem so important for her. It seemed that the immense shock of her daughter's death had unsettled the introjects she had lived by for so many years.

During this session Alice expressed a wish to remember aspects of her childhood. At the same time she was apprehensive and as we worked together she came up with an image of her opening a door, into herself and her past. We established that she had control over the door: when she opened it and with whom she opened it. This was the strengthening of self-regulation.

Alice appeared to use retroflection of blame and feelings of guilt to distance herself from her feelings. I suggested that, between this and the next session, when she felt guilty about the kind of life she gave her daughter, she remember that her daughter had said recently what a lovely mother Alice had been. I also asked Alice to think about what other feelings she might have, if she was not feeling guilty.

Second Session

'Is this wasting your time?' Alice asked me within a couple of minutes. I asked her if I was doing anything that made her think that she was wasting my time. Alice said that in the first session I had asked her if she had someone else to talk to, and she had heard it as a suggestion that she find someone other than me. She used deflection in her language, such as 'People don't want to listen to other people.' When I asked if anyone in her past would have treated her like that she became sad and said, 'That's the way you're bought up.'

During the previous week she had brought to her house the sewing machine that Fiona had owned. She took the cover off, and felt that she could have hugged it. It was as if she could smell Fiona. I continued gently to invite her to focus on what she was experiencing. She was mainly aware of her middle zone – her thoughts and introjects and feelings associated with a fixed gestalt of guilt – and her outer zone, in particular a focus on others' needs. She seemed not in contact with her inner zone at all and I frequently used my own body as a clue to when she might be desensitising, occasionally asking her to pay attention to her bodily sensations, tensions and emotions.

She discussed death and attitudes about death. About her own death she said, 'I think it would be very nice; the manner of it is quite scary but I think oblivion would be nice.' This was the session in which we discussed suicide and I asked her to undertake not to harm herself or anyone else, intentionally or unintentionally, while she was in therapy with me. She agreed. Strange as it may seem to ask someone to make sure that they will not do something unintentionally, I believed that, by including this notion, Alice was agreeing to remain alert to the possibilities of 'accidentally' hurting herself and was committing to making her safety a central figure.

It was at this time that Alice went on to say, 'As a small child you have had enough pain and you can't cope anymore.' The time that she was speaking about was during the time of the troubles in Belfast: her mother worked in a hospital; there was often a visible presence of the army; she witnessed violence on the streets which had terrified her; and as a child she used to dream of dead bodies. In hindsight, I believe her decision to deflect pain was also related to her very shallow breathing pattern, a creative adjustment she may have used to diminish the level of physical pain she experienced through the childhood abuse which Alice was to reveal in a later session. Alice described her numbness at Fiona's funeral, which I saw as another manifestation of her ability to desensitise.

Third Session

In the third session, Alice said that she had been able to really be with a grieving patient. For Alice this was progress, in that she felt less fearful of patients' feelings, and felt more able to cope at work.

She said that the night after the second session she had dreamt about Fiona and had given her a hug. Alice had tried to put a beautiful necklace around her neck, but realised that Fiona 'wasn't really there' and the necklace would not stay put. In the dream she knew that Fiona was dead, but nonetheless, she had enjoyed it a great deal. As she described the dream she looked warm and happy.

I felt that such a dream was significant, because in it Alice knew Fiona was dead, while in the previous session she had still expected Fiona to come back. It seemed that, gradually, Alice was beginning to accept the reality of her loss.

Alice went on to say that she was doing things without much enthusiasm. When she tried to do things that she did not want to do, she felt sick: 'I should be doing something much more reasonable . . . like the housework, or something more useful.' Here Alice appeared to be beginning to reject, emotionally and physically, the introjects of her life which made her feel validated if she was taking care of others: 'I felt very dry and arid if I was not doing things for others.'

Alice again began to talk of her childhood. In between the therapy sessions she had had vague recollections of being told by someone kind, 'When you're a grown girl, come home.' She connected to this as a memory of her father. She was aware of a 'comforting feeling'. This was the first time in her current awareness that she had any memory of her father.

She then began to talk about her mother and her memories. I include this passage as I think it graphically describes some of her experiences:

> You take it [Alice as a child] out of its home, you dump it down among strangers, you leave it, it's exposed to all sorts of dreadful things . . . and then a mother comes back and pats you on the head, and says 'I miss you' and 'I love you', . . . and I was always very grateful to my mother for rescuing me from something . . . she was working hard to support us, and she told us what she had given up for us.

Alice reported that she had felt angry with her mother during the week for the way she treated her. Previously she had only felt guilt about her, and she actually enjoyed feeling her anger. I said that I thought she was becoming more aware of her feelings. This growing awareness may have been the result of questioning her introjects. Alice also said that I was the only person that she did not feel responsible for.

Looking back on this episode, I feel that it was a true 'I–Thou' moment – that 'special moment of insight or illumination whenever the participants confirm each other in their unique being' (Jacobs, 1989: 29).

ALICE: I sort of think I don't have any responsibility for you.
ME: No, you don't.

> **ALICE:** Because you said it was a bereavement service, I don't feel I owe you anything . . . I don't have to think, what does she need? . . . I don't have to worry about you . . . I'm not responsible for you, I'm very pleased to see you . . . I just come here and talk for an hour about myself.

Her eyes lit up, her face broke into a broad smile and she truly seemed to revel in the idea that she was not responsible for me. I too felt the impact of her delight. It was a special moment for both of us.

Fourth Session

'I've been good and I think it's time she came back, it's long enough. I don't really believe she is dead . . . I've been awfully good, I haven't cried this week, I've got on with my work . . . please can I have my daughter back now?' Alice was distressed to discover that she still thought Fiona would come back. We spent time exploring this normal process of grieving and as we talked, Alice said that, even though the sessions were very painful for her, she could now think about Fiona without having to push her memories away.

She was aware that childhood memories were emerging increasingly in and between the sessions and I encouraged her to stay true to what became figural for her as she sat with me. She remembered 'aunties' who were paid by her mother to look after her and her brother, when she went to work in the hospital. These aunties would hit her with a belt when she wet the bed (which she often did). Alice was between five and eight years old at the time. They were often moved to new aunties, because of her bed-wetting.

'In those days, children were there, if you got angry, you hit them. If dirty old men felt like feeling them up, they did.' She said. As Alice spoke she became distressed. She told me of the decision she made that she must have been a very bad child when so many bad things happened to her. She described her three different childhoods: a family and a safe home; the 'Dickensian time' where 'people couldn't cope with me because I was a very bad child'; and then boarding school.

Alice's grief over Fiona was re-stimulating memories and unfinished gestalts that possessed similar affects, such as the death of her parents and the experiences she had had at the hands of aunties, teachers and others. As we explored the 'It' of her life's story, I stayed as far as possible in here-and-now I–Thou contact with Alice as she brought past into present between us.

Fifth Session

This session occurred on the day before the first anniversary of Fiona's death. As Alice approached this anniversary, she described what she was experiencing. The previous day she had been 'very, very sad', because she had seen someone who looked like her daughter: 'It's like a physical pain; it affects the whole of you,' she said, as she curled her body inwards and held herself still. I thought that Alice was showing an increasing awareness of her body sensations and also how her body voiced her psychological pain.

Almost immediately, she began to express a variety of introjects, such as that she was 'wallowing, self-indulgent' and so on. I said I did not know how much worse pain there is than to watch someone grow for 30 years and then see them die. I told her I did not think she was wallowing, and that I saw that she was in great pain. Her body seemed to relax a little as she heard my words and, I believe, allowed them in. Then she wailed 'But I don't want this pain' in such heartfelt desperation that I felt the truth of her words in my own belly.

Later in the session, Alice described her plans for the following day. She had decided to go to work on the anniversary of her daughter's death. I said that I was concerned about her working on that day, as she seemed so distressed. I felt that it was not useful or self-caring to be working with her patients on that anniversary. My impression was that Alice was attempting to deflect her feelings.

As she went on talking, she described her husband, who appeared to feel nothing, and her own grief which she said was 'the most tiring thing I've come across'. Alice's loneliness in the present seemed intense. She said she had come to me because 'I wanted to hold someone's hand, because I'm too damned childish to do it on my own.' I asked Alice whose hand she would like to hold. She replied that she did not know, but then began to talk about her husband. She said that in the past she had come to terms with the fact that her husband would never be what she wanted, but now she was having difficulty with the relationship when he appeared to be so unfeeling.

During and after this session I found myself at times almost overwhelmed by the level of pain that Alice was manifesting. At this point I was unsure whether I was experiencing co-transference or resonating with Alice's process. I did not wish to appear to be unable to cope with Alice's feelings, in the way that she had described with her patients at the clinic and the way that, I hypothesised, her husband felt in the face of her pain. Because I was unclear, I did not disclose my feelings. I was fortunate in that I went from this session to supervision, where I became aware that I had been re-stimulated to some extent in relation to my own experiences of early separation. In hindsight, I believe that my response was (as always) a blend of feelings about my own experiences and the feelings I experienced as the result of resonances and inclusion with Alice. I was thinking of Jacobs (1989) citing Buber exploring the concepts of inclusion: 'the therapist must feel the other side, the patient's side of the relationship; as a bodily touch to know how the patient feels it' (Buber, cited in Jacobs, 1989: 45).

Looking back on this session, it was very hard for us both, and I think that was to be expected in some way, because of the proximity of the anniversary of Alice's daughter's death.

Sixth Session

'I went up to the grave on Sunday. I felt much clearer for going . . . I put on my coat and went. I bought her some pink geraniums in a pot.' Then Alice talked about the previous session. She felt 'dreadful' and had taken the rest of the week off. A colleague had taken her some flowers and Alice 'cried all over her'. I thought that this was an enormous shift for Alice. She was no longer able to desensitise or deflect her need to express her feelings and she had also been open to the support of a colleague.

'I think that last week was some sort of . . . it was very bad last week you know . . . like when you burst, lance a boil or something.' She talked about her reactions to the session and the fact that, after it, she had felt as she did when Fiona had died. But instead of telling herself that she had to carry on (as she did over the funeral) she let herself cry.

Alice then went on to talk about her childhood relationship with her mother: 'It was important to think that we were friends with her [because they did not see her very often] and we got a hug. When you have a little bit of time then you want that time to be really good. And if she was displeased, you'd just be left with just the displeasure. If she was pleased with me, then I could go on through the week.' I said that children will take whatever they can and survive, and she responded, 'Poor little thing, though . . .'.

Stern (1985) describes the function of the 'evoked companion' of the child, where, when the child is alone, they have the capacity to bring into their reality the parent, to counteract the feelings of aloneness. With Alice this seemed to operate in two ways. When she had a memory of her mother that was nurturing, she could evoke the nurturing parent; when she remembered times that her mother was displeased, she could only evoke the displeased parent. Alice took what nurturing she could from a variety of sources. 'Given a certain amount of parenting, the child is not beyond hope and does have choice' (Yontef, 1983: 69).

Seventh Session

That week, Alice had realised more fully that Fiona would not be coming back. She had also realised that she was trying to find someone to blame for her daughter's death. I think this was a significant step forward, because for the first time (in the sessions) she was trying to find somebody else to blame instead of blaming herself. She remembered thinking of Fiona's boyfriend and had found a reason to blame him, as he had not been with Fiona when she had had the attack. When she alighted on a possible reason related to the boyfriend, she felt 'released in her whole body', as though in finding someone else to blame she could let go of the self-blame. She went on to repeat that she had blamed herself since Fiona's death.

This undoing of her retroflection reflects Perls' idea that 'an over-stern conscience can be cured only when self-reproach changes into object approach' (Perls, 1992 [1947]: 159), where 'object' refers to another person. Besides Alice's anger with Fiona's boyfriend, she also disclosed for the first time that soon after Fiona's death she had felt angry with her. Again, I saw Alice making significant changes in the way she was contacting her feelings and thoughts. My concern was to ensure that the undoing of the retroflections took place very slowly. Perls et al. (1972 [1951]) are very clear in stating that the undoing of a retroflective pattern must be carried out with care, otherwise the personality of the client 'comes to its defence as if to head off catastrophe'.

However, further on in the session, Alice began blaming herself again, this time for being the kind of mother her mother was. I was aware that she was angry and was also retroflecting anger and blame again. I also thought that she was being angry with herself in a way that had not been possible with her own mother. I told Alice what I thought was happening. Alice responded by beginning to feel physically sick and faint. I realised that this intervention was premature, even though Alice had repeatedly brought up issues of her childhood and parenting. She 'coped' by feeling sick, which resulted in our concern moving away from the issue and onto carrying out strategies to make her feel more comfortable, such as opening a window.

Alice's behaviour led me to think that she had very powerful introjects about not expressing anger to her mother or others. If such introjects are not adhered to, a high level of anxiety can occur. Smith (1988) reminds us that, when an introject is not obeyed, the experience can feel as if something awful, terrible, is threatened which will result in catastrophe. In light of such an observation, Alice's reaction seems very understandable. She had touched a 'limit situation' (Levin, 1991), a point beyond which she could not go, and had regulated herself in the best way she knew how, by feeling sick. Alice began to use the analogy of digging too deep and her wish to keep the door closed. So I reminded her that she had every right to close the door whenever she wished. She also had the right to open the door as and when she wanted, knowing she could close it at any time.

I had gone too fast and made an intervention which was inappropriate. I asked her how she felt about my clumsy comment and she said she didn't like it. I wondered aloud if at that moment, in her mind, I had become the person who was supposed to be caring for her and was instead hurting her. She became thoughtful and then looked at me intensely for a while. She said, 'But you didn't mean to hurt me. And I think you might have been right in what you said.'

Eighth Session

'I won't take my coat off, I'm not stopping' was how Alice opened her eighth session. She said that she was quoting from an old radio comedy programme. She admitted that there was a part of her that did not want to 'stop'. She had again felt physically unwell after the previous session. She did not go to the doctor, as she said it was 'a thing that I recognise when I am quite stressed'. I knew that she had been checked over by her doctor and no organic cause had been found for the feelings of sickness, which had started after Fiona's death. She said that her body tells her what is happening much more than her brain does. I felt that her level of desensitisation was markedly lower. I said I appreciated her ability to listen to her body and acknowledge her needs.

During the week Alice had found that she could think about her mother 'with a different sort of love, not a guilty sort of thing, and I really felt quite warm towards her'. She disclosed that she did get very angry the previous week: 'I even got a little bit angry with Fiona.' As Alice said this she became sad and tearful. I acknowledged that she could experience her feelings of sadness and anger and still function. She described what happened when she allowed her feelings to 'take over': 'My hands get very big and my head grows. Everything goes grey, distances change and I feel very scared . . . my head gets woozy.'

She described how occasionally she had become a 'screaming whimpering heap'. I suggested that, as soon as she started to feel like that, she could bring herself back by using specific strategies and talked to her about the effects of hyperventilation, which I suspected might be caused by emotional breathing that might be shallower than her usual habit. I emphasised her choice in this, and her level of control which she appeared to have over whether 'it' happened or not. Alice asked, 'Is it a memory of being ill as a child, because that is when it first started?'

Ninth Session

Alice expressed concern that she was forgetting her daughter. I had an impression that she was resting after what had been a very painful time. I said this to her. She took a deep breath and visibly relaxed. Her face changed and she smiled, 'that's what it feels like.' Clark (1982) describes the cycle of grief and states that, as a method of organismic self-regulation, there are times to take an emotional rest, to 'retire into isolation for recuperation'.

Alice began to hint more and more about something that had happened to her and how she felt. She used the term 'sexual abuse' for the first time, and said that she had been eight years old. I made no attempt to direct her in her disclosure. She went on to say, 'If I know it wasn't my fault, I'd be very angry at people, not my mother, I'd want to kill . . .'. I was very touched that she had the courage to look into her past, after so many years, and to see so clearly the function of her self-blame. I acknowledged that the capacity to kill another human being is in each one of us and that being aware of our potential for violence makes it far less likely to happen.

Alice talked of her shock at crying about her father's death, something she had never done. She described looking at his death certificate. She felt that it was the only tangible proof that he had existed. She said that the certificate had the number of children he had. I said that she was one of his children and she became tearful saying, 'I want to be somebody's child.' She quickly dismissed this, reminding herself that she was 58 years old.

Tenth Session

Two weeks later, as soon as Alice sat down, she began to describe a dream she had had two nights previously; she said she had dreamt about me. In the dream she saw a huge white bird, which she decided was a dove. She saw that the bird was me, and in the dream she was able to rest her head against the bird's breast and drop everything (her burden).

Alice was excited about the dream and its relevance to what she was doing with me. I was moved by the image but did not suggest exploring possible projections. Instead I chose to focus on her feeling associated with the dream, as her face was so animated at remembering the way she let her 'burden' down. She then noticed my voice (I was still croaking following a cold). I assured her that I was well taken care of, and that I felt fine to be with her. Alice immediately expressed relief that she did not have to take care of me and then went on to disclose her feelings of relief associated with her daughter's death. She did not have to worry about Fiona as she used to. She had worried, for example, about whether Fiona was well, whether she took her medication, whether she crossed the roads carefully and so on. I understood her feeling of relief and said so.

Alice then made yet another revealing statement about her experience of the sessions and of me. She said she wanted me to decide whether she should take two days off work to go away with a friend. She wanted me to make the decision because then she could blame me if her boss complained about her taking more time from work! Alice then went on to say, jokingly, 'I want mum to decide.' For me this was a fascinating moment of insight. Throughout the work I had been aware of the possible co-transference issues which might occur. In the knowledge that I am about the age that Alice's daughter was, I had assumed that I might have represented Fiona for Alice. I had never thought about the fact that Alice could see me as her mother. What was so interesting was that, apparently, age and gender are irrelevant to the transference in the therapeutic relationship. For Alice I became what was developmentally needed, her mother. The fact that I was her daughter's age did not matter.

With Alice, the unfinished business of her past became the pressing figure against the ground of her recent experience. I think that, in the striving towards health, clients will find what they need in order to be healed. And, as Alice said in the ninth session, 'I want to be somebody's child.'

Thinking about the times I listened to and tracked what Alice was saying, I feel that such 'empathic attunement', while totally located within and appropriate to an I–Thou relationship between two adults, echoes the parenting behaviours to a baby. Both Stern (1985) and Trevarthen (2008) describe the reflective mannerisms and vocalisations of parents. I suggest that the therapist, offering this sort of resonance and empathy, may evoke in the client either times when they were responded to by another with such mirroring – or times when need for it was unmet. This can cause a swift development of transference (which Joyce and Sills call 'introjective transference'), which the Gestalt therapist addresses, either overtly or covertly.

As Alice made contact with me in that emotional way, I felt the co-transferential pull to step into that mother role. I experienced warmth and protective feelings. Had our relationship been a long-term one, I might have chosen to allow this form of relating to deepen, in order to help Alice fully experience herself. However, she had only two sessions left, so I made an intervention which I hoped would reduce the level of transference and possible dependence on me. I asked her to be her own mum and see what her answer would be. She very quickly said that she would like the two days' break, and would request them.

Alice described some warm and happy memories of Fiona and then said how she wished she really knew how Fiona was now. I asked what difference that would make to her life and Alice said that she would feel great. I experienced her as searching for the answer in the hope that, with the answer, she would feel good again. Spinelli talks about the activity that individuals take up, in order to avoid the 'not knowingness of life': 'To be authentic, we must concede that all our being-related knowledge is, and will remain, incomplete and uncertain, whatever meaning life may seem to have for us is our construction and that hence in an ultimate sense, our existence is meaning-less' (Spinelli, 1989: 113).

With Spinelli's words in mind, I told Alice that I experienced her as searching for an answer, and making herself dependent on an answer that she would never ever really know. Again, Alice impressed me with the level of her insight. She responded, 'Maybe I'm still avoiding the fact that Fiona is dead. As long as I keep searching I don't need to face it ... It's very difficult to live in the now, maybe it's easier to be searching for something that doesn't exist, than look at life as it is.' If Spinelli needed an example to illustrate his concept Alice had just given it.

Alice began to talk about her husband, who had cried a few times recently. She seemed puzzled by his crying, as he had not cried during most of the year after Fiona's death. I suggested that he might be picking up changes in her and feeling more able to cry with her. I said that people change as they are with each other; I had changed by being with Alice, as she might change by being with me: 'being' with another is in itself a change process. Alice agreed and said that she had changed and was changing. She said that recently she had been more friendly towards her husband.

Eleventh Session

Alice had had a good Christmas and had also felt sad at times. She realised that she could have a good time and still feel sad. She described her sadness as moving into warmth. She also talked of the kindness of others, 'half saddening and half warming'.

In this session I affirmed Alice's courage and motivation in coming to the sessions with me. She stopped breathing for a few seconds; such positive feedback was over-whelming for her, and I remembered earlier sessions when she had also deflected positive comments of mine. I was reminded through this interaction that compliments given to someone who is not accustomed to receiving them, can be as threatening as criticisms, if not more so.

Alice seemed to be withdrawing, and beginning to look at the future. She was showing self-support, and talked about joining a women's group. The energy level of the session was calm and I felt she was moving well towards closure.

Twelfth Session

'So this is your last session,' I said. Alice spent some of the time looking to the future, at how she wanted to prepare for retirement, perhaps with the future support of more therapy. I do not think that she was deflecting from the reality of the last session, rather she was using me as a resource to discuss other possible forms of therapy, for example, in a group.

She reviewed her time with me, remembering how deeply she cried about her daughter in the first session, which had truly surprised her. She talked about the pain she had experienced and the depths that she had gone to. She described her difficulty in trusting anyone to see her; that she would rather run away. I asked her what it was like to be with me. She said it was different with me.

I reminded Alice of her contract in our second session – to keep safe while she was in therapy. Before I had finished she smiled and stated firmly that she had no intention of dying until she was of a good, old age.

As the session moved to a close I asked her if she wanted to say anything or wanted anything from me. She did not believe she did. She felt that she had said everything she needed to say.

I told her that I had learnt from her. She was surprised and asked what. Remembering her difficulty in hearing positives, I gently said that I had learnt about the level of motivation someone can have for working in the 12 sessions. And I said I had learnt about courage. She looked down and was silent. She then returned my gaze, her face warmed and her eyes sparkled.

This was really a lovely moment, a moment of 'pure contact'. Minutes later, I said goodbye.

I was very excited. Alice had come to me saying that she wanted someone's hand to hold and I assumed she was talking unconsciously about her mother. In the light of what happened I believe that we had co-created what she had been searching for, a mother to hold her hand. And when it was time to say goodbye she dropped the hand, saw me as me, and moved on.

Discussion

Throughout this work the therapist was guided by a statement of Gary Yontef (cited in Mulgrew and Mulgrew, 1987: 68) who said that a goal of Gestalt practice is 'to enable distressed individuals to experience fuller contact with their worlds so that they can assemble or reject experiences appropriately'. Alice 'wanting someone to hold her hand' had been a very clear request. She approached the therapist five weeks before the first anniversary of her daughter's death. The issues of her childhood, the way she had learned to be, to express feelings, to behave in the world at large – all impinged on her present life experience.

The therapist judged that the relationship between them would be the most important vehicle for healing, recalling Stern's (1985) concept of the 'evoked companion'. Alice had established fixed patterns of relating to people in her world which had prevented her from being fully in touch with her own feelings and needs while also making her unable to accept support from her friends: Some of those fixed gestalts were changed in the therapy relationship in the movement towards a more healthy structure of self.

Making acceptance of her client's position the highest priority, the therapist chose not to use many experiments. It is frequently useful in bereavement therapy to invite clients to undertake two-chair dialogues with the dead person. However, the therapist thought it was more appropriate to allow Alice to talk *about* her daughter and her memories of what she was like rather than invite her to do two-chair work. To ask her to imagine Fiona in the room whenever she talked about her might surely have increased her strong introjects against expressing feelings. What is more, it might also have supported her disbelief in Fiona's death and her hope that, if she behaved well, her daughter would 'come back'.

Alice was in contact with her distress and identified her wants very clearly. She manifested a high degree of self-regulation in the sessions, being able to express some of her pain, then move into closure and withdrawal.

Janice writes: 'Perhaps the most important ingredient of the therapy was Alice's motivation' (a hypothesis fully supported by psychotherapy outcome research – e.g. see Norcross, 2011; Wampold, 2001). A client with low motivation will disempower the most skilled therapist. Jacobs (1989) states that the therapist is 'powerless to change the patient'. Janice again: 'Alice approached her therapy session with commitment and courage. She may wish to have further therapy at some time in the future. However, the process of the therapy seemed complete; it progressed fluidly through the gestalt cycle of awareness. Alice came knowing what she wanted, addressed it and, to all intents and purposes, got what she wanted and finally withdrew.'

Author's Note

The original case study by Janice Scott is a chapter in *Gestalt Counselling* (Sills et al., 1995), on which much of this volume is based. We have kept it in this edition, because we feel it is a beautiful example of Gestalt therapy in a short-term context. With Janice's permission, we have simply edited the story a little in order to more fully illustrate some of the concepts we have introduced into this book and to bring the references up-to-date.

14

Gestalt in Organisations: With the Gestalt Coach or Consultant

Leaders and members of organisations continually grapple with facilitating change in our increasingly complex and networked world. People in organisations are required to possess or develop the intra- and interpersonal resources to make informed decisions when ambiguity prevails. These demands take their toll on people in organisations. Complexity can be overwhelming and sometimes undermine a person's confidence. Sometimes leaders and groups feel under-resourced and require outside support. Others realise that to maintain their current level of performance, time to retreat, reflect and renew is critical to sustaining a healthy organisation.

Such situations, and of course there are many more, present opportunities for Gestalt practitioners who are executive coaches and consultants but our theory, methods and practice may be a challenge for those procuring services such as coaching and organisation development interventions like team building, culture change, strategy engagement and executive team development. We often find we need to invest time and energy in helping organisations understand the benefits of working from a Gestalt perspective. This may require us to make contact with several individuals to inquire into the organisation and offer support to heighten awareness of 'what is' at this time as our holistic approach is often contrary to some deeply held beliefs people have about the nature of an organisation and how it can be controlled and manipulated. This control is often exercised through structures, good technical systems and strong leadership but is built on the 'illusion that the world is created of separate, unrelated forces' (Senge, 1990: 3), promulgating the leader as hero (Binney et al., 2005), and looking at parts of the organisation and the people in isolation from the whole.

For example, in many organisations there is a view that change occurs by having a strong, charismatic leader who can provide clear direction and clearly stipulate what is required. The assumption is that a strong leader will motivate people as they put aside their own fears, concerns, and hopes in the service of the leader's vision. It is a form of top-down leadership, often associated with a sense of command and control. There is little attention given to how people are really experiencing the current situation, or of fostering trusting relationships between people across different levels of the organisations to move forward in a way that honours their current context and future hopes.

Another common experience at times of complex change programmes is the desire for clear project structure and governance. While some structure and processes are necessary, others may be a way of trying to exert control and to predetermine outcomes for what are essentially emerging and dynamic human processes of relating between team members, divisions, or individuals who come from different organisations.

For example, a local government office was looking at ways to improve the quality of their service to vulnerable senior citizens by integrating social care, housing services and building a partnership with a charity. This required different parts of the organisation and external stakeholders to come together to offer a more integrated service to clients and find a way of reducing costs in order to maintain their competitiveness (as private providers could now enter this market). They quickly set up a detailed project governance structure with sponsors, steering groups and detailed project plans with activities and milestones. There was an obsessional focus on activities, updating plans, all in the service of trying to meet deadlines. However, it did not take account of the time required by individuals to build good-enough working relationships to address important issues. Any resistance encountered (and understandably there was resistance, as people were concerned for their professional reputations and job security) was seen as something to be overcome rather than inquired into as a 'creative adjustment'. Hence, opportunities to understand and foster a better quality of relationships were missed. This resulted in the project not meeting its objectives, and individuals, teams and clients feeling dissatisfied.

This vignette illustrates ways of perceiving organisations that assume a linear cause-and-effect relationship, where the presenting problem or opportunity can be neatly identified, controlled, and then quickly dealt with! This is very different to a Gestalt view of organising with its emphasis on interdependent dynamic relationships, where the whole is different to the sum of the parts. Working from a Gestalt perspective, consultants are paying attention to what they are co-creating with their clients, noticing what 'wants to make itself known' (Carlson and Kolodny, 2009). Problems are seen as aspects of the current organisational field conditions and not allocated to just one particular person or part of the organisation. As Gestaltists, we can support a way of working with people in organisations honouring where they are, while also facilitating change through heightening awareness and building support for purposeful action. In the remainder of this chapter we will firstly redefine how we see organisations from a Gestalt perspective. Then, we will highlight the application of key Gestalt concepts and practices (discussed in Part II and III) fundamental to coaching and consulting in organisations. We will finally identify the qualities Gestalt practitioners need to develop when working in organisations.

Application of Gestalt Fundamentals for Executive Coaches and Organisational Consultants

What is an Organisation?

In Gestalt theory, persons are continually changing in relation to their context. In organisations, persons are simultaneously shaped by and shaping their team, divisions and organisational context.

Andrea, a consultant, was facilitating a team-building day. Individuals appeared energetic in their interactions yet what they were saying sounded rehearsed and carefully crafted. She noticed her senses dulling, feeling bored in one moment and excited at others when other managers showed interest in a topic of conversation. She informed the team that she could continue to make the same interventions with them as if she had also pre-planned and rehearsed everything, but she would prefer to do something different. She also shared her feeling of both excitement and boredom as she listened to their discussions. The team members started responding to her and each other with greater spontaneity sharing their own hopes and concerns. Andrea quietly sat back and noticed the unfolding vibrant conversation and exchanges among team members with renewed interest and curiosity. Both Andrea and the team were changing in this dynamic relational process.

Organisations are of course made up of people. Bentley describes organisations as 'groups of people in relationship (*ostensibly*) bounded by a common purpose' (2001: 14; our additional word in brackets). Within this context, individuals sometimes struggle to develop meaningful relationships, get stuck, or feel dissatisfied with the status quo. Organisations are ongoing dynamic processes of organising where individuals are continually engaging in interactions of I–It and I–Thou modes of relating with each other to get things done. Here, organisations are no longer entities with reified boundaries but 'people in relationships producing relationships, which produce them at the same time' (Stacey, 2003: 312). In our example above, Andrea noticed the roles certain individuals adopted in the team meeting and how they seemed to be developing alliances that were either supportive or undermining of the issues being explored. Habitual patterns of conversation ensued. She informed them of these relational interactions and invited the team to consider if re-enacting their relational histories (I–It) was in the service of what they needed to address.

This perspective of organising is a far cry from the view of the organisational leader as all-knowing hero or the organisation as machine-like in its careful management of activities.

We believe there are three fundamental theoretical components that can support the Gestalt coach or consultant when 'intervening' in organisations. Some of these theories and methods have previously been explored in different ways by Gaffney (2009), Mauer (2005), Nevis (1987) and Stevenson (2010).

Gestalt Fundamentals for Working in Organisations

Angelita and Adam (the consulting team) were about to start a consulting assignment with the executive board and senior management teams of a housing association, Open Doors. The housing association's aim was to provide safe, affordable and quality social housing for people living in an inner city, multi-cultural environment that had high unemployment. The board members were a chief executive and five directors, and there were twelve senior managers. The chief executive and some of the board realised that the current way of operating was not going to deliver their ambitious plans for growth and quality improvement. They felt stuck. No matter what change initiatives or compelling communication plans they put in place, people seemed unable to 'step up' – a term used by the chief executive. They invited several providers to tender for a consulting assignment to help them develop their capability as a senior leadership team when working on strategy. Angelita and Adam won the assignment after a rather long tendering process. After the final presentation to secure the work, they noted how it had felt like an inquisition. While excited with the opportunity to work with Open Doors they also felt anxious about engaging. As Gestalt practitioners they were aware that the work had already started from the very first moment of contact with Open Doors when they responded to the tender.

Interconnectedness and Field Theory
Supports Staying with the Complexity of Organisations

When we enter organisations as coaches or consultants, the very anticipation of our participation affects the relational field and the field in turn affects us. Consultants and coaches are constantly engaged in co-creating experiences from the time of their very first contact with clients. As all are interconnected there is no such thing as objectivity that beholds a single truth. Coaches or consultants cannot stand outside the field of any organisation. They are embedded within it once they make contact. All they can offer are different perspectives to clients depending on their position and experience of being part of the organisational field.

Adapting Parlett's principles of field theory can support the consultant or coach working with the individual or group within an organisational context. They provide orientation to make sense of what the practitioner is doing when working in complex environments. They also provide a sound theoretical base for interventions. This can instil confidence in the practitioner, which in turn can enable him to stay alert and aware of the emerging phenomena.

The Whole is Different from the Sum of the Parts

Wollants (2007) describes the importance of the 'total situation', which means the relational field created by the interactions between the organisational context, the individuals and the consultants. This is a real challenge given the complexity of organisations and the social contexts in which they are embedded. In their assignments, practitioners are seeking to notice and understand how people self-organise to support themselves in getting things done within their current context. Angelita and Adam undertook the assignment on the condition that they could hold a co-inquiry process with all board members, the senior management team, some employees, and key stakeholders such as community groups and tenants. As much as possible they were trying to understand the whole organisation, not only the individual parts. They were curious to see how the leadership teams were organising themselves to meet their strategic objectives of growth and quality improvement. They 'hung out' in the organisation and noticed the quality of contact people had with each other within teams and across divisions. They noticed that the anxiety they experienced on winning the tender was also evident in the people they engaged in dialogue. At planned small-group events they invited people to draw an image in response to the question: 'How do you in Open Doors organise yourselves and your tasks to meet these objectives of growth and quality improvement?' Different images emerged which made apparent some of the formal and informal processes that shaped the whole Open Doors culture. They noticed the formal processes of strategic planning, project planning, technological processes and work schedules as well as the informal processes of corridor and coffee machine conversation where business got done, and the interaction between these. As Parlett says, '"structure" and "function" are not rigidly separated but are both attempts to convey qualities of the interrelated whole' (1991: 70). Here, the procedures were bureaucratic (i.e. structure), risk averse and onerous and, in the context of a highly politicised environment with a diverse, multi-cultural client base, this was stultifying their ability to be more agile and locally responsive. It was as if the people had become cogs in a wheel. Together with participants, the consulting team were developing a sense of the Open Doors as a whole. It seemed more like Inaccessible Doors than Open Doors!

All is Occurring in the Here and Now

The principle of contemporaneity indicates that it is only from the present influence of the organisation and wider field that individuals can make sense of their current experience. Whatever the situation, all that is happening is happening simultaneously now. In organisations the remembering of the past and the anticipation of the future in the current conversations are occurring in the present moment. It is the patterns of relating and contacting that explains current behaviour. A two-day team retreat was held for the Open Doors board and the senior management team at a rural conference centre, to explore their ways of working. During the morning of the first day, Angelita asked them to organise themselves into groups to explore how they currently worked on their strategy. They self-organised into three groups. The board was one, and the senior management team self-organised into two different groups: those in external-facing roles, for example, call centre, housing repairs, community development, and those in internal-facing roles, such as finance and corporate services.

Angelita and Adam were focusing on what was emerging in the here and now. Once people had self-organised, they invited them to firstly explore their current constellation, rather than proceed with the initial task. This division of resources reflected what they did in the organisation. They remained in their silos to do their thinking and only once they had decided what was most relevant and important for their function, did they engage with others. The board and senior team were slowly becoming aware of how their current way of working inhibited them from truly engaging with the strategy as a dynamic and exciting opportunity for the whole organisation.

Multiple Perspectives Are Honoured

The principle of singularity is where each person's experience and the organisational context they are part of is considered unique, depending on their history, current role, function, future expectations and so on. Consultants and coaches are genuinely curious about what is unique to this particular situation, perceiving the present organisational experience as a figure of the organisational field, specific to this moment, without making generalisations. It is a reminder for consultants and coaches to refrain from the role of expert who translates these specific experiences into generalisations for the whole organisation. As Angelita and Adam facilitated the group in exploring their current way of organising in the here and now, multiple and different experiences emerged. They remained curious about what was unique about this particular situation. The CEO informed his team that he was clear on the strategic direction required but felt worried that there was little action being taken to deliver it. As she listened to the discussion, Angelita noticed that when a new opinion was offered it seemed as if it plopped into the middle of the room, like a stone into a swamp. There was a lack of spontaneity. The team seemed to withdraw their energy. People's breathing seemed to be shallow and they appeared to turn inwards on themselves. Yet, Adam felt a sense of hyper-alertness as he noticed his body tensing and his heart anxiously beating faster. Of all aspects of the present situation he decided to reflect back this process, sharing his own feelings as a current aspect of the field. Now other members of the group spoke hesitantly of their fear in expressing different views as they had heard that the chief executive had dismissed board members in his previous organisation when his strategic perspective was challenged. In that moment, it seemed that this history and the differing hopes for a new future were inhibiting a more spontaneous and honest conversation.

Organisations Are in a State of Constant Flux

The principle of changing process identifies that nothing is static. Nothing is permanent. Life is always in process. Change is occurring all the time. In organisations, both people and the groups or divisions they belong to are also changing. This principle cautions consultants against categorising and labelling, even though the temporary feeling of certainty that labelling produces is attractive. If categories are attributed to patterns it is important to remain open to these changing as soon as they are named. It is a way of seeing the organising activities as processes where people are creatively adjusting and doing the best they can with the current level of support.

At the end of first retreat day, Angelita and Adam were reflecting on the work with Open Doors. They noticed that the level of support they offered had changed during the day. In the early part of the day they had deliberately taken on leadership roles as facilitators of the retreat. They collated ideas and wrote them on flip charts and invited the members of the group to attend to what was happening between them. In the latter part of the day, particularly after Adam's intervention, they noticed the groups now had mixed membership when working on tasks relating to the strategy, each group including board members and internal and external focused senior managers. Conversation was less hesitant and some members were starting to share their thoughts, feelings and 'gut reactions' to the strategy which was now being re-explored. Changes were occurring with more open and honest participation. Angelita and Adam could see that Open Doors was becoming a different kind of organisation at this moment in time; and they also wondered what perhaps was being consistently being missed in the work.

All Events, Experiences and Encounters Are Potentially Relevant

The principle of possible relevance suggests everything in the organisation has possible meaning. According to this principle, consultants cannot arbitrarily ignore the relevance of anything in the organisation and its context. They notice how people are consulted around changes, who initiates the process, how individuals participate and what happens as a result. They also observe and engage with the physical environment people work in and keep attuned to external and internal communications and how messages are disseminated, all the while paying attention to their phenomenology. Instead of trying to track and make sense of every possible aspect of the field, which of course would be impossible, consultants are interested in the obvious and what is pressing or calling for attention. They are noticing what is really captivating their interest. They are open to recurring themes or patterns emerging from the organisational ground. Sometimes this means paying attention to an aspect of organisational life and relationships that are often overlooked or persistently omitted.

Late on the second morning of the retreat, a theme best described as 'quality of care' became figural. Angelita noticed how group members seemed to describe their clients (tenants and some external stakeholders), as if they were objects or tasks to be dealt with. She also noticed how they took little care of themselves: working through breaks, checking emails and mobile phones. They chose not to take time to walk and talk in the warm and beautiful outdoors, to reflect on the previous day's work. She also noticed how she and Adam seemed to be less caring towards each other this morning, unusually not checking in with each other before the day started. She wondered if the 'quality of care' that the team exhibited towards each other was persistently overlooked in the pressure to be a 'caring-for-others' organisation. Perhaps they were never able to explore the opposite polarity of being less caring that was emerging in the work. Was this 'quality of care' sufficient to enable the whole team to feel more engaged and committed to the new strategy? Angelita offered her experience and wondered aloud if this was also an aspect of Open Doors' organisational field. People from the senior management team responded and shared their sense of relief that this was now in the open. They also expressed their awkwardness as they acknowledged the current lack of care they experienced from the board in hearing their views on the strategy. They became aware that this was now something they were co-creating in their relationships with clients, and agreed that the strategy process must involve tenant representatives if it was to energise the whole organisation.

In summary, field principles support the Gestalt consultant and coach in recognising they are co-inquirers participating within an organisation where all is interconnected. The attention for Gestalt practitioners in organisations is on the ongoing process of interactions between people in the here-and-now. The here-and-now also includes the there-and-then, where the organisational history is being retold in the present moment. Expectations and hopes for the future are shaping how the stories of the past are being retold in the present.

Heightening Awareness to Facilitate Purposeful Action

Working as Gestalt coaches and consultants, we emphasise heightening the awareness of our clients – whether an individual, group or whole organisation. Often individuals and organisations may have over-developed particular zones of awareness as creative adjustments that have supported them in being successful. In an increasingly complex world, people need to be more adaptable and capable of being highly attuned to their environments. What previously worked may now be contributing to a feeling of being stuck or recreating patterns of relating and doing things that seem less effective. Educating our clients to develop their different zones of awareness (inner, middle, outer and co-created, see Chapter 4) enables them to access alternative ways of experiencing and knowing, leading to greater choice of behaviour. This relationship between awareness and behaviour change is unique to Gestalt (Simon, 2009). Clients become more mindful in deciding which course of action is appropriate to take in their context, which is timely, relevant and congruent with who they are and what they hope to become.

Engaging the 'External' World through the Senses (Outer Zone)

Our internal and external worlds are inextricably linked. Within an organisational context, 'external' is referring to the psychological and physical boundary where one person's role or organisation ends and another begins. These boundaries are permeable, and are the ways individuals, teams and organisations interact to express their autonomy as well as their sense of being interconnected. Often individuals in organisations appear to overly rely on some senses at the expense of others. Important data can get missed that is sometimes critical for successful contact and subsequent purposeful action.

Della, an executive coach recommended by Angelita and Adam, noticed that Jamie the chief executive of Open Doors was very articulate and listened well but she experienced him as aloof and felt invisible when coaching him. She observed that he rarely seemed interested in his environment. When she inquired into what he saw in the organisation, he found it difficult to remember or describe the environment his colleagues worked in. He seemed unaware of people's ethnicity, cultural heritage or their facial or bodily expressions. Della suggested experiments where he would visit people in their offices and closely observe what he saw so he could describe it in detail. Also, she invited him in the here-and-now of the work to notice gestures such as hand or body movements, facial expressions, and so on. Later, when he discussed the experiment, he said that the renewed awareness was helping him to understand why people were unable to 'step up' to the new strategy. He recognised his gaze of care and interest was absent in his meetings with them. He listened but was not sensitive to their context or what was going on for them. He was slowly developing his ability to use his senses to 'read the person and their situation' before engaging with them on his agenda.

Trusting the Integrity of their Experience (Inner Zone)

In organisations, feelings and bodily sensations are often mistrusted or ignored as they are deemed irrelevant. This is particularly so when organisations are bureaucratic in their structure and processes. In such environments, individuals may numb their bodies and suppress expression of emotions, creating a rather formal and 'professional' culture. As we saw earlier, Open Doors was such an organisation at the beginning of the retreat when the people self-organised into their own teams. Their feelings of fear were not expressed as they seemed to move rigidly into their pre-configured groups. The deeply held beliefs and values that brought people into the social housing sector was unacknowledged, and the inner somatic sensations accompanying these cherished values of pride, compassion and hope were quelled.

A few weeks after the retreat, in a group coaching session, Angelita and Adam invited the board members to notice their physical sensations and emotions as they worked together. Mindful of the potential for vulnerability and even shame when executives are learning something new, Angelita and Adam went first in sharing their sensations and associated feelings. At one point, Adam said, 'I feel a tightening of my chest, a slight difficulty in breathing and I notice a sense of alarm when I hear of health and safety issues being avoided.' He hoped that over time the group would become more aware of physical sensations and associated feelings, trusting these as an integral part of the co-created experience. They hoped that this would support appropriate self-disclosure and purposeful action that would unlock energy for renewing the strategy.

Inquiring into the World of Thought, Planning and Imagining (Middle Zone)

This is the zone familiar to many people in organisations of remembering, imagining, rationalising. However, for many leaders it is also the zone of their 'quiet demons' – the part of them that carries their deeply held introjects or unexamined beliefs about how things should be done. Often, patterns of thought, planning and implementa-tion are habituated. Organisational decisions are made and activities completed in the same way regardless of the current context. This was an aspect of Open Doors' strategy development and implementation processes. In the coaching session with Jamie, Della helped him explore his belief that as leader, he was solely responsible for setting the strategic direction and needed to have all the answers to any unan-ticipated problems that emerged. She invited him to imagine what it would be like if he did not hold these beliefs so dearly. He said he felt lighter, supple, and imagined that he could gracefully move around the organisation engaging others to support him in problem solving. Inquiring into his belief that he 'should' have all the answers, it transpired that all through his career his previous bosses rewarded him for his quick intellect and he believed it was his only way of being credible as board level. However, when he reminded himself of what he had previously imagined as possible, this started to open up new possibilities as to how he would take up his chief executive role in the future.

Highlighting Interconnectedness (Co-creating Zone)

This zone of awareness invites clients to be open to the possibilities that emerge within collaborative relationships. It requires people to dwell in their current organ-isational experience, reflected in the here-and-now relationship with each other, and trust what emerges as belonging to both the co-created relationship and wider organisational field. For example, it is the zone where a forgotten, historical hurt remains as unfinished business only to re-emerge in the form of stories or metaphors in the work. Or, it could be a struggle, past or present that is held in the private sphere of offices or meetings – yet to be reawakened.

Two months into the work with Open Doors, Angelita was facilitating an action-learning group of six members of the senior leadership team. The purpose was to provide an opportunity for members to work on real leadership and strategy chal-lenges in a supportive learning environment. Action learning is described as both self-development and organisational-development where there is no learning without action and no action without learning (Pedler, 1997). The consulting team believed this would foster collaborative working that could be experimented with outside the groups and experienced in the wider organisation. During the work, a persistent image of a stagnant pond kept occurring to Angelita, particularly when the group were talking about their leadership challenges. Angelita wondered what was calling for attention with the emergence of this metaphor as it seemed unrelated to the here-and-now conversation. She told the group about it and wondered aloud if this had any resonance with current or past organisational experiences.

After a few minutes' silence, one of the team spoke and recalled that four years previously a tragic accident occurred when two young family members drowned in a water-fountain feature in one of Open Doors' social housing projects. The incident had been quickly pushed aside and never discussed. It was remembered as a time when some board members did not accept the responsibility of their roles and instead looked for scapegoats among the senior management team.

While all seemed alive with life on the surface of the pond (just like the developing strategy conversations) the waters underneath were dark, murky and still. It seemed some of the senior managers in the group did not trust the board members and these conversations were buried in the depths of the organisational history. With this renewed awareness the team believed it was important to raise this at the next away day.

In summary, heightening clients' awareness promotes greater choice and offers opportunities for responding and behaving differently in distinctive contexts. With greater awareness individuals and organisations develop new ways of knowing and experiencing which informs action that is supportive of the organisation's purpose.

Gestalt Interactive Cycle: a Way to Support Effective Interventions

The interactive cycle is a way of conceptualising the cycle of experience for individuals (Chapter 6) *and* their interactions with others in a group, team and organisation. Each person and part of the organisation is not only required to be aware of their cycle of experience but also to notice, listen and respond to others' cycles. The phases translated for a consulting or coaching assignment can be described as follows:

- Sensation – The multiple and random events and associated sensations people experience;
- Recognition – A heightened shared awareness of problem/issue that is calling for attention;
- Appraisal and Planning – Conversations to explore how best to move forward on the issue and identify some options;
- Action – Starting to experiment with different ways of addressing the issue;
- Contact – Individuals invest themselves fully with each other around a common objective. All other issues are temporarily put to one side;
- Assimilation and Completion – The team/pair reviews the work together, checking for common understanding on what was achieved, or not, and why. They reflect on their learning as they discuss what went well and less well;
- Withdrawal – The meeting or conversation ends and time is allowed for new tasks and priorities to emerge.

Coaches and consultants attend to *both* the interplay between the different cycles of experience of individuals and parts of the organisation *and* how they progress through these stages within their organisational context. The interactive cycle concept supports coaches and consultants to understand how clients (whether individuals, teams or organisations) integrate the different 'awareness, energy and contact patterns' (Nevis, 1987: 31) into effective team or organisational function. For example, Figure 14.1 illustrates the interactive cycle of Open Doors at the outset of the consulting assignment with Angelita and Adam. As you may recall, the chief executive and the five board members were feeling stuck, unable to instil confidence or energy for the new strategy and change ways of working that would deliver their ambitious plans for

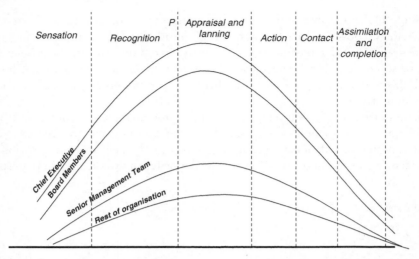

Figure 14.1 Open Doors' interactive cycle – beginning of consulting assignment

growth and quality improvement. You will notice that the chief executive and the board member had a similar progress through the sensation and recognition stages. However, the management team have a different trajectory of the sensation and recognition stage, and hence have a different level of awareness of the issues that the board and chief executive had already identified.

Angelita and Adam noticed that, despite having had plenty of time to gather data, the board had been discussing the organisational challenges for the past three months. However, the management team and other colleagues had not been invited to participate in this process and were now seen to be resisting. It seemed that any action taken lacked energy and cohesion resulting in much 'busy-ness' but poor and ineffective outcomes. Reflecting on these interactive cycles, Angelita and Adam realised that many people in Open Doors needed more time and support to immerse themselves in conversations in the way the board had been able to do. Hence, they suggested a two-day strategy engagement process where people selected representatives from various roles and functions to attend. The purpose was to better understand what was required and why, in order to build awareness and support for mobilising energy around the strategic challenges in the hope that good quality contact could be experienced when working together in the future.

Of course, the coach or consultant must also pay attention to their own awareness as well as others. The interactive cycle provides some important orienting principles when supporting clients to move purposefully through the cycle of experience. The aim of the consultant/coach–client relationship is to facilitate work being completed satisfactorily, while better equipping clients to address unexpected challenges and opportunities in the future. With a greater understanding of the interactive cycle, the consultant or coach can then decide how best to intervene to support their client's development. Next, we will briefly outline some of these orienting principles.

Principle One: Use the Interactive Cycle
as a Way of Assessing What is Going on in the Organisation

Attending to the interactive cycle of experience between people in the here-and-now coaching or consulting relationship can illuminate the organisational dynamics at play.

In the coaching session with Jamie, Della noticed that each time an issue was just about to be agreed and contracted for the session, Jamie introduced another topic. The figure was one of dissipating figures! Wheeler says 'the *meaning of the figure* (of behaviour – the gesture itself) will be given in the *structure of the ground* – i.e., the norms, goals, values' (1991: 103; emphasis in original). It seemed in Open Doors the ability to quickly identify issues was valued. It was expected that board members were the custodians of this activity, which they then delegated to others to implement. Della and Jamie explored this pattern. They realised that one of the reasons quality was slow to improve was because there was insufficient support to ensure options were explored (appraisal and planning stage) and agreement achieved on what to do.

Principle Two: Determining where Interruptions
and Modifications Occur Can Facilitate Change

Critchley and Casey (1989) suggest that impediments to organisational change are created within the organisation, resulting in them getting stuck at a particular stage of the cycle of experience. It can be helpful to notice how different individuals and parts of the organisation modify their contact in the interactive cycle of experience and seem to get stuck in habitual patterns of relating. Rather than trying to manipulate or push, adopting the paradoxical theory of change facilitates movement.

One week before the strategy engagement process, Della was in a coaching session with Jamie. She noticed that they appeared to be interrupting at the stage between appraisal/planning and action. Della invited Jamie to identify with this interruption and fully experience his current state. Jamie became aware that he was really clear on the options for Open Doors but he felt paralysed with fear in case he chose the 'wrong' option. It became evident that he held an unexamined assumption about his responsibility to find the 'right' answer. This was contrary to the upcoming strategy-engagement process where he would be open to new emerging strategic options. Decisions would include others' opinions and ultimately rest with the board, not only with him. Once he acknowledged this, he noticed a weight lift off his shoulders and the conversation flowed. He started to focus on ways he could position the two-day strategy process to build sufficient support for good connections and conversation.

Principle Three: Staying Close to Where People Are

In every organisation, people and parts of the organisation will often be at different places on the interactive cycle. It is important that consultants and coaches don't get ahead of clients on the cycle, otherwise their interventions are experienced as inappropriate and possibly insensitive. It is the role of the consultant to heighten awareness of these differences and foster the conditions in the organisational field to support conversations about them.

In Open Doors we have already seen how the board were ahead of the rest of the organisation in deciding what they believed needed to be done (Figure 14.1) leaving others feeling disengaged, with little energy to focus on the strategic objectives. Angelita and Adam saw the engagement process was necessary if they were to be trusted by the whole organisation and not perceived to be serving the self-interests of the board.

Principle Four: Developing Clients' Ability to Learn Utilising the Interactive Cycle

Creating sustainable and healthy organisations requires them to fully experience each stage of the cycle. This will help them develop, learn and grow into more responsive and adaptable organisations. To assist this process, the coach or consultant enters the relationship as a co-inquirer and learner. Both the client and consultant/coach are open to being changed as they develop a greater awareness of self and other by using the interactive cycle of experience to reflect on their work together.

One afternoon at the end of a meeting, the board and consulting team were reflecting on the process. They recognised that investing themselves in their respective expert roles was a way of desensitising themselves to the lived experience of the tenants who were Open Doors' clients and who were not held in mind during the meeting. Many of their clients were living in urban environments with high unemployment and poor community relationships. Both the board and consulting team realised that they were feeling shame because of their privileged backgrounds and roles. This got in the way of truly understanding the complexity of their context and resulted in rushing to simplified solutions as a way of reducing their felt sense of shame.

The consulting team invited the board members to pair up and share an aspect of them that was probably hitherto unknown. Angelita and Adam modelled this by informing each other about something in their backgrounds that was not known to the other.

Using the interactive cycle of experience to reflect on their work, the consulting team supported Open Doors in identifying what they were avoiding or missing. They developed the confidence to use it as a way of reflecting on their interactions with each other in meetings. This provided a way of monitoring their progress – an important aspect of organisational life.

Qualities of a Gestalt Coach and Consultant

Having defined what an organisation is from a Gestalt perspective and shown the applicability of key Gestalt concepts for working in organisations, we now highlight some of the core qualities effective Gestalt coaches and consultants need to develop. This is far from exhaustive. We see these particular qualities as support for the Gestalt practitioner to make timely and effective interventions that are in the service of clients' development.

Presence that Supports Healthy Connection

Presence is a stance rather than a quality. It is something that cannot be applied as a technique. Paradoxically, when the consultant or coach tries to be present, it is then that he is least present. In trying to become present it evades him. Presence can be defined as a 'turning toward the other' (Buber, 1965b: 22). It requires a momentary letting go of the agreed contract and objectives of the work to be fully available to meet the client in the here-and-now. Presence is a relational process requiring the organisational practitioner to offer a quality of contact that supports heightening awareness for the client. The quality of presence requires modifying. Too little and the client feels missed, too much and the client may feel overly exposed, particularly at the outset of assignments. This requires practitioners to stay aware of their embodied experience, utilising this to attune to what is missing or required in the client system, and make timely interventions. An appropriate presence is experienced by the client when they feel confirmed and understood by the coach or consultant.

Genuine Curiosity and Being Comfortable with Not Knowing

Practitioners need to allow themselves to be lost, to flow with the emerging conversation and see what unfolds in the co-created relationship. When exploring, the practitioner needs to be 'tuned in order to be responsive to the ever-changing rhythms of the human encounter' (Hycner, 1991: 13). This requires courage and involves risk-taking on behalf of the consultant or coach and a willingness to genuinely inquire without judgement or attachment to any particular outcome. Within a coaching or consulting assignment it is important that all aspects of the organisational field are explored. Once in the organisation, the consultant and coach become part of the organisational field, so that when inquiring with a genuine curiosity they refrain from taking up the role of change agent. They adopt a stance of co-inquirer into the current reality of the clients' context. Their focus of attention moves between what is happening for them and what is happening for clients, without drawing conclusions too quickly. The practitioners trust that the conversation will take them where it needs to take them, moving between I–It and I–Thou modes of relating.

Holding an Experimental Attitude

In a coaching session or organisational development intervention, all parties 'are not only reflecting on how to do things differently but really do things differently, this is, more jointly and generatively, enacting more relational quality' (Lambrechts et al., 2009: 46). Experimentation can provide opportunities for clients to experience new ways of behaving and relating. Holding an experimental attitude, the consultant or coach trusts his creativity and ability to sense into the organisational field. The experiment is an intervention that emerges from the here-and-now context. The role of consultant or coach is to offer 'bold, creative, well articulated interventions and withdrawals to allow their [clients'] process to continue' (Zinker, 1994: 287).

The consultant or coach co-designs an experiment with their client that is relevant to the current situation and the emerging figure or issue of interest. The intention and goal is one of enhancing the client's awareness, rather than moving or changing the client to a pre-determined outcome or to behaving in a different pre-determined way. Maintaining a stance of creative indifference, the consultant and coach continue to reject the role of change agent and become a co-inquirer to heighten awareness, not knowing where this may lead or what may emerge. Holding an experimental attitude, the consultant or coach trusts the client's autonomy and resources to develop and grow.

Commitment to Learning

Working within a dialogical relationship coaches and consultants are vulnerable, as they too are open to being changed in their encounter with clients. Growth and learning occur for clients when practitioners are most open to being changed in the relational encounter. The consultant/coach and client are co-learners. While the practitioners are not paid-up members of the organisation, they are part of the organisational field, joining people as they work on the contract of their work together. This requires a practitioner to be both reflective and reflexive, exploring the part he plays in the co-created relationship. It will require a continuing commitment to self-development as this is 'the single most useful means of becoming an effective consultant' (Nevis, 1987: 58). However, many individuals and executives in organisations may feel exposed when being invited to learn and change, when much of their work identity and affirmation has been about knowing. The coach and consultant who model openness to learning and changing in the work can offer support to clients to do the same. It is a way of minimising the potential for shame that is part of the organisational field when people start to learn new skills, behaviours and ways of working.

Additional Reading

Coffey, F. and Cavicchia, S. (2005) 'Revitalising feedback – an organisational case study', *British Gestalt Journal*, 14 (1): 15–25.
Handlon, J.H. and Fredericson, I. (1998) 'What changes the individual in gestalt groups? A proposed theoretical model', *Gestalt Review*, 2 (4): 275–94.
Wollants, G. (2007) 'Therapy of the situation', *British Gestalt Journal*, 14 (2): 91–102.

Afterword

We are born into a world that is rich in its diversity; a diversity that is visible in a myriad of characteristics such as our ethnicities, genders and sexualities, each enveloped in our different cultures and nationalities and experienced in the political and daily routines and rituals of our lives. In addition, there is the unique and awe-inspiring topography of our planet Earth where different plant and animal species co-exist in interdependent relationships and eco-systems.

However, due to the rapid pace of development in the name of human advancement, the diverse Earth we inhabit is being damaged. We know intuitively from the moment we allow ourselves to fully experience the beauty of a flower, the changing of the seasons, a loving gaze between friends or parent and child, the delight in different cultures, that we are interconnected. And this is also true for the painful moments in life when we see and experience suffering in the world, whether due to food shortages as a result of drought, or at times of war, disease or other natural disasters when people's lives and livelihoods are decimated. As we go to press, we are aware of the aftermath of devastating earthquakes in Japan and elsewhere, floods in Asia, famine in Somalia, war in North Africa, conflict in Syria – and much more. People reach out to others in different ways as an expression of care in times of such adversity – demonstrating our connectedness to fellow humankind and the world we inhabit.

Yet, as human beings, we often seem to engage in living as if we are separate, sometimes disconnected in our humanity.

Our innate human capacity to grow, advance and become more socially adept in adapting constructively to change is becoming distorted. Rather than using resources responsibly and creatively, we tend to focus on ourselves, embracing the individualistic as opposed to the relational paradigm. In the latter we would be more mindful of the potential impact of our intentions and actions on others; in the former we lose sight of the reality of 'other'. As sensate persons, we have the capacity to see, feel and sense the scars our actions are leaving on the Earth and her inhabitants. Yet something in us as humans is invested in choosing to ignore the unfolding realities of these scars as manifested in events such as climate change, the clambering for energy resource and the ever-increasing social economic divide between the rich and the poor.

It appears as a species that we are more human 'doings' than human 'beings'. In our 'doing' we seem engaged and focused on output. In contrast, in 'being' we could immerse ourselves in our experience and be more reflective and discerning in our understanding. Perhaps our focus on 'doing things' is a fixed gestalt. We live with limited awareness and engaged in contacting processes in a way that sometimes appears to be one of self-interest as opposed to self-in-relationship. Examples of this contacting process at a political level can be seen when our respective national leaders meet to discuss the issues of climate change and world poverty.

The wider social, political and ecological contexts shape our experiences and affect how we interact with each other in our co-created relationships, whether in therapy, coaching or in the communities where we live and work. In recent times, even with the renewed awareness that we are stewards of our communities and planet for future generations, we seem to continue to make decisions and take action with potentially damaging consequences. Perls et al. said:

> The case is that, by and large, we exist in a chronic emergency and that most of our forces of love and wit, anger and indignation, are repressed or dulled. Those who see more sharply, feel more intensely, and act more courageously, mainly waste them-selves and are in pain, for it is impossible for anyone to be extremely happy until we are happy more generally. Yet if we get into contact with this terrible actuality, there exists in it also a creative possibility. (1972 [1951]: 252)

We believe that Gestalt provides a theory and method where we can consider and care for both our own interests and the interests of the wider field at the same time, thereby embracing the diversity of our lived lives and the world in which we participate. According to Stoehr (1994), Goodman's ideal of therapy includes therapy of society. We would take this further and say that working as Gestalt practitioners we have opportunities to consider the whole wider ecological perspective that also includes our planet, our environment, our communities and the political systems we live within. This requires a dialogical relationship where we genuinely inquire into the wider and ever-changing field. It is Gestalt's insistence that we human beings cannot be understood in isolation but only as part of our context (as we know from field theory), that supports us to include the cultural, societal and environmental aspects of our experience. Creative possibilities are discovered through heightening awareness, maintaining healthy contact and developing support within our dialogical person-to-person relationships. We believe that such creative possibilities nurture the diverse communities and ecologies within which we live and ensure a hopeful future of generations to come.

Appendix I: Client Intake Sheets (Therapy)

Sheet 1

Name:	
Address:	
Tel: Mobile: Email:	
DOB:	Age:
Family doctor: Address/Tel:	
Date first seen:	
Referred by:	

(This sheet must be stored separately from case notes.)
© P. Joyce, 1992

Sheet 2

First name or code:	
Date started counselling:	
Occupation:	
Culture/ethnicity:	
Relationship status:	Children:
Parents:	
Siblings:	
Medical/Psychiatric history:	
Drink/Drugs/Suicide attempts/Self-harm history:	
Current level of functioning and stress:	
Previous therapy/counselling:	
Presenting issues/problems:	
Expectations and desired outcome of therapy:	
Contract frequency and duration:	Fee:

(1) No violence to self, therapist or consulting room. (2) Limits of my confidentiality: (a) supervision; (b) danger. (3) Four-week notice of stopping therapy where possible. (4) Cancellation policy. (5) Recorded and/or written material can be used only for therapist's development. Discussed and agreed with client.

Sheet 3

Contact functions: Talking: Hearing: Seeing: Touching: Movement:
Support: Self – organismic; postural; patterns of living: Environmental:
Modifications to contact:
Unfinished business:
Impressions and reactions to client:
Assessment and agreements:
Points to remember:

Reproduced and adapted with permission, from P. Joyce (1992) 'Client intake', *Gestalt Psychotherapy Student Handbook*. London: Metanoia Institute.

Appendix II: Coaching Client-Contact, Assessing and Contracting, Reflection Sheets

A: Client Contact Details

(This sheet must be stored separately from contracting and co-assessing sheet and coaching session reflection notes.)

Name: Role: How long in role/organisation: Reports to:	
Organisation name and address: Contact name for coaching contract: Agreed number of sessions: Agreed locations for sessions: Cost per session or for whole contract: Agreed method of payment:	
Client contact Tel. (Mobile): (Work): Email:	
Date of birth: Age:	Family relationships:
Date of first session: Anticipated finishing date:	
Any other administrative notes:	

B: Initial Contracting and Co-assessing

Date of coaching session:
Client's first name:
Nature of confidentiality discussed and agreed:
Beginning the coaching relationship: How and why did client choose you? Previous coaching relationships and what worked well/less well: Agreed 'contract' of working with each other in the session:
Objectives for coaching sessions:
Description of Line Manager involvement (if any or mid-way/at end in coaching session with client):
Organisational, cultural, socio-economic aspects of field:
Coach–client co-assessing:
Zones of awareness (inner, middle, outer, co-created):
Contact functions (talking, hearing, seeing, touching, moving):
Support: Self (e.g. breathing, eye contact, pace and tone of voice, body posture, sitting in chair etc.):
Other (relational networks inside and outside of organisation):
Modifications to contact (e.g. introjection, projection, deflection, egotism, retroflection, desensitisation, confluence):
Interactive cycle of experience (in which phase or phases does modification tend to happen?):
Unfinished business (e.g. previous issues still unresolved, fixed gestalts etc.):
Impressions and responses to client (thoughts, feelings, sensations, images, etc.):

C: Post Coaching Session Reflection 'Checklist'

Name:	Date:	Session No:

Agreed objective(s) for session:
Zones of awareness (inner, middle, outer, co-created):
Contact functions (talking, hearing, seeing, touching, moving):
Support (Describe quality of support): Self (e.g. breathing, eye contact, pace and tone of voice, body posture, sitting in chair etc.): Other (describe quality of relationships):
Modifications to contact (e.g. introjection, projection, deflection, egotism, retroflection, desensitisation, confluence):
Interactive cycle of experience with you/others (in which phase or phases does modification tend to happen?):
Unfinished business (what is figural/ground):
Organisational, cultural, socio-economic aspects of field:
Impressions and responses to client (including co-transferring processes):
Potential issues for supervision:

Bibliography

Aspling, A. (2010) 'Wind of change', *Global Responsibility*. 3 (June): 20–1.

Asay, T.P. and Lambert, M.J. (1999) 'The empirical case for the common factors in therapy: quantitative findings', in M.A. Hubble, B.L. Duncan and S.D. Miller (eds), *The Heart and Soul of Change: What Works in Therapy*. Washington, DC: APA Press. pp. 33–56.

Beaumont, H. (1991) 'Fragile self process', Workshop Presentation, Metanoia, London.

Beaumont, H. (1993) 'Martin Buber's "I–Thou" and fragile self-organisation: Gestalt couples therapy', *British Gestalt Journal*, 2 (2): 85–95.

Beisser, A.R. (1970) 'The paradoxical theory of change', in J. Fagan and I. Shepherd (eds), *Gestalt Therapy Now*. Palo Alto, CA: Science and Behavior Books. pp. 77–80.

Bentley, T. (2001) 'The emerging system: gestalt approach to organisational interventions', *British Gestalt Journal*, 10 (1): 13–19.

Bettelheim, B. (1986 [1960]) *The Informed Heart*. London: Peregrine.

Binney, G., Wilke, G. and Williams, C. (2005) *Living Leadership: A Practical Guide for Ordinary Heroes*. London: FT Prentice Hall.

Bion, W.R. (1959) *Experiences in Groups*. New York: Basic Books.

Bion, W. (1967) 'Notes on memory and desire', *The Psychoanalytic Forum*, 2: 272–3; 279–80.

Brownell, P. (2008) *Handbook for Theory, Research and Practice in Gestalt Therapy*. Cambridge: Cambridge Scholars Publishing.

Brownell, P. (2010) *A Guide to Contemporary Practice: Gestalt Therapy*. New York: Springer Publishing.

Buber, M. (1958 [1923]) *I and Thou* (Trans. R.G. Smith). New York: Charles Scribner and Sons.

Buber, M. (1965a) *The Knowledge of Man*. New York: Harper and Row.

Buber, M (1965b) *Between Man and Man* (Trans. R.G. Smith). New York: Macmillan.

Carlson, C. and Kolodny, R. (2009) 'Embodying field theory in how we work with groups and organizations', in D. Ullman and G. Wheeler (eds), *Co-Creating the Field: Intention and Practice in the Age of Complexity*. New York: Routledge.

Chinnock, K. (2011) 'Relational supervision in relational transactional analysis', in H. Fowlie and C. Sills (eds), *Relational Transactional Analysis: Principles in Practice*. London: Karnac. pp. 293–303.

Clark, A. (1982) 'Grief and gestalt therapy', *The Gestalt Journal*, 5 (1): 49–63.

Clarkson, P. (1989) *Gestalt Counselling in Action*. London: Sage.

Clarkson, P. (1992) *Transactional Analysis Psychotherapy: An Integrated Approach*. London: Routledge.

Clarkson, P. (2003) *The Therapeutic Relationship* (2nd edn). London: Whurr Publishers.

Clarkson, P. and Mackewn, J. (1993) *Fritz Perls*. Key Figures in Counselling and Psychotherapy Series. London: Sage.

Clemmens, M. and Bursztyn, A. (2005) 'Culture and the body', in T. Levine Bar-Yoseph (ed.), *The Bridge: Dialogue Across Cultures*. USA: Gestalt Institute Press.

Coffey, F. and Cavicchia, S. (2005) 'Revitalising feedback – an organisational case study', *British Gestalt Journal*, 14 (1): 15–25.

Cooper, M. (2008) *Essential Research Findings in Counselling and Psychotherapy: The Facts are Friendly*. London: Sage.

Cornell, W. (2003) 'The impassioned body: erotic vitality and disturbance in psychother- apy', *British Gestalt Journal*, 12 (2): 97–104.

Critchley, B. (2008) 'A relational approach to counselling'. Paper delivered at the 15th Annual EMCC Conference, Prague.

Critchley, B. (2012) 'Relational coaching: dancing on the edge', in E. de Haan and C. Sills, *Coaching Relationships*. London: Libri. pp. 19–30.

Critchley, B. and Casey, D. (1989) 'Organisations get stuck too', *Training Journal*, 10 (4): 3–12.

Crocker, S. (2008) 'A unified theory', in P. Brownell (ed.), *A Guide to Contemporary Practice: Gestalt Therapy*. New York: Springer Publishing. pp. 124–50.

Delisle, G. (1999) *Personality Disorders*. Quebec: Les Editions du Reflet.

Erikson, E. (1950) *Childhood and Society*. New York: W.W. Norton.

Faraday, A. (1973) *Dreamwork*. London: Pan Books.

Fish, S. and Lapworth, P. (1994) *Understand and Use Your Dreams*. Bath: Dormouse Press.

Frank, R. (2001) *Body of Awareness: A Somatic and Developmental Approach to Psychotherapy*. Cambridge, MA: Gestalt Press.

Frank, R. and La Barre, F. (2011) *The First Year and the Rest of Your Life: Movement, Development and Psychotherapeutic Change*. New York: Taylor & Francis Group.

Frankl, V. (1964) *Man's Search for Meaning*. London: Hodder & Stoughton.

Friedlander, S. (1918) *Schopferische Indifjerenz*. Munich: Georg Muller.

Friedman, M.S. (1985) *The Healing Dialogue in Psychotherapy*. New York: Jason Arson.

Gaffney, S. (2009) 'The cycle of experience re-cycled: then, now . . . next?', *Gestalt Review*, 13 (1): 7–23.

Gelso, C.J. and Carter, J.A. (1985) 'The relationship in counseling and psychotherapy: components, consequences and theoretical antecedents', *Counselling Psychologist*, 13 (2): 155–243.

Gerhardt, S. (2004) *Why Love Matters*. Hove and New York: Brunner-Routledge.

Goldstein, K. (1940) *Human Nature in the Light of Psychopathology*. Cambridge, MA: Harvard University Press.

Greenberg, E. (2003) 'Love, admiration, or safety: a system of gestalt diagnosis of borderline, narcissistic, and schizoid adaptations that focuses on what is figure for the client', *Gestalt!*, 6 (3) (accessed 20 May 2011 from: www.g-gej.org/6-3/ diagnosis.html).

Greenway, I. (1992) *Assessment Checklist*. Nottingham: Sherwood Institute.

Handlon, J.H. and Fredericson, I. (1998) 'What changes the individual in gestalt groups? A proposed theroetical model', *Gestalt Review*, 2 (4): 275–94.

Harris, J. (1989) *Gestalt: An Idiosyncratic Introduction*. Manchester: Gestalt Centre.

Heidegger, M. (1962) *Being and Time* (Trans. J. McQuarrie and E. Robinson). New York: Harper and Row.

Hycner, R.A. (1990) 'The I–Thou relationship and gestalt therapy', *The Gestalt Journal*, 13 (1): 41–54.

Hycner, R.A. (1991) *Between Person and Person: Toward a Dialogical Psychotherapy*. Highland, NY: Gestalt Journal Press.

Hycner, R.A. and Jacobs, L. (1995) *The Healing Relationship in Gestalt Therapy*. Highland, NY: Gestalt Journal Press.

Hycner, R.A. and Jacobs, L. (2008) *Relational Approaches in Gestalt Therapy*. New York: Routledge, Taylor and Francis.

Jacobs, L. (1989) 'The dialogue in theory and therapy', *The Gestalt Journal*, 12 (1): 25–67.

Jacobs, L. (1996) 'Shame in the therapeutic dialogue', in R.G. Lee and G. Wheeler (eds), *The Voice of Shame: Silence and Connection in Psychotherapy*. San Francisco, CA: Jossey-Bass. pp. 297–314.

Jacobs, L. (2005) 'For whites only', in T. Levine Bar-Yoseph (ed.), *The Bridge: Dialogues Across Cultures*. New Orleans, LA: Gestalt Institute Press. pp. 225–44.

Joyce, P. (1992) *Gestalt Psychotherapy Student Handbook*. London: Metanoia Institute.

Joyce, P. and Sills, C. (2001) *Skills in Gestalt Counselling and Psychotherapy*. London: Sage.

Joyce, P. and Sills, C. (2010) *Skills in Gestalt Counselling and Psychotherapy* (2nd edn). London: Sage.

Keenan, B. (1992) *An Evil Cradling*. London: Hutchinson.

Kennedy, D. (2005) 'The lived body', *British Gestalt Journal*, 14 (2): 109–17.

Kepner, J. (1993) *Body Process: Working with the Body in Psychotherapy*. San Francisco, CA: Jossey-Bass.

Kepner, J. (1996) *Healing Tasks: Psychotherapy with Adult Survivors of Child Abuse*. Hillsdale, NJ: Analytic Press.

Kepner, J. (2003) 'The embodied field', *British Gestalt Review*, 12 (1): 6–14.

Koestenbaum, P. and Block, P. (2001) *Freedom and Accountability at Work: Applying Philosophical Insight to the Real World*. San Francisco, CA: Jossey-Bass/Pfeiffer.

Kolodny, R. (2004) 'Why awareness works and other insights from spiritual practice', *British Gestalt Journal*, 12 (2): 92–9.

Korzybski, A.H.S. (1931/1933) 'A non-Aristotelian system and its necessity for rigour in mathematics and physics'. Paper presented before the American Mathematical Society at the New Orleans, Louisiana, meeting of the American Association for the Advancement of Science, 28 December 1931. (Reprinted in *Science and Sanity*, 1933, pp. 747–61.)

Lambrechts, F., Grieten, S., Bouwen, R. and Corthouts, F. (2009) 'Process consultation revisited: taking a relational practice perspective', *Journal of Applied Behavioural Science*, 45 (1): 39–58.

Latner, J. (1992) 'The theory of gestalt therapy', in E. Nevis (ed.), *Gestalt Therapy: Perspectives and Applications*. Cambridge, MA: Gestalt Press.

Latner, J. (2000) 'The theory of Gestalt therapy', in E. Nevis (ed.), *Gestalt Therapy Perspectives and Applications*. New York: Gestalt Institute of Cleveland Press/Gardner Press. pp. 13–56.

Levin, J. (1991) 'Perls, Hefferline and Goodman', *Workshop Presentation*, Metanoia, London.

Levin, P. (1974) *Becoming the Way We Are*. San Francisco, CA: Transpubs.

Lewin, K. (1935) *A Dynamic Theory of Personality*. New York: McGraw-Hill.

Lewin, K. (1952) *Field Theory in Social Science: Selected Theoretical Papers*. London: Tavistock.

Lichtenberg, P. (1990) *Community and Confluence: Undoing the Clinch of Oppression*. Cambridge, MA: Gestalt Press.

Lovelock, J.E. (1987) *Gaia: A New Look at Life on Earth*. Oxford: Oxford University Press.

Mackewn, J. (1994) 'Modern gestalt – an integrative and ethical approach to counselling and psychotherapy', *Counselling: The Journal of the British Association for Counselling*, 5 (2): 105–8.

Mackewn, J. (1997) *Developing Gestalt Counselling*. London: Sage.

Mahler, M.S., Pine, F. and Bergman, A. (1975) *The Psychological Birth of the Human Infant*. New York: Basic Books.

Mandela, N. (1995) *A Long Walk to Freedom*. New York: Little, Brown and Co.

Martin, D.J., Garske, J.P. and Davis, M.K. (2000) Relational of the therapeutic alliance with outcome and other variables; and meta-analytic review', *Journal of Consulting and Clinical Psychology*, 68 (3): 438–50.

Mauer, R. (2003) 'Using the paradoxical theory of change in organisations', *Gestalt Review*, 7 (3): 252–60.

Mauer, R. (2005) 'Gestalt approaches with organisations and large systems', in A.L. Woldt and S.M. Toman (eds), *Gestalt Therapy: History, Theory and Practice*. Thousand Oaks, CA: Sage. pp. 237–56.

Melnick, J. (2003) 'Countertransference and the gestalt approach', *The British Gestalt Journal*, 12 (1): 40–8.

Melnick, J. (2009) 'Interview on creativity with Joseph C. Zinker, PhD', *Gestalt Review*, 13 (2): 119–22.

Melnick, J. and Nevis, S. (1997) 'Gestalt diagnosis and DSM–IV', *British Gestalt Journal*, 6 (2): 97–106.

Melnick, J. and Nevis, E.C. (2009) *Mending the World: Social Healing Interventions by Gestalt Practitioners Worldwide*. Gestalt International Study Centre.

Mencken, H.L. (1994) *The Little Zen Companion* (Ed. D. Schiller). New York: Workman Publishing Company.

Menninger, K. (1958) *The Theory of Psychoanalytic Technique*. New York: Basic Books.

Mulgrew, E. and Mulgrew, J. (1987) 'Awareness of self and other in gestalt therapy', *The Gestalt Journal*, 10 (2): 67–72.

Naranjo, C. (1970) 'Present-centeredness: techniques, prescriptions and ideal', in J. Fagan and I.L. Shepherd (eds), *Gestalt Therapy Now*. New York: Harper and Row. pp. 47–69.

Nevis, E. (1987) *Organisational Consulting: A Gestalt Approach*. New York: Gestalt Institute of Cleveland Press/Gardner Press.

Nevis, E. (ed.) (1992) *Gestalt Therapy Perspectives and Applications*. New York: Gestalt Institute of Cleveland Press/Gardner Press.

Nevis, S., Backman, S. and Nevis, E. (2003) 'Connecting strategic and intimate interactions: the need for balance', *Gestalt Review*, 7 (2): 134–46.

Nhat, Hanh, T. (1975) *The Miracle of Mindfulness: A Manual on Meditation*. Boston, MA: Beacon Press.

Nhat, Hahn, T. (2008) *Thich Nhat Hanh: Essential Writings* (Ed. R. Ellsberg). London: Darton, Longman and Todd.

Norcross, J.C. (2011) *Psychotherapy Relationships that Work: Evidence-based Responsiveness*. New York: Oxford University Press.

O'Neill, B. and Gaffney, S. (2008) 'Field theoretical strategy', in P. Brownell (ed.), *A Guide to Contemporary Practice: Gestalt Therapy*. New York: Springer Publishing. pp. 228–56.

O'Shea, L. (2003) 'The erotic field', *British Gestalt Journal*, 12 (2): 105–10.

Palmer, P. (1997) 'The grace of great things: reclaiming the sacred in knowing, teaching and learning', *Holistic Education Review*, 10 (3): 8–16.

Panksepp, J. (1998) *Affective Neuroscience: The Foundations of Human and Animal Emotions*. Oxford: Oxford University Press.

Parlett, M. (1991) 'Reflections on field theory', *British Gestalt Journal*, 1 (2): 69–81.

Parlett, M. (1997) 'The unified field in practice', *Gestalt Review*, 1 (1): 10–33.

Parlett, M. (2005) 'Contemporary gestalt therapy: field theory', in A.L. Woldt and S.M. Toman (eds), *Gestalt Therapy: History, Theory and Practice*. Thousand Oaks, CA: Sage. pp. 41–64.

Pedler, M. (ed.) (1997) *Action Learning Practice* (3rd edn). Gower: Aldershot.

Perls, F.S. (1969) *Gestalt Therapy Verbatim*. Moab, UT: Real People Press.

Perls, F.S. (1976) *The Gestalt Approach and Eye Witness to Therapy*. New York: Bantam.

Perls, F.S. (1992 [1947]) *Ego, Hunger and Aggression: A Revision of Freud's Theory and Method*. New York: Gestalt Journal Press.

Perls, F.S., Hefferline, R. and Goodman, P. (1972 [1951]) *Gestalt Therapy*. London: The Julian Press.

Perls, L. (1992) *Living at the Boundary*. New York: Gestalt Journal.

Philippson, P. (2001) *Self in Relation*. New York: The Gestalt Journal Press.

Philippson, P. (2009) *The Emergent Self*. London: Karnac Books.

Polster, E. (1987) *Every Person's Life is Worth a Novel*. New York: W.W. Norton.

Polster, E. (1991) 'Tight therapeutic sequences', *British Gestalt Journal*, 1 (2): 63–8.

Polster, E. (2009) *The Population of Selves*. San Francisco, CA: Gestalt Journal Press.

Polster, E. and Polster, M. (1974) *Gestalt Therapy Integrated*. New York: Vintage Books.

Polster, E. and Polster, M. (2000) *From the Radical Centre: The Heart of Gestalt Therapy*. Cambridge, MA: Gestalt Press.

Polster, M. and Polster, E. (1990) 'Gestalt therapy', in J.K. Zeig and W.M. Munion (eds), *What is Psychotherapy? Contemporary Perspectives*. San Francisco, CA: Jossey-Bass. pp. 103–7.

Ransome, A. (2010/1930) *Swallows and Amazons*. London: Red Fox, Random House Books.

Reich, W. (1972 [1945]) *Character Analysis*. New York: Simon & Schuster.

Resnick, R. (1990) *Gestalt Therapy with Couples*. Workshop at Metanoia Institute, London.

Rogers, C. (1951) *Client-Centred Therapy*. London: Constable and Co.

Schiller, D. (ed.) (1994) *The Little Zen Companion*. New York: Workman Publishing Company.

Schore, A. (2003) *Affect, Regulation and Repair of the Self*. New York: W.W. Norton & Co.

Senge, P. (1990) *The Fifth Discipline: The Art and Practice of The Learning Organisation*. London: Random House.

Serline, I.A. and Shane, P. (1999) 'Laura Perls and gestalt therapy: her life and values', in D. Moss (ed.), *Humanistic and Transpersonal Psychology: A Historical and Biographical Source Book*. Westport, CT: Greenwood Press. pp. 375–84.

Siegel, D. (2010) *The Mindful Therapist*. New York: W.W. Norton.

Sills, C., Fish, S. and Lapworth, P. (1995) *Gestalt Counselling*. Oxon: Winslow Press. pp. 169–91.

Simon, S.N. (2009) 'Applying gestalt theory to coaching', *Gestalt Review*, 13 (3): 230–40.

Simon, S.N. and Geib, P. (1996) 'When therapists cause shame: rupture and repair at the contact boundary', in R. Lee and G. Wheeler (eds), *The Voice of Shame*. Cambridge, MA: Gestalt Press. pp. 315–36.

Smith, E. (1988) 'Self interruptions in the rhythm of contact and withdrawal', *The Gestalt Journal*, 11 (2): 37–57.

Smuts, H.C. (1996 [1926]) *Holism and Evolution*. New York: Macmillian.

Spagnuolo Lobb, M. (2005) 'Classical gestalt therapy theory', in A.L. Woldt and S.M. Toman (eds), *Gestalt Therapy: History, Theory and Practice*. Thousand Oaks, CA: Sage.

Spinelli, E. (1989) *The Interpreted World: An Introduction to Phenomenological Psychology*. London: Sage.

Stacey, R. (2003) *Strategic Management and Organisational Dynamics: The Challenge of Complexity*. Harlow: Prentice-Hall.

Staemmler, F.-M. (1993) 'Projective identification in gestalt therapy with severely impaired clients', *British Gestalt Journal*, 2 (2): 104–10.

Staemmler, F.-M. (1999) 'Dialogical diagnosis: changing through understanding', in R. Fuhr, M. Sreckovic and M. Gremmler-Fuhr (eds), *Handbook of Gestalt Therapy*. Göttingen: Hogrefe. pp. 673–87.

Staemmler, F.-M. (2009) *Aggression, Time, and Understanding: Contributions to the Evolution of Gestalt Therapy*. New York: Gestalt Press.

Stawman, S. (2008) 'Relational gestalt: four waves', in R.A. Hycner and L. Jacobs (eds), *Relational Approaches in Gestalt Therapy*. New York: Routledge, Taylor and Francis. pp. 11–36.

Steiner, C. (1984) 'Emotional literacy', *Transactional Analysis Journal*, 14 (3): 162–73.

Stern, D. (1985) *The Interpersonal World of the Infant*. New York: Basic Books.

Stevenson, H. (2010) 'Paradox: a gestalt theory of change for organisations', *Gestalt Review*, 14 (2): 111–26.

Stoehr, T. (1994) *Here Now Next: Paul Goodman and the Origins of Gestalt Therapy*. San Francisco, CA: Jossey-Bass.

Trevarthen, C. (2008) 'The musical art of infant conversation', *Musicae Sientie*, 12 (1): 15–46.

Wampold, B. (2001) *The Great Psychotherapy Debate*. Hove: Lawrence Erlbaum.

Wheeler, G. (1991) *Gestalt Reconsidered*. New York: Gestalt Institute of Cleveland Press/Gardner Press.

Wheeler, G. (1994) 'Compulsion and curiosity – a gestalt approach to obsessive compulsive disorder', *British Gestalt Journal*, 3 (1): 15–21.

Wheeler, G. (1996) 'Self and shame: a new paradigm for psychotherapy', in R. Lee and G. Wheeler (ed), *The Voice of Shame*. Cambridge, MA: Gestalt Press. pp. 23–58.

Wheeler, G. (2000) *Beyond Individualism: Toward Understanding of Self, Relationship and Experience*. Hillsdale, NJ: Gestalt Press.

Wheeler, G. (2005) 'Culture, self, and field', in T. Levine Bar-Yoseph (ed.), *The Bridge: Dialogues Across Cultures*. New Orleans, LA: Gestalt Institute Press.

Wheeler, G. (2009) 'New directions in gestalt theory: psychology and psychotherapy in the age of complexity', in D. Ullman and G. Wheeler (eds), *Co-Creating the Field: Intention and Practice in the Age of Complexity*. Cleveland: Gestalt Press. pp. 3–44.

Winnicott, D. (1958) *Collected Papers through Paediatrics to Psychoanalysis*. London: Tavistock.

Winnicott, D.W. (1965) *The Maturational Processes and the Facilitating Environment: Studies in the Theory of Emotional Development*. New York: International Universities Press.

Wollants, G. (2007) 'Therapy of the situation', *British Gestalt Journal*, 14 (2): 91–102.

Wollants, G. (2012) *Gestalt Therapy: Therapy of the Situation*. London: SAGE.

Yalom, I. (1980) *Existential Psychotherapy*. New York: Basic Books.

Yontef, G. (1983) 'The self in gestalt therapy: reply to Tobin', *The Gestalt Journal*, 6 (1): 55–70.

Yontef, G. (1991) 'Techniques in gestalt therapy-letter', *British Gestalt Journal*, 1 (2): 114–15.

Yontef, G. (1993) *Awareness, Dialogue and Process: Essays on Gestalt Therapy*. Highland, NY: The Gestalt Journal Inc.

Yontef, G. and Simkin, I.F. (1989) 'Gestalt therapy', in R. Corsini and D. Wedding (eds), *Current Psychotherapies* (4th edn). Itasca, IL: Peacock.

Zinker, J. (1975) 'On loving encounters: a phenomenological view', in F. Stephenson (ed.), *Gestalt Therapy Primer*. Chicago, IL: Charles Thomas. pp. 54–72.

Zinker, J. (1977) *Creative Process in Gestalt Therapy*. New York Brunner/Mazel.

Zinker, J. (1990) in R.L. Harman (ed.) *Gestalt Therapy Discussions with the Masters*. Springfield, IL: Charles C. Thomas.

Zinker, J. (1994) *In Search of Good Form*. San Francisco, CA: Jossey-Bass.

Zinker, J. and Nevis, S.M. (1981) *The Gestalt Theory of Couple and Family Interactions*, Working Paper, Centre for the Study of Intimate Systems, Gestalt Institute of Cleveland.

Index

Figures and tables are indicated by page numbers in **bold**.